THE
GREATEST
MAN
WHO EVER LIVED

Publishers
WATCHTOWER BIBLE AND TRACT SOCIETY
OF NEW YORK, INC.
Brooklyn, New York, U.S.A.

2006 Printing
This publication is provided as part of a worldwide Bible
educational work supported by voluntary donations.

Scripture quotations are from the modern-language
New World Translation of the Holy Scriptures, 1984 Edition

Picture Credits
Map preceding Chapter 1: based on a map copyrighted by
Pictorial Archive (Near Eastern History) Est. and Survey of Israel

The Greatest Man Who Ever Lived   English (*gt*-E)
Made in the United States of America

Contents

1 Messages From Heaven

2 Honored Before He Was Born

3 The Preparer of the Way Is Born

4 Pregnant but Not Married

5 Jesus' Birth—Where and When?

6 The Child of Promise

7 Jesus and the Astrologers

8 Escape From a Tyrant

9 Jesus' Early Family Life

10 Trips to Jerusalem

11 John Prepares the Way

12 Jesus' Baptism

13 Learning From Jesus' Temptations

14 Jesus' First Disciples

15 Jesus' First Miracle

16 Zeal for Jehovah's Worship

17 Teaching Nicodemus

18 John Decreases, Jesus Increases

19 Teaching a Samaritan Woman

20 Second Miracle While in Cana

21 In Jesus' Hometown Synagogue

22 Four Disciples Are Called

23 More Miracles in Capernaum

24 Why Jesus Came to Earth

25 Compassion for a Leper

26 Back Home in Capernaum

27 The Calling of Matthew

28 Questioned About Fasting

29 Doing Good Works on the Sabbath

30 Answering His Accusers

31 Plucking Grain on the Sabbath

32 What Is Lawful on the Sabbath?

33 Fulfilling Isaiah's Prophecy

34 Choosing His Apostles

35 The Most Famous Sermon Ever Given

36 An Army Officer's Great Faith

37 Jesus Dispels a Widow's Grief

38 Did John Lack Faith?

39 The Proud and the Lowly

40 A Lesson in Mercy

41 A Center of Controversy

42 Jesus Rebukes the Pharisees

43 Teaching With Illustrations

44 Silencing a Terrifying Storm

45 An Unlikely Disciple

46 She Touched His Garment

47 Tears Turned to Great Ecstasy

48 Leaving Jairus' Home and Revisiting Nazareth

49 Another Preaching Tour of Galilee

50 Preparation to Face Persecution

51 Murder During a Birthday Party

52 Jesus Miraculously Feeds Thousands

53 A Desired Superhuman Ruler

54 "True Bread From Heaven"

55 Many Disciples Quit Following Jesus

56 What Defiles a Man?

57 Compassion for the Afflicted

58 The Loaves and the Leaven

59 Who Really Is Jesus?

60 A Preview of Christ's Kingdom Glory

61 Possessed Boy Healed

62 A Lesson in Humility

63 Further Corrective Counsel

64 A Lesson in Forgiveness

65 A Secret Trip to Jerusalem

66 At the Festival of Tabernacles

67 They Fail to Arrest Him

68 Further Teaching on the Seventh Day

69 The Question of Fatherhood

70 Healing a Man Born Blind

71 Pharisees' Willful Unbelief

72 Jesus Sends Out the 70

73 A Neighborly Samaritan

74 Counsel to Martha, and Instruction on Prayer

75 The Source of Happiness

76 Dining With a Pharisee

77 The Question of Inheritance

78 Keep Ready!

79 A Nation Lost, but Not All

80 The Sheepfolds and the Shepherd

81 Further Attempts to Kill Jesus

82 Jesus Again Heads for Jerusalem

83 Entertained by a Pharisee

84 The Responsibility of Discipleship

85 Searching for the Lost

86 The Story of a Lost Son

87 Provide for the Future With Practical Wisdom

88 The Rich Man and Lazarus

89 A Mission of Mercy Into Judea

90 The Resurrection Hope

91 When Lazarus Is Resurrected

92 Ten Lepers Healed During Jesus' Final Trip to Jerusalem

93 When the Son of Man Is Revealed

94 The Need for Prayer and for Humility

95 Lessons on Divorce and on Love for Children

96 Jesus and a Rich Young Ruler

97 Workers in the Vineyard

98 The Disciples Argue as Jesus' Death Nears

99 Jesus Teaches at Jericho

100 The Illustration of the Minas

101 At Bethany, in the House of Simon

102 Christ's Triumphal Entry Into Jerusalem

103 Visiting the Temple Again

104 God's Voice Heard a Third Time

105 Beginning of a Crucial Day

106 Exposed by Vineyard Illustrations

107 Illustration of the Marriage Feast

108 They Fail to Entrap Jesus

109 Jesus Denounces His Opposers

110 Ministry at the Temple Completed

111 Sign of the Last Days

112 Jesus' Final Passover Is At Hand

113 Humility at the Last Passover

114 The Memorial Supper

115 An Argument Erupts

116 Preparing the Apostles for His Departure

117 Agony in the Garden

118 Betrayal and Arrest

119 Taken to Annas, Then to Caiaphas

120 Denials in the Courtyard

121 Before the Sanhedrin, Then to Pilate

122 From Pilate to Herod and Back Again

123 "Look! The Man!"

124 Handed Over and Led Away

125 Agony on the Stake

126 "Certainly This Was God's Son"

127 Buried Friday—An Empty Tomb Sunday

128 Jesus Is Alive!

129 Further Appearances

130 At the Sea of Galilee

131 Final Appearances, and Pentecost 33 C.E.

132 At God's Right Hand

133 Jesus Finishes All God Asks

The Greatest Man Who Ever Lived

C AN any man unquestionably be called the greatest man who ever lived? How do you measure a man's greatness? By his military genius? his physical strength? his mental prowess?

The historian H. G. Wells said that a man's greatness can be measured by 'what he leaves to grow, and whether he started others to think along fresh lines with a vigor that persisted after him.' Wells, although not claiming to be a Christian, acknowledged: "By this test Jesus stands first."

Alexander the Great, Charlemagne (styled "the Great" even in his own lifetime), and Napoleon Bonaparte were powerful rulers. By their formidable presence, they wielded great influence over those they commanded. Yet, Napoleon is reported to have said: "Jesus Christ has influenced and commanded His subjects without His visible bodily presence."

By his dynamic teachings and by the way he lived in harmony with them, Jesus has powerfully affected the lives of people for nearly two thousand years. As one writer aptly expressed it: "All the armies that ever marched, and all the navies that ever were built, and all the parliaments that ever sat, all the kings that ever reigned, put together have not affected the life of man upon this earth as powerfully."

A Historical Person

Yet, strangely, some say that Jesus never lived—that he is, in effect, a creation of some first-century men. Answering such skeptics, the respected historian Will Durant argued: "That a few simple men should in one generation have invented so powerful and appealing a personality, so lofty an ethic and so inspiring a vision of human brotherhood, would be a miracle far more incredible than any recorded in the Gospels."

Ask yourself: Could a person who never lived have affected human history so remarkably? The reference work *The Historians' History of the World* observed: "The historical result of [Jesus'] activities was more momentous, even from a strictly secular standpoint, than the deeds of any other character of history. A new era, recognised by the chief civilisations of the world, dates from his birth."

Yes, think about it. Even calendars today are based on the year that Jesus was thought to have been born. "Dates before that year are listed as B.C., or *before Christ*," explains *The World Book Encyclopedia*. "Dates after that year are listed as A.D., or *anno Domini* (in the year of our Lord)."

Critics, nevertheless, point out that all that we really know about Jesus is found in the Bible. No other contemporary records concerning him exist, they say. Even H. G. Wells wrote: "The old Roman historians ignored Jesus entirely; he left no impress on the historical records of his time." But is this true?

Although references to Jesus Christ by early secular historians are meager, such references do exist. Cornelius Tacitus, a respected first-century Roman historian, wrote: "The name [Christian] is derived from Christ, whom the procurator Pontius Pilate had executed in the reign of Tiberius." Suetonius and Pliny the Younger, other

Roman writers of the time, also referred to Christ. In addition, Flavius Josephus, a first-century Jewish historian, wrote of James, whom he identified as "the brother of Jesus, who was called Christ."

The New Encyclopædia Britannica thus concludes: "These independent accounts prove that in ancient times even the opponents of Christianity never doubted the historicity of Jesus, which was disputed for the first time and on inadequate grounds at the end of the 18th, during the 19th, and at the beginning of the 20th centuries."

Essentially, however, all that is known about Jesus was recorded by his first-century followers. Their reports have been preserved in the Gospels—Bible books written by Matthew, Mark, Luke, and John. What do these accounts say regarding the identity of Jesus?

Really, Who Was He?

Jesus' first-century associates pondered that question. When they saw Jesus miraculously calm a wind-whipped sea with a rebuke, they wondered in astonishment: "Who really is this?" Later, on another occasion, Jesus asked his apostles: "Who do you say I am?"—Mark 4:41; Matthew 16:15.

If you were asked that question, how would you answer? Was Jesus, in fact, God? Many today say that he was. Yet, his associates never believed that he was God. The apostle Peter's response to Jesus' question was: "You are the Christ, the Son of the living God."—Matthew 16:16.

Jesus never claimed to be God, but he acknowledged that he was the promised Messiah, or Christ. He also said he was "God's Son," *not God.* (John 4:25, 26; 10:36) Yet, the Bible does not say Jesus was a man like any other man. He was a very special person because he was created by God before all other things. (Colossians 1:15) For countless billions of years, before even the physical universe was created, Jesus lived as a spirit person in heaven and enjoyed intimate fellowship with his Father, Jehovah God, the Grand Creator.—Proverbs 8:22, 27-31.

Then, about two thousand years ago, God transferred his Son's life to the womb of a woman, and Jesus came to be a human son of God, born in the normal manner through a woman. (Galatians 4:4) When Jesus was developing in the womb and while he was growing up as a boy, he was dependent upon those whom God had selected to be his earthly parents. Eventually Jesus reached manhood, and he was granted full remembrance of his previous association with God in heaven.—John 8:23; 17:5.

What Made Him the Greatest

Because he carefully imitated his heavenly Father, Jesus was the greatest man who ever lived. As a faithful Son, Jesus copied his Father so exactly that he could tell his followers: "He that has seen me has seen the Father also." (John 14:9, 10) In every situation here on earth, he did just as his Father, Almighty God, would have done. "I do nothing of my own initiative," Jesus explained, "but just as the Father taught me I speak these things." (John 8:28) So when we study the life of Jesus Christ, we are, in effect, obtaining a clear picture of just what God is like.

Thus, even though the apostle John acknowledged that "no man has seen God," he could still write that "God is love." (John 1:18; 1 John 4:8) John could do this because he knew God's love through what he saw in Jesus, who was the perfect reflection of his Father. Jesus was compassionate, kind, humble, and approachable. The weak and downtrodden felt comfortable with him, as did people of all kinds—men, women, children, the rich, the poor, the powerful, even gross sinners. Only those with wicked hearts did not like him.

Indeed, Jesus did not merely teach his followers to love one another, but he showed them how. "Just as I have loved you," he said, "you also [should] love one another." (John 13:34) Knowing "the love of the Christ," explained one of his apostles, "surpasses knowledge." (Ephesians 3:19) Yes, the love Christ demonstrated ascends above academic head knowledge and "compels" others to respond to it. (2 Corinthians 5:14) Thus, Jesus' surpassing example of love, in particular, is what made him the greatest man who ever lived. His love has touched the hearts of millions through the centuries and has influenced their lives for the good.

Yet, some may object: 'Look at all the crimes that have been committed in the name of Christ—the Crusades, the Inquisition, and the wars that have seen millions who claim to be Christian kill one another on opposing battle lines.' But the truth is, these people belie their claim to be followers of Jesus. His teachings and way of life condemn their actions. Even a Hindu, Mohandas Gandhi, was moved to say: 'I love Christ, but I despise Christians because they do not live as Christ lived.'

Benefit by Learning About Him

Surely no study could be more important today than that of the life and ministry of Jesus Christ. "Look intently at . . . Jesus," urged the apostle Paul. "Indeed, consider closely [that] one." And God himself commanded regarding his Son: *"Listen to him."* This is what the book *The Greatest Man Who Ever Lived* will help you to do.—Hebrews 12:2, 3; Matthew 17:5.

An effort has been made to present every event in Jesus' earthly life that is set forth in the four Gospels, including the speeches he delivered and his illustrations and miracles. To the extent possible, everything is related in the order in which it occurred. At the end of each chapter is a list of the Bible texts upon which the chapter is based. You are encouraged to read these texts and to answer the review questions that are provided.

A scholar from the University of Chicago claimed recently: "More has been written about Jesus in the last twenty years than in the previous two thousand." Yet there is a vital need to consider personally the Gospel accounts, for as *The Encyclopædia Britannica* stated: "Many a modern student has become so preoccupied with conflicting theories about Jesus and the Gospels that he has neglected to study these basic sources by themselves."

After a close, unprejudiced consideration of the Gospel accounts, we feel you will agree that the greatest of all events in human history occurred in the reign of the Roman Caesar Augustus, when Jesus of Nazareth appeared in order to give his life in our behalf.

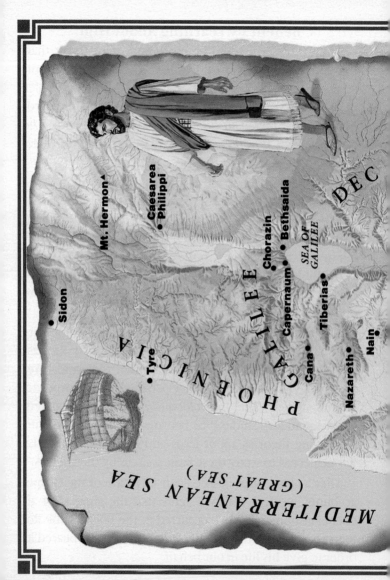

Sidon

Mt. Hermon

Caesarea
Philippi

Tyre

PHOENICIA

GALILEE

Chorazin

Capernaum

Bethsaida

SEA OF
GALILEE

DEC

Cana

Tiberias

Nazareth

Nain

MEDITERRANEAN SEA
(GREAT SEA)

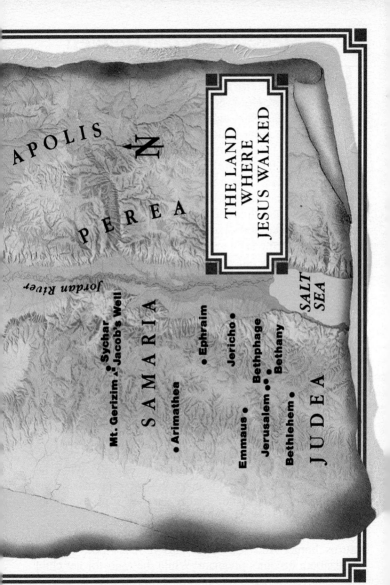

Messages From Heaven

THE entire Bible is, in effect, a message from heaven, having been provided by our heavenly Father for our instruction. However, two special messages were delivered nearly 2,000 years ago by an angel who "stands near before God." His name is Gabriel. Let us examine the circumstances of these two important visits to earth.

The year is 3 B.C.E. In the Judean hills, probably not too far from Jerusalem, lives a priest of Jehovah by the name of Zechariah. He has grown old, and so has his wife, Elizabeth. And they have no children. Zechariah is taking his turn at priestly service in God's temple in Jerusalem. Suddenly Gabriel appears at the right side of the incense altar.

Zechariah is very much afraid. But Gabriel quiets his fears, saying, "Have no fear, Zechariah, because your supplication has been favorably heard, and your wife Elizabeth will become mother to a son to you, and you are to call his name John." Gabriel goes on to proclaim that John "will be great before Jehovah" and that he will "get ready for Jehovah a prepared people."

However, Zechariah cannot believe it. It seems so impossible that he and Elizabeth could have a child at their age. So Gabriel tells him: "You will be silent and not able to speak until the day that these things take place, because you did not believe my words."

Well, in the meantime, the people outside are wondering why Zechariah is taking so long in the temple. When he finally comes out, he cannot speak but can only make signs with his hands, and they realize he has seen something supernatural.

After Zechariah finishes his period of temple service, he returns home. And soon afterward it really does happen —Elizabeth becomes pregnant! While she waits for her child to be born, Elizabeth stays at home away from people for five months.

Later Gabriel appears again. And to whom does he speak? It is to a young unmarried woman by the name of Mary from the town of Nazareth. What message does he deliver this time? Listen! "You have found favor with God," Gabriel tells Mary. "Look! you will conceive in your womb and give birth to a son, and you are to call his name Jesus." Gabriel adds: "This one will be great and will be called Son of the Most High; . . . and he will rule as king over the house of Jacob forever, and there will be no end of his kingdom."

We can be sure that Gabriel feels privileged to deliver these messages. And as we read more about John and Jesus, we will see more clearly just why these messages from heaven are so important.   **2 Timothy 3:16; Luke 1:5-33.**

■ What two important messages are delivered from heaven?
■ Who delivers the messages, and to whom are they delivered?
■ Why are the messages so difficult to believe?

Honored Before He Was Born

AFTER the angel Gabriel tells the young woman Mary that she will give birth to a baby boy who will become an everlasting king, Mary asks: "How is this to be, since I am having no intercourse with a man?"

"Holy spirit will come upon you," Gabriel explains, "and power of the Most High will overshadow you. For that reason also what is born will be called holy, God's Son."

To help Mary believe his message, Gabriel continues: "And, look! Elizabeth your relative has also herself conceived a son, in her old age, and this is the sixth month for her, the so-called barren woman; because with God no declaration will be an impossibility."

Mary accepts Gabriel's word. And what is her response? "Look! Jehovah's slave girl!" she exclaims. "May it take place with me according to your declaration."

Soon after Gabriel leaves, Mary gets ready and goes to visit Elizabeth, who lives with her husband, Zechariah, in the

mountainous country of Judea. From Mary's home in Nazareth, this is a long trip of perhaps three or four days.

When Mary finally arrives at Zechariah's house, she enters and offers a greeting. At that, Elizabeth is filled with holy spirit, and she says to Mary: "Blessed are you among women, and blessed is the fruit of your womb! So how is it that this privilege is mine, to have the mother of my Lord come to me? For, look! as the sound of your greeting fell upon my ears, the infant in my womb leaped with great gladness."

At hearing this, Mary responds with

heartfelt gratitude: "My soul magnifies Jehovah, and my spirit cannot keep from being overjoyed at God my Savior; because he has looked upon the low position of his slave girl. For, look! from now on all generations will pronounce me happy; because the powerful One has done great deeds for me." Yet, despite the favor she is shown, Mary directs all honor to God. "Holy is his name," she says, "and for generations after generations his mercy is upon those who fear him."

Mary continues praising God in inspired prophetic song, proclaiming: "He has performed mightily with his arm, he has scattered abroad those who are haughty in the intention of their hearts. He has brought down men of power from thrones and exalted lowly ones; he has fully satisfied hungry ones with good things and he has sent away empty those who had wealth. He has come to the aid of Israel his servant, to call to mind mercy, just as he told to our forefathers, to Abraham and to his seed, forever."

Mary stays with Elizabeth for about three months, and no doubt she is a big help during these final weeks of Elizabeth's pregnancy. It is indeed fine that these two faithful women, both carrying a child with God's help, can be together at this blessed time of their lives!

Did you notice the honor that was paid Jesus even before he was born? Elizabeth called him "my Lord," and her unborn child leapt with gladness when Mary first appeared. On the other hand, others later treated Mary and her yet-to-be-born child with little respect, as we shall see. Luke 1:26-56.

- What does Gabriel say to help Mary understand how she would become pregnant?

- How was Jesus honored before he was born?

- What does Mary say in a prophetic song in praise of God?

- How long does Mary stay with Elizabeth, and why is it appropriate that Mary stay with Elizabeth during this time?

The Preparer of the Way Is Born

ELIZABETH is almost ready to have her baby. For these past three months, Mary has been staying with her. But now it is time for Mary to say good-bye and to make the long trip back home to Nazareth. In about six months she too will have a baby.

Soon after Mary leaves, Elizabeth gives birth. What joy there is when the birth is successful and Elizabeth and the baby are in good health! When Elizabeth shows the little one to her neighbors and relatives, they all rejoice with her.

The eighth day after his birth, according to God's Law, a baby boy in Israel must be circumcised. For this occasion friends and relatives come to visit. They say that the boy should be named after his father,

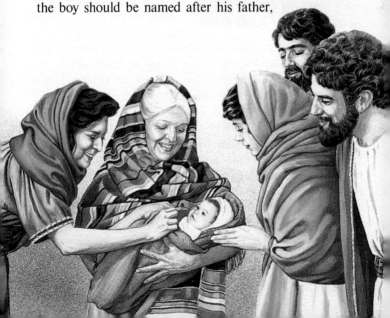

Zechariah. But Elizabeth speaks up. "No, indeed!" she says, "but he shall be called John." Remember, that is the name the angel Gabriel said should be given to the child.

Their friends, however, protest: "There is no one among your relatives that is called by this name." Then, using sign language, they ask what his father wants to name the boy. Asking for a writing tablet, Zechariah, to the astonishment of all, writes: "John is its name."

With that, Zechariah's speech is miraculously restored. You will recall that he lost his ability to speak when he did not believe the angel's announcement that Elizabeth would have a child. Well, when Zechariah speaks, all those living in the neighborhood are amazed and say to themselves: "What really will this young child be?"

Zechariah is now filled with holy spirit, and he exults: "Blessed be Jehovah the God of Israel, because he has turned his attention and performed deliverance toward his people. And he has raised up a horn of salvation for us in the house of David his servant." This "horn of salvation," of course, is the Lord Jesus, who is yet to be born. By means of him, Zechariah says, God will "grant us, after we have been rescued from the hands of enemies, the privilege of fearlessly rendering sacred service to him with loyalty and righteousness before him all our days."

Then Zechariah foretells regarding his son, John: "But as for you, young child, you will be called a prophet of the Most High, for you will go in advance before Jehovah to make his ways ready, to give knowledge of salvation to his people by forgiveness of their sins, because of the tender compassion of our God. With this compassion a daybreak will visit us from on high, to give light to those sitting in darkness and death's shadow, to direct our feet prosperously in the way of peace."

By this time Mary, who evidently is still an unmarried woman, has arrived home in Nazareth. What will happen to her when it becomes obvious that she is pregnant? **Luke 1: 56-80; Leviticus 12:2, 3.**

- How much older is John than Jesus?
- What things happen when John is eight days old?
- How has God turned his attention to his people?
- What work is John foretold to do?

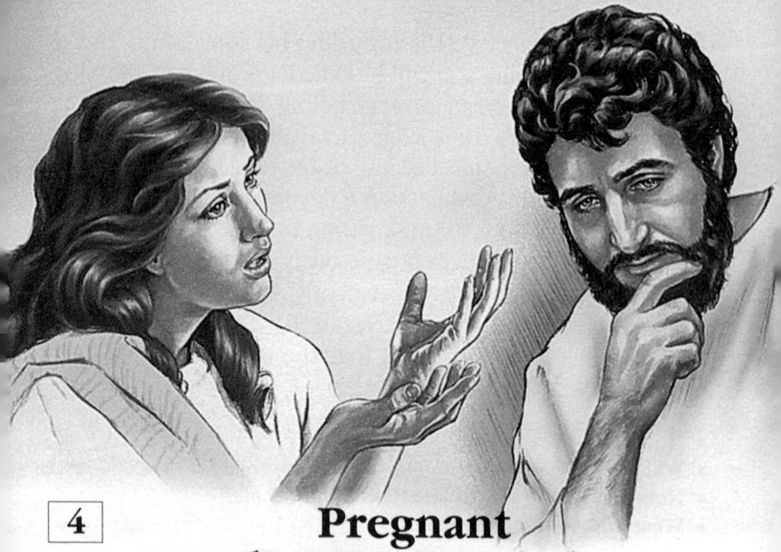

4

Pregnant but Not Married

MARY is in the third month of pregnancy. You will remember that she spent the early part of her pregnancy visiting Elizabeth, but now she has returned home to Nazareth. Soon her condition will become public knowledge in her hometown. She, indeed, is in a distressing situation!

What makes the situation worse is that Mary is engaged to become the wife of the carpenter Joseph. And she knows that, under God's law to Israel, a woman who is engaged to one man but who willingly has sexual relations with another man is to be stoned to death. How can she explain her pregnancy to Joseph?

Since Mary has been gone three months, we can be sure Joseph is eager to see her. When they meet, likely Mary breaks the news to him. She may do her best to explain that it is by means of God's holy spirit that she is pregnant.

But, as you can imagine, this is a very difficult thing for Joseph to believe.

Joseph knows the fine reputation Mary has. And apparently he loves her dearly. Yet, despite what she may claim, it really seems she is pregnant by some man. Even so, Joseph does not want her to be stoned to death or to be disgraced publicly. So he makes up his mind to divorce her secretly. In those days, engaged persons were viewed as married, and a divorce was required to end an engagement.

Later, as Joseph is still considering these matters, he goes to sleep. Jehovah's angel appears to him in a dream and says: "Do not be afraid to take Mary your wife home, for that which has been begotten in her is by holy spirit. She will give birth to a son, and you must call his name Jesus, for he will save his people from their sins."

When Joseph wakes up, how grateful he is! Without delay he does just what the angel directed. He takes Mary to his home. This public action serves, in effect, as a marriage ceremony, giving notice that Joseph and Mary are now officially married. But Joseph does not have sexual relations with Mary as long as she is pregnant with Jesus.

Look! Mary is heavy with child, yet Joseph is putting her on a donkey. Where are they going, and why are they making a trip when Mary is about ready to give birth? **Luke 1:39-41, 56; Matthew 1:18-25; Deuteronomy 22:23, 24.**

- What is Joseph's state of mind when learning of Mary's pregnancy, and why?
- How can Joseph divorce Mary when they are not yet married?
- What public action serves as Joseph and Mary's marriage ceremony?

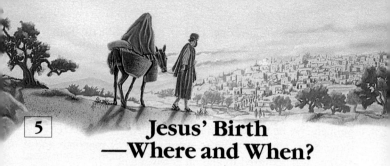

Jesus' Birth
—Where and When?

THE emperor of the Roman Empire, Caesar Augustus, has decreed that everyone must return to the city of his birth to be registered. So Joseph travels to his birthplace, the city of Bethlehem.

A lot of people are in Bethlehem to register, and the only place that Joseph and Mary can find to stay is in a stable. Here, where donkeys and other animals are kept, Jesus is born. Mary wraps him in strips of cloth and lays him in a manger, the place that holds the food for the animals.

Surely it was at God's direction that Caesar Augustus made his registration law. This made it possible for Jesus to be born in Bethlehem, the city the Scriptures had long before foretold would be the birthplace of the promised ruler.

What an important night this is! Out in the fields a bright light gleams around a group of shepherds. It is Jehovah's glory! And Jehovah's angel tells them: "Have no fear, for, look! I am declaring to you good news of a great joy that all the people will have, because there was born to you today a Savior, who is Christ the Lord, in David's city. And this is a sign for you: you will find an infant bound in cloth bands and lying in a manger." Suddenly many more angels appear and sing: "Glory in the heights above to God, and upon earth peace among men of goodwill."

When the angels leave, the shepherds say to one another: "Let us by all means go clear to Bethlehem and see this thing that has taken place, which Jehovah has made known to us." They go in a hurry and find Jesus just where the angel said they would. When the shepherds relate what the angel told them, all who hear about it marvel. Mary safeguards all these sayings and cherishes them in her heart.

Many people today believe that Jesus was born on December 25. But December is a rainy, cold season in Bethlehem. Shepherds would not be out in the fields overnight with their flocks at that time of the year. Also, the Roman Caesar would not likely have required a people who were already inclined to revolt against him to make that trip in the dead of winter to register. Evidently Jesus was born sometime in the early autumn of the year. *Luke 2:1-20; Micah 5:2.*

- Why do Joseph and Mary travel to Bethlehem?
- What marvelous thing happens the night Jesus is born?
- How do we know that Jesus was not born on December 25?

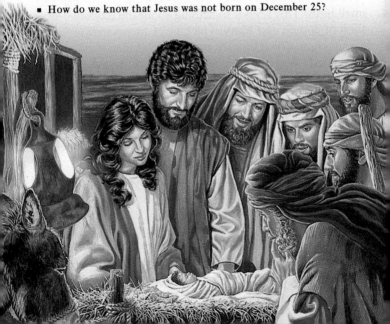

The Child of Promise

INSTEAD of returning to Nazareth, Joseph and Mary remain in Bethlehem. And when Jesus is eight days old, they have him circumcised, as God's Law to Moses commands. It is apparently the custom also to give a baby boy his name on the eighth day. So they name their child Jesus, as the angel Gabriel had directed earlier.

More than a month passes, and Jesus is 40 days old. Where do his parents now take him? To the temple in Jerusalem, which is only a few miles from where they are staying. According to God's Law to Moses, 40 days after giving birth to a son, a mother is required to present a purification offering at the temple.

That is what Mary does. As her offering, she brings two small birds. This reveals something about the economic situation of Joseph and Mary. The Law of Moses indicates that a young ram, which is much more valuable than birds, should be offered. But if the mother could not afford this, two turtledoves or two pigeons would suffice.

In the temple an old man takes Jesus into his arms. His name is Simeon. God has revealed to him that he will not die before he has seen Jehovah's promised Christ, or Messiah. When Simeon comes to the temple on this day, he is directed by holy spirit to the child carried by Joseph and Mary.

As Simeon holds Jesus he thanks God, saying: "Now, Sovereign Lord, you are letting your slave go free in peace according to your declaration; because my eyes have seen your means of saving that you have made ready in the sight of all the peoples, a light for removing the veil from the nations and a glory of your people Israel."

Joseph and Mary are amazed when they hear this. Then Simeon blesses them and says to Mary that her son "is laid for the fall and the rising again of many in Israel" and that sorrow, like a sharp sword, will pierce her soul.

Present on this occasion is the 84-year-old prophetess named Anna. In fact, she is never missing from the temple. In that very hour she comes near and begins giving thanks to God and speaking about Jesus to all those who will listen.

How Joseph and Mary rejoice over these events at the temple! Surely, all of this confirms to them that the child is the Promised One of God. **Luke 2:21-38; Leviticus 12:1-8.**

■ When was it apparently the custom to give a baby Israelite boy his name?

■ What was required of an Israelite mother when her son was 40 days old, and how does the fulfilling of this requirement reveal Mary's economic situation?

■ Who recognize the identity of Jesus on this occasion, and how do they show this?

Jesus and the Astrologers

A NUMBER of men come from the East. They are astrologers—people who claim to interpret the position of stars. While they were at home in the East, they saw a new star, and they have followed it hundreds of miles to Jerusalem.

When the astrologers get to Jerusalem, they ask: "Where is the one born king of the Jews? For we saw his star when we were in the east, and we have come to do him obeisance."

When King Herod at Jerusalem hears about this, he is very upset. So he calls the chief priests and asks where the Christ is to be born. Basing their reply on the Scriptures, they answer: "In Bethlehem." At that, Herod has the astrologers brought to him and tells them: "Go make a careful search for the young child, and when you have found it report back to me, that I too may go and do it obeisance." But, actually, Herod wants to find the child to kill him!

After they leave, an amazing thing happens. The star they had seen when they were in the East travels ahead of them. Clearly, this is no ordinary star, but it has been specially provided to direct them. The astrologers keep following it

until it stops right above the house where Joseph and Mary are staying.

When the astrologers enter the house, they find Mary with her young child, Jesus. At that they all bow down to him. And they take out of their bags gifts of gold, frankincense, and myrrh. Afterward, when they are about to return and tell Herod where the child is, they are warned by God in a dream not to do that. So they leave for their own country by another way.

Who do you think provided the star that moved in the sky to guide the astrologers? Remember, the star did not guide them directly to Jesus in Bethlehem. Rather, they were led to Jerusalem where they came in touch with King Herod, who wanted to kill Jesus. And he would have done so if God had not stepped in and warned the astrologers not to tell Herod where Jesus was. It was God's enemy, Satan the Devil, who wanted Jesus killed, and he used that star to try to accomplish his purpose.   **Matthew 2:1-12; Micah 5:2.**

- What shows that the star the astrologers saw was no ordinary star?
- Where is Jesus when the astrologers find him?
- Why do we know that Satan provided the star to guide the astrologers?

Escape From a Tyrant

JOSEPH wakes up Mary to give her urgent news. Jehovah's angel has just appeared to him, saying: "Get up, take the young child and its mother and flee into Egypt, and stay there until I give you word; for Herod is about to search for the young child to destroy it."

Quickly, the three of them make their escape. And it is just in time because Herod has learned that the astrologers have tricked him and have left the country. Remember, they were supposed to report back to him when they found Jesus. Herod is furious. So in an attempt to kill Jesus, he gives orders to put to death all the boys in Bethlehem and its districts who are two years of age and younger. He bases this age calculation on the information that he obtained earlier from the astrologers who had come from the East.

The slaughter of all the baby boys is something horrible to see! Herod's soldiers break into one home after another. And when they find a baby boy, they grab him from his mother's arms. We have no idea how many babies they kill, but the

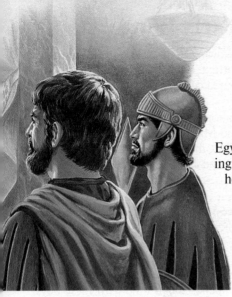

great weeping and wailing of the mothers fulfills a prophecy in the Bible by God's prophet Jeremiah.

In the meantime, Joseph and his family have safely made it to Egypt, and they are now living there. But one night Jehovah's angel again appears to Joseph in a dream. "Get up, take the young child and its mother," the angel says, "and be on your way into the land of Israel, for those who were seeking the soul of the young child are dead." So in fulfillment of another Bible prophecy that says God's Son would be called out of Egypt, the family return to their homeland.

Apparently Joseph intends to settle in Judea, where they were living in the town of Bethlehem before they fled to Egypt. But he learns that Herod's wicked son Archelaus is now the king of Judea, and in another dream he is warned by Jehovah of the danger. So Joseph and his family travel north and settle in the town of Nazareth in Galilee. Here in this community, away from the center of Jewish religious life, Jesus grows up. **Matthew 2:13-23; Jeremiah 31:15; Hosea 11:1.**

■ When the astrologers do not return, what terrible thing does King Herod do, but how is Jesus protected?

■ On returning from Egypt, why does Joseph not again stay in Bethlehem?

■ What Bible prophecies are fulfilled during this period of time?

Jesus' Early Family Life

WHEN Jesus is growing up in Nazareth, it is a rather small, unimportant city. It is located in the hill country of an area called Galilee, not far from the beautiful Jezreel Valley.

When Jesus, perhaps about two years old, is brought here from Egypt by Joseph and Mary, he is evidently Mary's only child. But not for long. In time, James, Joseph, Simon, and Judas are born, and Mary and Joseph become parents to girls also. Eventually Jesus has, at the very least, six younger brothers and sisters.

Jesus has other relatives too. We already know about his older cousin John, who lives many miles away in Judea. But living closer by in Galilee is Salome, who apparently is Mary's sister. Salome is married to Zebedee, so their two boys, James and John, would be Jesus' cousins. We do not know whether, while growing up, Jesus spends much time with these boys, but later they become close companions.

Joseph has to work very hard to support his growing family. He is a carpenter. Joseph raises Jesus as his own son, so Jesus is called "the carpenter's son." Joseph teaches Jesus to be a carpenter too, and he learns well. That is why people later say of Jesus, "This is the carpenter."

The life of Joseph's family is built around the worship of Jehovah God. In keeping with God's Law, Joseph and Mary give their children spiritual instruction 'when they sit in their house, when they walk on the road, when they lie down, and when they get up.' There is a synagogue in Nazareth, and we can be sure that Joseph also regularly takes his family along to worship there. But no doubt they find their greatest enjoyment in regular trips to Jehovah's temple in Jerusalem.

Matthew 13:55, 56; 27:56; Mark 15:40; 6:3; Deuteronomy 6:6-9.

■ At least how many younger brothers and sisters does Jesus have, and what are the names of some of them?

■ Who are three well-known cousins of Jesus?

■ What secular occupation does Jesus eventually take up, and why?

■ What vital instruction does Joseph provide for his family?

Trips to Jerusalem

SPRING has arrived. And it is time for Joseph's family, along with friends and relatives, to make their yearly springtime trip to Jerusalem to celebrate the Passover. As they leave on what is about a 65-mile journey, there is the usual excitement. Jesus is now 12 years old, and he looks forward with special interest to the festival.

To Jesus and his family, the Passover is not just a one-day affair. They also stay for the following seven-day Festival of Unfermented Cakes, which they consider part of the Passover season. As a result, the entire trip from their home in Nazareth, including the stay in Jerusalem, takes about two weeks. But this year, because of something that involves Jesus, it takes longer.

The problem comes to light on the return trip from Jerusalem. Joseph and Mary assume that Jesus is in the group of relatives and friends traveling together. Yet he does not show up when they stop for the night, and they go hunting for him among their traveling companions. He is nowhere to be found. So Joseph and Mary go all the way back to Jerusalem to look for him.

For a whole day they hunt, but without success. The second day they cannot find him either. Finally, on the third day, they go to the temple. There, in one of its halls, they see Jesus sitting in the midst of the Jewish teachers, listening to them and asking questions.

"Child, why did you treat us this way?" Mary asks. "Here your father and I in mental distress have been looking for you."

Jesus is surprised that they did not know where to find him. "Why did you have to go looking for me?" he asks. "Did you not know that I must be in the house of my Father?"

Jesus cannot understand why his parents would not know this. At that, Jesus returns home with his parents and contin-

ues subject to them. He goes on progressing in wisdom and in physical growth and in favor with God and men. Yes, from his childhood on, Jesus sets a fine example not only in seeking spiritual interests but also in showing respect to his parents. Luke 2:40-52; 22:7.

■ What springtime trip does Jesus regularly make with his family, and how long is it?

■ What happens during the trip they make when Jesus is 12 years old?

■ What example does Jesus set for youths today?

John Prepares the Way

SEVENTEEN years have passed since Jesus was a child of 12 questioning the teachers in the temple. It is the spring of the year 29 C.E., and everybody, it seems, is talking about Jesus' cousin John, who is preaching in all the country around the Jordan River.

John is indeed an impressive man, both in appearance and in speech. His clothing is of camel hair, and he wears a leather girdle around his loins. His food is insect locusts and wild honey. And his message? "Repent, for the kingdom of the heavens has drawn near."

This message excites his listeners. Many realize their need to repent, that is, to change their attitude and to reject their past course of life as undesirable. So from all the territory around the Jordan, and even from Jerusalem, the people come out to John in great numbers, and he baptizes them, dipping them beneath the waters of the Jordan. Why?

John baptizes people in symbol, or acknowledgment, of their heartfelt repentance for sins against God's Law covenant. Thus, when some Pharisees and Sadducees come out to the Jordan, John condemns them. "You offspring of vipers," he says. "Produce fruit that befits repentance; and do not presume to say to yourselves, 'As a father we have Abraham.' For I say to you that God is able to raise up children to Abraham from these stones. Already the ax is lying at the root of the trees; every tree, then, that does not produce fine fruit is to be cut down and thrown into the fire."

Because of all the attention John is receiving, the Jews send out priests and Levites to him. These ask: "Who are you?"

"I am not the Christ," John confesses.

"What, then?" they inquire. "Are you Elijah?"

"I am not," he answers.

"Are you The Prophet?"

"No!"

So they become insistent: "Who are you? that we may give an answer to those who sent us. What do you say about yourself?"

John explains: "I am a voice of someone crying out in the wilderness, 'Make the way of Jehovah straight,' just as Isaiah the prophet said."

"Why, then, do you baptize," they want to know, "if you yourself are not the Christ or Elijah or The Prophet?"

"I baptize in water," he answers. "In the midst of you one is standing whom you do not know, the one coming behind me."

John is preparing the way by getting people in a proper heart condition to accept the Messiah, who will become King. Of this One, John says: "The one coming after me is stronger than I am, whose sandals I am not fit to take off." In fact, John even says: "The one coming behind me has advanced in front of me, because he existed before me."

Thus, John's message, "the kingdom of the heavens has drawn near," serves as a public notification that the ministry of Jehovah's appointed King, Jesus Christ, is about to begin. **John 1:6-8, 15-28; Matthew 3:1-12; Luke 3:1-18; Acts 19:4.**

- What kind of man is John?
- Why does John baptize people?
- Why can John say that the Kingdom has drawn near?

Jesus' Baptism

ABOUT six months after John begins preaching, Jesus, who is now 30 years old, comes to him at the Jordan. For what reason? To pay a social visit? Is Jesus simply interested in how John's work is progressing? No, Jesus asks John to baptize him.

Right away John objects: "I am the one needing to be baptized by you, and are you coming to me?" John knows that his cousin Jesus is God's special Son. Why, John had jumped with gladness in his mother's belly when Mary, pregnant with Jesus, visited them! John's mother, Elizabeth, no doubt later told him about this. And she would also have told him about the angel's announcement of Jesus' birth and about the appearance of angels to shepherds the night Jesus was born.

So Jesus is no stranger to John. And John knows that his baptism is not for Jesus. It is for those repenting of their sins, but Jesus is without sin. Yet, despite John's objection, Jesus insists: "Let it be, this time, for in that way it is suitable for us to carry out all that is righteous."

Why is it right for Jesus to be baptized? Because Jesus' baptism is a symbol, not of repentance for sins, but of his presenting himself to do the will of his Father. Jesus has been a carpenter, but now the time has come for him to begin the ministry that Jehovah God sent him to earth to perform. Do you think John expects anything unusual to happen when he baptizes Jesus?

Well, John later reports: "The very One who sent me to baptize in water said to me, 'Whoever it is upon whom you see the spirit coming down and remaining, this is the one that baptizes in holy spirit.'" So John is expecting God's spirit to come upon someone he baptizes. Perhaps, therefore, he is not really surprised when, as Jesus comes up from the water, John sees "like a dove God's spirit coming upon him."

But more than that happens as Jesus is baptized. 'The heavens are opened up' to him. What does this mean? Evidently it means that while he is being baptized, the memory of his prehuman life in heaven returns to him. Thus, Jesus now fully recalls his life as a spirit son of Jehovah God, including all the things that God spoke to him in heaven during his prehuman existence.

In addition, at the time of his baptism, a voice from heaven proclaims: "This is my Son, the beloved, whom I have approved." Whose voice is that? Jesus' own voice? Of course not! It is God's. Clearly, Jesus is God's Son, not God himself, as some people claim.

However, Jesus is a human son of God, even as was the first man, Adam. The disciple Luke, after describing Jesus' baptism, writes: "Jesus himself, when he commenced his work, was about thirty years old, being the son, as the opinion was, of Joseph, son of Heli, . . . son of David, . . . son of Abraham, . . . son of Noah, . . . son of Adam, son of God."

As Adam was a human "son of God," so is Jesus. Jesus is the greatest man who ever lived, which becomes evident when

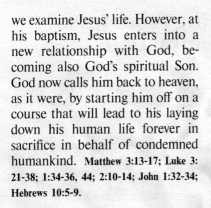

we examine Jesus' life. However, at his baptism, Jesus enters into a new relationship with God, becoming also God's spiritual Son. God now calls him back to heaven, as it were, by starting him off on a course that will lead to his laying down his human life forever in sacrifice in behalf of condemned humankind. **Matthew 3:13-17; Luke 3: 21-38; 1:34-36, 44; 2:10-14; John 1:32-34; Hebrews 10:5-9.**

- Why is Jesus no stranger to John?

- Since he has committed no sins, why is Jesus baptized?

- In view of what John knows about Jesus, why might he not be surprised when God's spirit comes upon Jesus?

Learning From Jesus' Temptations

IMMEDIATELY after his baptism, Jesus is led by God's spirit into the Judean wilderness. He has a lot to think about, for at his baptism "the heavens were opened up," so that he could discern heavenly things. Indeed, there is much for him to meditate on!

Jesus spends 40 days and 40 nights in the wilderness and eats nothing during this time. Then, when Jesus is very hungry, the Devil approaches to tempt him, saying: "If you are a son of God, tell these stones to become loaves of bread." But Jesus knows it is wrong to use his miraculous powers to satisfy his personal desires. So he refuses to be tempted.

But the Devil does not give up. He tries another approach. He challenges Jesus to leap off the temple wall so that God's angels will rescue him. But Jesus is not tempted to make such a spectacular display. Quoting from the Scriptures, Jesus shows that it is wrong to put God to the test in this way.

In a third temptation, the Devil shows Jesus all the kingdoms of the world in some miraculous way and says: "All these things I will give you if you fall down and do an act of worship to me." But again Jesus refuses to yield to temptation to do wrong, choosing to remain faithful to God.

We can learn from these temptations of Jesus. They show, for example, that the Devil is not a mere quality of evil, as some people claim, but that he is a real, invisible person. The temptation of Jesus also shows that all the world governments are the Devil's property. For how could the Devil's offering them to Christ have been a real temptation if they were not really his?

And think of this: The Devil said he was willing to reward Jesus for one act of worship, even giving him *all the kingdoms of the world*. The Devil may well try to tempt us in a similar

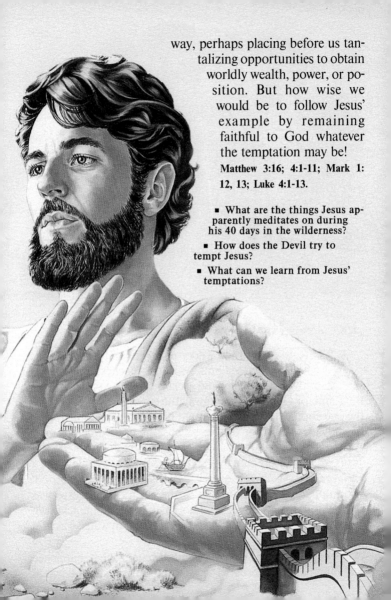

way, perhaps placing before us tantalizing opportunities to obtain worldly wealth, power, or position. But how wise we would be to follow Jesus' example by remaining faithful to God whatever the temptation may be!

Matthew 3:16; 4:1-11; Mark 1: 12, 13; Luke 4:1-13.

■ What are the things Jesus apparently meditates on during his 40 days in the wilderness?

■ How does the Devil try to tempt Jesus?

■ What can we learn from Jesus' temptations?

14   **Jesus' First Disciples**

AFTER 40 days in the wilderness, Jesus returns to John, who had baptized him. As he approaches, John apparently points to him and exclaims to those present: "See, the Lamb of God that takes away the sin of the world! This is the one about whom I said, Behind me there comes a man who has advanced in front of me, because he existed before me." Although John is older than his cousin Jesus, John knows that Jesus existed before him as a spirit person in heaven.

Yet, a few weeks earlier, when Jesus came to be baptized, John apparently did not know with certainty that Jesus was to be the Messiah. "Even I did not know him," John acknowledges, "but the reason why I came baptizing in water was that he might be made manifest to Israel."

John goes on to explain to his listeners what happened when he baptized Jesus: "I viewed the spirit coming down as

a dove out of heaven, and it remained upon him. Even I did not know him, but the very One who sent me to baptize in water said to me, 'Whoever it is upon whom you see the spirit coming down and remaining, this is the one that baptizes in holy spirit.' And I have seen it, and I have borne witness that this one is the Son of God."

The next day John is standing with two of his disciples. Again, as Jesus approaches, he says: "See, the Lamb of God!" At this, these two disciples of John the Baptizer follow Jesus. One of them is Andrew, and the other is evidently the very person who recorded these things, who was also named John. This John, according to indications, is also a cousin of Jesus, apparently being a son of Mary's sister, Salome.

Turning and seeing Andrew and John following him, Jesus asks: "What are you looking for?"

"Rabbi," they ask, "where are you staying?"

"Come, and you will see," Jesus answers.

It is about four o'clock in the afternoon, and Andrew and John stay with Jesus the rest of that day. Afterward Andrew is so excited that he hurries to find his brother, who is called Peter. "We have found the Messiah," he tells him. And he takes Peter to Jesus. Perhaps John at the same time finds his brother James and brings him to Jesus; yet, characteristically, John omits this personal information from his Gospel.

The next day, Jesus finds Philip, who is from Bethsaida, the same city Andrew and Peter were originally from. He invites him: "Be my follower."

Philip then finds Nathanael, who is also called Bartholomew, and says: "We have found the one of whom Moses, in the Law, and the Prophets wrote, Jesus, the son of Joseph, from Nazareth." Nathanael is doubtful. "Can anything good come out of Nazareth?" he asks.

"Come and see," Philip urges. When they are coming toward Jesus, Jesus says about Nathanael: "See, an Israelite for a certainty, in whom there is no deceit."

"How does it come that you know me?" Nathanael asks.

"Before Philip called you, while you were under the fig tree, I saw you," Jesus answers.

Nathanael is amazed. "Rabbi [meaning Teacher], you are the Son of God, you are King of Israel," he says.

"Because I told you I saw you underneath the fig tree do you believe?" Jesus asks. "You will see things greater than these." Then he promises: "Most truly I say to you men, You will see heaven opened up and the angels of God ascending and descending to the Son of man."

Very soon after this, Jesus, along with his newly acquired disciples, leaves the Jordan Valley and travels to Galilee. John 1:29-51.

- Who are the first disciples of Jesus?
- How is Peter, as well as perhaps James, introduced to Jesus?
- What convinces Nathanael that Jesus is the Son of God?

15   **Jesus' First Miracle**

IT HAS been only a day or two since Andrew, Peter, John, Philip, Nathanael, and perhaps James became Jesus' first disciples. These now are on their way home to the district of Galilee, where all of them originated. Their destination is Cana, the hometown of Nathanael, located in the hills not far from Nazareth, where Jesus himself grew up. They have been invited to a wedding feast in Cana.

Jesus' mother too has come to the wedding. As a friend of the family of the ones getting married, Mary appears to have been involved in ministering to the needs of the many guests. So she is quick to note a shortage, which she reports to Jesus: "They have no wine."

When Mary thus, in effect, suggests that Jesus do something about the lack of wine, Jesus at first is reluctant. "What have I to do with you?" he asks. As God's appointed King, he is not to be directed in his activity by family or friends. So Mary wisely leaves the matter in her son's hands, simply saying to those ministering: "Whatever he tells you, do."

Well, there are six large stone water jars, each of which can hold over ten gallons. Jesus instructs those ministering: "Fill the water jars with water." And the attendants fill them to the brim. Then Jesus says: "Draw some out now and take it to the director of the feast."

The director is impressed by the fine quality of the wine, not realizing that it has been miraculously produced. Calling the bridegroom, he says: "Every other man puts out the fine wine first, and when people are intoxicated, the inferior. You have reserved the fine wine until now."

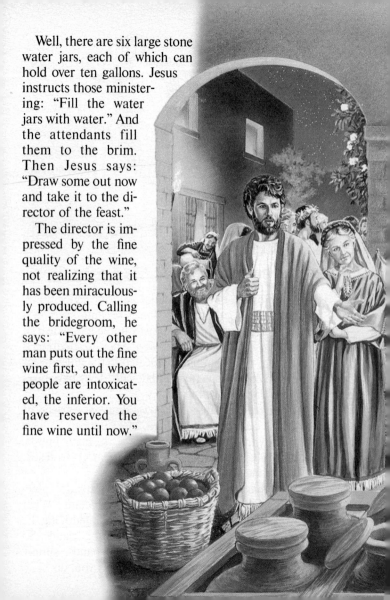

This is the first miracle of Jesus, and on their seeing it, the faith of his new disciples is strengthened. Afterward, along with his mother and his half brothers, they travel to the city of Capernaum near the Sea of Galilee. **John 2:1-12.**

- When during Jesus' ministry does the wedding in Cana occur?

- Why does Jesus object to his mother's suggestion?

- What miracle does Jesus perform, and what effect does it have on others?

16

Zeal for Jehovah's Worship

JESUS' half brothers—Mary's other sons—are James, Joseph, Simon, and Judas. Before these all travel with Jesus and his disciples to Capernaum, a city near the Sea of Galilee, perhaps they stop at their home in Nazareth so that the family can pack the things they will need.

But why does Jesus go to Capernaum rather than carry on his ministry in Cana, in Nazareth, or in some other place in the hills of Galilee? For one thing, Capernaum is more prominently situated and is evidently a larger city. Also,

most of Jesus' newly acquired disciples live in or near Capernaum, so they will not have to leave their homes to receive training from him.

During his stay in Capernaum, Jesus performs marvelous works, as he himself testifies some months later. But soon Jesus and his companions are on the road again. It is spring, and they are on their way to Jerusalem to attend the Passover of 30 C.E. While there, his disciples see something about Jesus that they have perhaps not seen before.

According to God's Law, Israelites are required to make animal sacrifices. So, for their convenience, merchants in Jerusalem sell animals or birds for this purpose. But they are selling right inside the temple, and they are cheating the people by charging them too much.

Filled with indignation, Jesus makes a whip of ropes and drives the sellers out. He pours out the coins of the money changers and overturns their tables. "Take these things away from here!" he cries out to those selling the doves. "Stop making the house of my Father a house of merchandise!"

When Jesus' disciples see this, they remember the prophecy about God's Son: "The zeal for your house will eat me up." But the Jews ask: "What sign have you to show us, since you are doing these things?" Jesus answers: "Break down this temple, and in three days I will raise it up."

The Jews assume that Jesus is talking about the literal temple, and so they ask: "This temple was built in forty-six years, and will you raise it up in three days?" However, Jesus is talking about the temple of his body. And three years later, his disciples remember this saying of his when he is raised from the dead. **John 2:12-22; Matthew 13:55; Luke 4:23.**

- After the wedding in Cana, to what places does Jesus travel?
- Why is Jesus indignant, and what does he do?
- What do Jesus' disciples recall on seeing his actions?
- What does Jesus say about "this temple," and what does he mean?

17

Teaching Nicodemus

WHILE he is attending the Passover of 30 C.E., Jesus performs remarkable signs, or miracles. As a result, many people put their faith in him. Nicodemus, a member of the Sanhedrin, the Jewish high court, is impressed and wants to learn more. So he visits Jesus during the darkness of night, probably fearing that his reputation with other Jewish leaders will be damaged if he is seen.

"Rabbi," he says, "we know that you as a teacher have come from God; for no one can perform these signs that you perform unless God is with him." In reply, Jesus tells Nicodemus that in order to enter the Kingdom of God, a person must be "born again."

Yet, how can a person be born again? "He cannot

enter into the womb of his mother a second time and be born, can he?" Nicodemus asks.

No, that is not what being born again means. "Unless anyone is born from water and spirit," Jesus explains, "he cannot enter into the kingdom of God." When Jesus was baptized and holy spirit descended upon him, he was thus born "from water and spirit." By the accompanying declaration from heaven, 'This is my Son whom I have approved,' God announced that he had brought forth a spiritual son having the prospect of entering into the heavenly Kingdom. Later, at Pentecost 33 C.E., other baptized ones will receive holy spirit and will thus also be born again as spiritual sons of God.

But the role of God's special human Son is

vital. "Just as Moses lifted up the serpent in the wilderness," Jesus tells Nicodemus, "so the Son of man must be lifted up, that everyone believing in him may have everlasting life." Yes, as those Israelites bitten by poisonous snakes had to look at the copper serpent to be saved, so all humans need to exercise faith in God's Son to be saved from their dying condition.

Stressing Jehovah's loving role in this, Jesus next tells Nicodemus: "God loved the world so much that he gave his only-begotten Son, in order that everyone exercising faith in him might not be destroyed but have everlasting life." Thus, here in Jerusalem just six months after beginning his ministry, Jesus makes clear that he is Jehovah God's means for saving humankind.

Jesus goes on to explain further to Nicodemus: "For God sent forth his Son into the world, not for him to judge the world," that is, not to judge it adversely, or condemn it, sentencing the human race to destruction. Rather, as Jesus says, he was sent "for the world to be saved through him."

Nicodemus has fearfully come to Jesus under cover of darkness. So it is interesting that Jesus closes his conversation with him by saying: "Now this is the basis for judgment, that the light [which Jesus personified in his life and teachings] has come into the world but men have loved the darkness rather than the light, for their works were wicked. For he that practices vile things hates the light and does not come to the light, in order that his works may not be reproved. But he that does what is true comes to the light, in order that his works may be made manifest as having been worked in harmony with God." **John 2:23–3:21; Matthew 3:16, 17; Acts 2:1-4; Numbers 21:9.**

- What prompts Nicodemus' visit, and why does he come at night?
- What does it mean to be "born again"?
- How does Jesus illustrate his role in our salvation?
- What does it mean that Jesus did not come to judge the world?

18

John Decreases, Jesus Increases

FOLLOWING the Passover in the spring of 30 C.E., Jesus and his disciples leave Jerusalem. However, they do not return to their homes in Galilee but go into the country of Judea, where they do baptizing. John the Baptizer has been doing the same work for about a year now, and he still has disciples associating with him.

Actually, Jesus does not do any baptizing himself, but his disciples do it under his direction. Their baptism has the same significance as that performed by John, it being a symbol of a Jew's repentance of sins against God's Law covenant. However, after his resurrection, Jesus instructs his disciples to do baptizing that has a different significance. Christian baptism today is a symbol of a person's dedication to serve Jehovah God.

At this early point in Jesus' ministry, however, both John and he, although working separately, are teaching and baptizing repentant ones. But John's disciples become jealous and complain to him regarding Jesus: "Rabbi, . . . see, this one is baptizing and all are going to him."

Rather than being jealous, John rejoices in Jesus' success and also wants his disciples to rejoice. He reminds them: "You yourselves bear me witness that I said, I am not the Christ, but, I have been sent forth in advance of that one." Then he uses a beautiful illustration: "He that has the bride is the bridegroom. However, the friend of the bridegroom, when he stands and hears him, has a great deal of joy on account of the voice of the bridegroom. Therefore this joy of mine has been made full."

John, as the friend of the Bridegroom, rejoiced some six months earlier when he introduced his disciples to Jesus. Certain ones of them became prospective members of Christ's heavenly bride class to be made up of Christians anointed with the spirit. John wants his present disciples also to follow Jesus, since his purpose is to prepare the way for Christ's successful ministry. As John the Baptizer explains: "That one must go on increasing, but I must go on decreasing."

Jesus' new disciple John, who earlier had also been a disciple of John the Baptizer, writes regarding Jesus' origin and His important role in human salvation, saying: "He that comes from heaven is over all others. . . . The Father loves the Son and has given all things into his hand. He that exercises faith in the Son has everlasting life; he that disobeys the Son will not see life, but the wrath of God remains upon him."

Not long after John the Baptizer discusses the decrease of his own activity, he is arrested by King Herod. Herod has taken Herodias, the wife of Philip his brother, as his own, and when John publicly exposes his actions as improper, Herod has him put in prison. When Jesus hears about John's arrest, he leaves Judea with his disciples for Galilee.

John 3:22–4:3; Acts 19:4; Matthew 28: 19; 2 Corinthians 11:2; Mark 1:14; 6:17-20.

∎ What is the significance of baptisms done under Jesus' direction prior to his resurrection? And after his resurrection?

∎ How does John show that his disciples' complaint is unwarranted?

∎ Why is John put in prison?

19

Teaching a Samaritan Woman

ON THEIR way from Judea to Galilee, Jesus and his disciples travel through the district of Samaria. Tired from the journey, about noon they stop to rest by a well near the city of Sychar. This well was dug centuries before by Jacob, and it remains even down until today, near the modern-day city of Nablus.

While Jesus rests here, his disciples go into the city to buy some food. When a Samaritan woman comes to draw water, he requests: "Give me a drink."

Jews and Samaritans generally have no dealings with one another because of deep-seated prejudices. So, in astonishment, the woman asks: "How is it that you, despite being a Jew, ask me for a drink, when I am a Samaritan woman?"

"If you had known," Jesus answers, "who it is that says to you, 'Give me a drink,' you would have asked him, and he would have given you living water."

"Sir," she replies, "you have not even a bucket for drawing water, and the well is deep. From what source, therefore, do you have this living water? You are not greater than our forefather Jacob, who gave us the well and who himself together with his sons and his cattle drank out of it, are you?"

"Everyone drinking from this water will get thirsty again," Jesus observes. "Whoever drinks from the water that I will give him will never get thirsty at all, but the water that I will give him will become in him a fountain of water bubbling up to impart everlasting life."

"Sir, give me this water, so that I may neither thirst nor keep coming over to this place to draw water," the woman responds.

Jesus now says to her: "Go, call your husband and come to this place."

"I do not have a husband," she answers.

Jesus verifies her statement. "You said well, 'A husband I do not have.' For you have had five husbands, and the man you now have is not your husband."

"Sir, I perceive you are a prophet," the woman says in amazement. Revealing her spiritual interest, she notes that the Samaritans "worshiped in this mountain [Gerizim, which stands nearby]; but you people [the Jews] say that in Jerusalem is the place where persons ought to worship."

Yet, the place of worship is not the important thing, Jesus points out. "The hour is coming," he says, "when the true worshipers will worship the Father with spirit and truth, for, indeed, the Father is looking for suchlike ones to worship him. God is a Spirit, and those worshiping him must worship with spirit and truth."

The woman is deeply impressed. "I know that Messiah is coming, who is called Christ," she says. "Whenever that one arrives, he will declare all things to us openly."

"I who am speaking to you am he," Jesus declares. Think of it! This woman who comes at midday to draw water, perhaps in order to avoid contact with townswomen who despise her for her way of life, is favored in a wonderful way by Jesus. Point-blank he tells her what he has not confessed openly to anyone else. With what consequences?

Many Samaritans Believe

On returning from Sychar with food, the disciples find Jesus at Jacob's well where they left him, and where he is now talking with a Samaritan woman. When the disciples arrive, she departs, leaving her water jar, and heads for the city.

Interested deeply in the things Jesus told her, she tells the men in the city: "Come here, see a man that told me all the things I did." Then, in such a way as to arouse curiosity, she asks: "This is not perhaps the Christ, is it?" The question accomplishes its purpose—the men go to see for themselves.

Meanwhile, the disciples urge Jesus to eat the food that they have brought from the city. But he replies: "I have food to eat of which you do not know."

"No one has brought him anything to eat, has he?" the disciples ask one another. Jesus explains: "My food is for me to do the will of him that sent me and to finish his work. Do you not say that there are yet four months before the harvest comes?" However, pointing to the spiritual harvest, Jesus

says: "Lift up your eyes and view the fields, that they are white for harvesting. Already the reaper is receiving wages and gathering fruit for everlasting life, so that the sower and the reaper may rejoice together."

Perhaps Jesus can already see the grand effect of his encounter with the Samaritan woman—that many are putting faith in him on account of her testimony. She is witnessing to the townspeople, saying: "He told me all the things I did." Therefore, when the men of Sychar come to him at the well, they ask him to stay and talk to them more. Jesus accepts the invitation and remains for two days.

As the Samaritans listen to Jesus, many more believe. Then they say to the woman: "We do not believe any longer on account of your talk; for we have heard for ourselves and we know that this man is for a certainty the savior of the world." Surely the Samaritan woman provides a fine example of how we can witness about Christ by arousing curiosity so that listeners will search further!

Recall that it is four months before the harvest—evidently the barley harvest, which in Palestine occurs in the spring. So it is now probably November or December. This means that following the Passover of 30 C.E., Jesus and his disciples spent eight months or so in Judea teaching and baptizing. They leave now for their home territory of Galilee. What awaits them there? John 4:3-43.

- Why is the Samaritan woman surprised that Jesus spoke to her?
- What does Jesus teach her about living water and where to worship?
- How does Jesus reveal to her who he is, and why is this disclosure so amazing?
- What witnessing does the Samaritan woman do and with what result?
- How is Jesus' food related to the harvest?
- How can we determine the length of Jesus' ministry in Judea following the Passover of 30 C.E.?

20

Second Miracle
While in Cana

WHEN Jesus returns to his home territory after an extended preaching campaign in Judea, it is not to rest up. Rather, he begins an even greater ministry in Galilee, the land where he grew up. But his disciples, instead of staying with him, return home to their families and their former occupations.

What message does Jesus begin preaching? This: "The kingdom of God has drawn near. Be repentant, you people, and have faith in the good news." And the response? The Galileans receive Jesus. He is held in honor by all. However, this is not particularly due to his message but, rather, because many of them were at the Passover in Jerusalem months before and saw the remarkable signs he performed.

Jesus apparently begins his great Galilean ministry in Cana. Earlier, you may recall, on returning from Judea, he turned water into wine at a wedding feast there. On this second occasion, the child of a government official of King Herod Antipas is very sick. Hearing that Jesus has come from Judea to Cana, the official travels all the way from his home in Capernaum to find Jesus. Grief-stricken, the man urges: 'Please come immediately, before my child dies.'

Jesus responds: 'Go back home. Your son is healed!' Herod's official believes and starts on the long trip home. On the way he is met by his servants, who have hurried to tell him that all is well—his son has recovered! 'When did he get better?' he asks.

'Yesterday at 1:00 p.m.,' they answer.

The official realizes that this is the very hour when Jesus said, 'Your son is healed!' After that, the man and his entire household become disciples of Christ.

Cana thus became favored as the place where, signaling his return from Judea, Jesus twice performed miracles. These, of course, are not the only miracles he performed up to this time, but they are significant because they marked his return to Galilee.

Jesus now heads home to Nazareth. What awaits him there?   John 4:43-54; Mark 1:14, 15; Luke 4:14, 15.

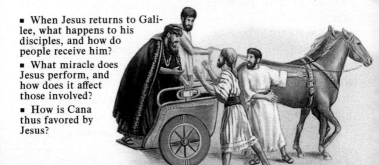

■ When Jesus returns to Galilee, what happens to his disciples, and how do people receive him?

■ What miracle does Jesus perform, and how does it affect those involved?

■ How is Cana thus favored by Jesus?

21

In Jesus' Hometown Synagogue

THERE is no doubt a stir of excitement in Nazareth when Jesus returns home. Before he left to be baptized by John a little over a year before, Jesus was known as a carpenter. But now he is known far and wide as a miracle worker. The local residents are eager to see him do some of these marvelous works among them.

Their anticipation rises as Jesus, according to his custom, goes to the local synagogue. During the services, he stands up to read, and the scroll of the prophet Isaiah is handed to him. He finds the place where it tells of the One anointed by Jehovah's spirit, which place in our Bible today is chapter 61.

After reading about how this One would preach a release to the captives, a recovery of sight to the blind, and about Jehovah's acceptable year, Jesus hands the scroll back to the attendant and sits down. All eyes are intently fixed upon him. Then he speaks, probably at some length, explaining: *"Today this scripture that you just heard is fulfilled."*

The people marvel at his "winsome words" and say to one another: "This is a son of Joseph, is it not?" But knowing that they want to see him perform miracles, Jesus continues: "No doubt you will apply this illustration to me, 'Physician, cure yourself; the things we heard as having happened in Capernaum do also here in your home territory.'" Evidently, Jesus' former neighbors feel that healing should begin at home, for

the benefit of his own people first. So they feel they have been slighted by Jesus.

Realizing their thinking, Jesus relates some applicable history. There were many widows in Israel during the days of Elijah, he notes, but Elijah was sent to none of those. Rather, he went to a non-Israelite widow in Sidon, where he performed a lifesaving miracle. And in the days of Elisha, there were many lepers, but Elisha cleansed only Naaman from Syria.

Angered by these unfavorable historical comparisons that expose their selfishness and lack of faith, those in the synagogue rise up and rush Jesus outside the city. There, on the brow of the mountain upon which Nazareth is built, they try to throw him over the edge. But Jesus escapes from their grasp and gets away safely. **Luke 4:16-30; 1 Kings 17:8-16; 2 Kings 5:8-14.**

- Why is there a stir of excitement in Nazareth?
- What do the people think of Jesus' speech, but then what makes them so angry?
- What do the people try to do to Jesus?

22

Four Disciples Are Called

AFTER the murderous attempt on Jesus' life in his hometown of Nazareth, he moves to the city of Capernaum near the Sea of Galilee. This fulfills another prophecy of Isaiah. It is the one that foretold that people of Galilee dwelling by the sea would see a great light.

As Jesus carries on his light-bearing work of Kingdom preaching here, he locates four of his disciples. These had traveled with him earlier but went back to their fishing business when they returned with Jesus from Judea. Likely, Jesus now searches them out, since it is time to have steady, regular helpers whom he can train to carry on the ministry after he is gone.

So as Jesus is walking along the seashore and sees Simon Peter and his companions washing their nets, he goes over to them. He climbs into Peter's boat and asks him to pull away

from land. When they get out a little distance, Jesus sits down in the boat and begins teaching the crowds on the shore.

Afterward, Jesus says to Peter: "Pull out to where it is deep, and you men let down your nets for a catch."

"Instructor," Peter replies, "for a whole night we toiled and took nothing, but at your bidding I will lower the nets."

When the nets are lowered, such a great multitude of fish are caught that the nets begin to rip. Urgently, the men motion to their partners in a boat nearby to come and help. Soon both boats are filled with so many fish that they begin to sink. Seeing this, Peter falls down before Jesus and says: "Depart from me, because I am a sinful man, Lord."

"Stop being afraid," Jesus answers. "From now on you will be catching men alive."

Jesus also invites Peter's brother Andrew. "Come after me," he urges them, "and I will make you fishers of men." Their fishing partners James and John, the sons of Zebedee, are given the same invitation, and they too respond without hesitation. So these four abandon their fishing business and become the first four of Jesus' steady, regular followers. **Luke 5:1-11; Matthew 4:13-22; Mark 1:16-20; Isaiah 9:1, 2.**

- Why does Jesus call his disciples to follow him, and who are these?
- What miracle frightens Peter?
- What type of fishing does Jesus invite his disciples to do?

23

More Miracles in Capernaum

THE Sabbath after Jesus called his first four disciples —Peter, Andrew, James, and John—they all go to a local synagogue in Capernaum. There Jesus begins to teach, and the people are astounded because he teaches them as one having authority and not as the scribes.

On this Sabbath a demonized man is present. After a while, he shouts with a loud voice: "What have we to do with you, Jesus you Nazarene? Did you come to destroy us? I know exactly who you are, the Holy One of God."

The demon controlling the man is actually one of Satan's angels. Rebuking the demon, Jesus says: "Be silent, and come on out of him!"

Well, the demon throws the man into a convulsion and yells at the top of its voice. But it comes out of the man without hurting him. Everyone is simply astonished! "What is this?" they ask. "He authoritatively orders even the unclean spirits, and they obey him." The news about this spreads throughout the surrounding area.

Leaving the synagogue, Jesus and his disciples go to the home of Simon, or Peter. There Peter's mother-in-law is very sick with a high fever. 'Please help her,' they beg. So Jesus goes over, takes her by the hand, and raises her up. Right away she is cured and begins to prepare a meal for them!

Later, when the sun has set, people from all over start coming to Peter's house with their sick ones. Soon the whole city is gathered at the door! And Jesus cures all their sick ones, no matter what their diseases are. He even frees the demon-possessed. As they come out, the demons that he expels shout: "You are the Son of God." But Jesus rebukes them and does not allow them to speak because they know he is the Christ. **Mark 1:21-34; Luke 4:31-41; Matthew 8:14-17.**

- What happens in the synagogue on the Sabbath after Jesus calls his four disciples?

- Where does Jesus go when leaving the synagogue, and what miracle does he perform there?

- What happens later that same evening?

24 Why Jesus Came to Earth

JESUS' day in Capernaum with his four disciples has been a busy one, concluding with the people of Capernaum bringing him all their sick ones to be cured during the evening. There has been no time for privacy.

Now it is early the following morning. While it is still dark, Jesus gets up and goes outside by himself. He travels to a lonely place where he can pray to his Father in private. But Jesus' privacy is short-lived because when Peter and others realize that he is missing, they go out searching for him.

When they find Jesus, Peter says: "All are looking for you." The people of Capernaum want Jesus to stay with them. They truly appreciate what he has done for them! But did Jesus

come to earth primarily to perform such miraculous healings? What does he say about this?

According to one Bible account, Jesus answers his disciples: "Let us go somewhere else, into the village towns nearby, that I may preach there also, for it is for this purpose I have gone out." Even though the people urge Jesus to stay, he tells them: "Also to other cities I must declare the good news of the kingdom of God, because for this I was sent forth."

Yes, Jesus came to earth particularly to preach about God's Kingdom, which will vindicate his Father's name and permanently solve all human ills. However, to give evidence that he is sent by God, Jesus performs miraculous healings. In the same way Moses, centuries before, performed miracles to establish his credentials as God's servant.

Now, when Jesus leaves Capernaum to preach in other cities, his four disciples go with him. These four are Peter and his brother Andrew, and John and his brother James. You will recall that just the week before, they had been invited to be Jesus' first traveling coworkers.

Jesus' preaching tour of Galilee with his four disciples is a wonderful success! In fact, the report about his activities spreads even into all Syria. Great crowds from Galilee, Judea, and across the Jordan River follow Jesus and his disciples. **Mark 1:35-39; Luke 4:42, 43; Matthew 4:23-25; Exodus 4:1-9, 30, 31.**

- **What happens the morning after Jesus' busy day in Capernaum?**
- **Why was Jesus sent to earth, and what purpose do his miracles serve?**
- **Who go with Jesus on his preaching tour of Galilee, and what is the response to Jesus' activities?**

25   Compassion for a Leper

AS JESUS and his four disciples visit the cities of Galilee, news about the wonderful things he is doing spreads throughout the district. Word of his deeds reaches one city where there is a man sick with leprosy. The physician Luke describes him as being "full of leprosy." In its advanced stages, this dreadful disease slowly disfigures various parts of the body. So this leper is in a pitiful condition.

When Jesus arrives in the city, the leper approaches him. According to God's Law, a leper is to call out in warning,

"Unclean, unclean!" to protect others from coming too close and risking infection. The leper now falls upon his face and begs Jesus: "Lord, if you just want to, you can make me clean."

What faith the man has in Jesus! Yet, how pitiful his disease must make him appear! What will Jesus do? What would you do? Moved with compassion, Jesus stretches out his hand and touches the man, saying: "I want to. Be made clean." And immediately the leprosy vanishes from him.

Would you like someone as compassionate as this for your king? The way Jesus treats this leper gives us confidence that during His Kingdom rule, the Bible prophecy will be fulfilled: "He will feel sorry for the lowly one and the poor one, and the souls of the poor ones he will save." Yes, Jesus will then fulfill his heart's desire to help *all* afflicted ones.

Even prior to the healing of the leper, Jesus' ministry has been creating great excitement among the people. In fulfillment of Isaiah's prophecy, Jesus now orders the healed man: "See that you tell nobody a thing." He then instructs him: "Go show yourself to the priest and offer in behalf of your cleansing the things Moses directed, for a witness to them."

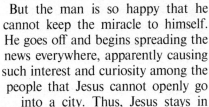

But the man is so happy that he cannot keep the miracle to himself. He goes off and begins spreading the news everywhere, apparently causing such interest and curiosity among the people that Jesus cannot openly go into a city. Thus, Jesus stays in lonely places where nobody lives, and people from all over come to listen to him and to be cured of their sicknesses. **Luke 5:12-16; Mark 1:40-45; Matthew 8:2-4; Leviticus 13:45; 14:10-13; Psalm 72:13; Isaiah 42:1, 2.**

■ What effect can leprosy have, and what warning was a leper to give?

■ How does a leper appeal to Jesus, and what can we learn from Jesus' response?

■ How does the healed man fail to obey Jesus, and what are the consequences?

Back Home in Capernaum

B Y NOW Jesus' fame has spread far and wide, and many people travel to the out-of-the-way places where he is staying. After some days, however, he returns to Capernaum by the Sea of Galilee. Quickly the news spreads through the city that he is back home, and many come to the house where he is. Pharisees and Law teachers come from as far away as Jerusalem.

The crowd is so great that they jam the doorway, and there is no room for anyone else to get inside. The stage is set for a truly remarkable event. What occurs on this occasion is of vital importance, for it helps us to appreciate that Jesus has the power to remove the cause of human suffering and restore health to all whom he chooses.

While Jesus is teaching the crowd, four men bring to the house a paralyzed man on a cot. They want Jesus to heal their friend, but because of the crowd, they cannot get inside. How disappointing! Yet they do not give up. They climb up on the flat roof, make a hole in it, and lower the cot with the paralyzed man on it down next to Jesus.

Is Jesus angry because of the interruption? Not at all! Rather, he is deeply impressed by their faith. He says to the paralytic: "Your sins are forgiven." But can Jesus actually forgive sins? The scribes and the Pharisees do not think so. They reason in their hearts: "Why is this man talking in this manner? He is blaspheming. Who can forgive sins except one, God?"

Knowing their thoughts, Jesus says to them: "Why are you reasoning these things in your hearts? Which is easier, to say to the paralytic, 'Your sins are forgiven,' or to say, 'Get up and pick up your cot and walk'?"

Then, Jesus allows the crowd, including his critics, to see a remarkable demonstration that will reveal he has authority to

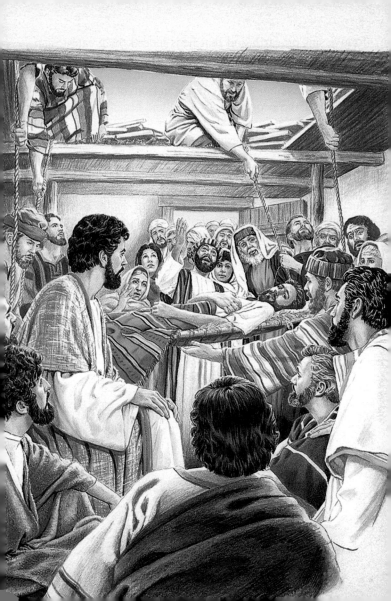

forgive sins on earth and that he is indeed the greatest man who ever lived. He turns to the paralytic and commands: "Get up, pick up your cot, and go to your home." And he immediately does, walking out with his cot in front of all of them! In amazement the people glorify God and exclaim: "We never saw the like of it"!

Did you notice that Jesus mentions sins in connection with sickness and that forgiveness of sins is related to the gaining of physical health? The Bible explains that our first parent, Adam, sinned and that all of us have inherited the consequences of that sin, namely, sickness and death. But under the rule of God's Kingdom, Jesus will forgive the sins of all who love God and serve Him, and then all sickness will be removed. How fine that will be! **Mark 2:1-12; Luke 5:17-26; Matthew 9:1-8; Romans 5:12, 17-19.**

■ What was the setting for a truly remarkable event?

■ How did the paralytic reach Jesus?

■ Why are all of us sinful, but how did Jesus provide hope that forgiveness of our sins and perfect health are possible?

27　The Calling of Matthew

SHORTLY after healing the paralytic, Jesus goes out from Capernaum to the Sea of Galilee. Again crowds of people come to him, and he begins teaching them. As he walks on, he sees Matthew, who is also called Levi, sitting at the tax office. "Be my follower," is Jesus' invitation.

Likely, Matthew is already familiar with Jesus' teachings, even as were Peter, Andrew, James, and John when they were called. And like them, Matthew immediately responds to the invitation. He gets up, leaves his responsibilities as a tax collector behind, and follows Jesus.

Later, perhaps to celebrate the receiving of his call, Matthew holds a big reception feast in his house. In addition to Jesus and His disciples, former associates of Matthew are present. These men are generally despised by their fellow Jews because they collect taxes for the hated Roman authorities. Moreover, they often dishonestly exact more money from the people than the regular tax rate.

Observing Jesus at the feast with such persons, the Pharisees ask his disciples: "Why is it that your teacher eats with tax collectors and sinners?" Overhearing the question, Jesus answers the Pharisees: "Persons in health do not need a physician, but the ailing do. Go, then, and learn what this means, 'I want mercy, and not sacrifice.' For I came to call, not righteous people, but sinners."

Apparently, Matthew has invited these tax collectors to his home so that they can listen to Jesus and receive spiritual healing. So Jesus associates with them to help them attain a healthy relationship with God. Jesus does not despise such ones, as do the self-righteous Pharisees. Rather, moved with compassion he, in effect, serves as a spiritual physician to them.

Thus Jesus' exercise of mercy toward sinners is not a condoning of their sins but an expression of the same tender feelings he manifested toward the physically ill. Recall, for example, when he compassionately reached out and touched the leper, saying: "I want to. Be made clean." May we likewise show mercy by helping persons in need, especially assisting them in a spiritual way. Matthew 8:3; 9:9-13; Mark 2:13-17; Luke 5:27-32.

- Where is Matthew when Jesus sees him?
- What is Matthew's occupation, and why are such persons despised by other Jews?
- What complaint is made against Jesus, and how does he respond?
- Why does Jesus associate with sinners?

28 **Questioned About Fasting**

ALMOST a year has gone by since Jesus attended the Passover of 30 C.E. By now, John the Baptist has been imprisoned for several months. Although he wanted his disciples to become followers of Christ, not all of them have.

Now some of these disciples of the imprisoned John come to Jesus and ask: "Why is it that we and the Pharisees practice fasting but your disciples do not fast?" The Pharisees practice fasting twice a week as a ritual of their religion. And John's disciples perhaps follow a similar custom. It may also be

that they are fasting to mourn John's imprisonment and wonder why Jesus' disciples do not join them in this expression of grief.

In answer Jesus explains: "The friends of the bridegroom have no reason to mourn as long as the bridegroom is with them, do they? But days will come when the bridegroom will be taken away from them, and then they will fast."

John's disciples should recall that John himself spoke of Jesus as the Bridegroom. So while Jesus is present, John would not consider it appropriate to fast, and neither do Jesus' disciples. Later, when Jesus dies, his disciples do mourn and fast. But when he is resurrected and ascends to heaven, they have no further cause for mournful fasting.

Next, Jesus gives these illustrations: "Nobody sews a patch of unshrunk cloth upon an old outer garment; for its full strength would pull from the outer garment and the tear would become worse. Neither do people put new wine into old wineskins; but if they do, then the wineskins burst and the wine spills out and the wineskins are ruined. But people put new wine into new wineskins." What do these illustrations have to do with fasting?

Jesus was helping the disciples of John the Baptist to appreciate that no one should expect his followers to conform to the old practices of Judaism, such as ritual fasting. He did not come to patch up and prolong old worn-out systems of worship that were ready to be discarded. Christianity would not be made to conform to the Judaism of the day with its traditions of men. No, it would not be as a new patch on an old garment or as new wine in an old wineskin. **Matthew 9: 14-17; Mark 2:18-22; Luke 5:33-39; John 3:27-29.**

- Who practice fasting, and for what purpose?
- Why do Jesus' disciples not fast while he is with them, and afterward how will cause for fasting soon disappear?
- What illustrations does Jesus relate, and what do they mean?

29 **Doing Good Works on the Sabbath**

I T IS the spring of 31 C.E. A few months have passed since Jesus spoke to the woman at the well in Samaria while en route from Judea to Galilee.

Now, after teaching extensively throughout Galilee, Jesus again leaves for Judea, where he preaches in the synagogues. Compared with the attention the Bible gives to his Galilean ministry, it tells little of Jesus' activity in Judea during this visit and during the months he spent here following the previous Passover. Evidently his ministry did not receive as favorable a response in Judea as it did in Galilee.

Soon Jesus is on his way to Judea's principal city, Jerusalem, for the Passover of 31 C.E. Here, near the city's Sheep Gate, is the pool called Bethzatha, where many sick, blind, and lame come. They believe that people can be healed by getting into the waters of the pool when these are agitated.

It is the Sabbath, and Jesus sees a man at the pool who has been sick for 38 years. Being aware of the long duration of the man's sickness, Jesus asks: "Do you want to become sound in health?"

He answers Jesus: "Sir, I do not have a man to put me into the pool when the water is disturbed; but while I am coming another steps down ahead of me."

Jesus says to him: "Get up, pick up your cot and walk." With that the man immediately becomes sound in body, picks up his cot, and begins to walk!

But when the Jews see the man, they say: "It is Sabbath, and it is not lawful for you to carry the cot."

The man answers them: "The very one that made me sound in health said to me, 'Pick up your cot and walk.'"

"Who is the man that told you, 'Pick it up and walk'?" they ask. Jesus had turned aside because of the crowd, and the one who

was healed did not know Jesus' name. Later, however, Jesus and the man meet in the temple, and the man learns who it is that healed him.

So the healed man finds the Jews to tell them that it is Jesus who has made him sound in health. On learning this, the Jews go to Jesus. For what reason? To learn by what means he is able to do these wonderful things? No. But to find fault with him because he is doing these good things on the Sabbath. And they even begin persecuting him! Luke 4:44; John 5:1-16.

- About how long has it been since Jesus last visited Judea?
- Why is the pool that is called Bethzatha so popular?
- What miracle does Jesus perform at the pool, and what is the reaction of the Jews?

30

Answering His Accusers

WHEN the Jewish religious leaders accuse Jesus of breaking the Sabbath, he answers: "My Father has kept working until now, and I keep working."

Despite the claim of the Pharisees, Jesus' work is not of the type forbidden by Sabbath law. His work of preaching and healing is an assignment from God, and in imitation of God's example, he keeps on doing it daily. However, his answer makes the Jews even angrier than they were before, and they seek to kill him. Why?

It is because now they not only believe that Jesus is breaking the Sabbath but consider his claim of being God's personal Son to be blasphemy. However, Jesus is unafraid and answers them further regarding his favored relationship with God. "The Father has affection for the Son," he says, "and shows him all the things he himself does."

"Just as the Father raises the dead up," Jesus continues, "so the Son also makes those alive whom he wants to." Indeed, the Son is already raising the dead in a spiritual way! "He that hears my word and believes him that sent me," Jesus says, "has passed over from death to life." Yes, he continues: "The hour is coming, and it is now, when the dead will hear the voice of the Son of God and those who have given heed will live."

Although there is no record that Jesus has as yet literally raised anyone from the dead, he tells his accusers that such a literal resurrection of the dead will occur. "Do not marvel at this," he says, "because the hour is coming in which all those in the memorial tombs will hear his voice and come out."

Up to this time, Jesus has evidently never publicly described his vital role in God's purpose in such a distinct and definite way. But Jesus' accusers have more than his own witness

about these things. "You have dispatched men to John," Jesus reminds them, "and he has borne witness to the truth."

Just two years before, John the Baptizer told these Jewish religious leaders about the One coming after him. Reminding them of their once high regard for the now imprisoned John, Jesus says: "You for a short time were willing to rejoice greatly in his light." Jesus recalls this to their minds in hopes of helping, yes, saving, them. Yet he does not depend on the witness of John.

"The works themselves that I am doing [including the miracle he just performed] bear witness about me that the Father dispatched me." But besides that, Jesus continues: "The Father who sent me has himself borne witness about me." God bore witness about Jesus, for instance, at his baptism, saying: "This is my Son, the beloved."

Really, Jesus' accusers have no excuse for rejecting him. The very Scriptures they claim to be searching testify about him! "If you believed Moses you would believe me," Jesus concludes, "for that one wrote about me. But if you do not believe the writings of that one, how will you believe my sayings?" John 5:17-47; 1:19-27; Matthew 3:17.

- Why is Jesus' work not in violation of the Sabbath?
- How does Jesus describe his vital role in God's purpose?
- To prove that he is God's Son, to whose witness does Jesus point?

31

Plucking Grain
on the Sabbath

SOON Jesus and his disciples leave Jerusalem to return to Galilee. It is springtime, and in the fields there are ears of grain on the stalks. The disciples are hungry. So they pluck heads of grain and eat. But since it is a Sabbath, their actions do not go unobserved.

Religious leaders in Jerusalem had just sought to kill Jesus for alleged violations of the Sabbath. Now Pharisees bring an accusation. "Look! Your disciples are doing what it is not lawful to do on the sabbath," they charge.

The Pharisees claim that picking grain and rubbing it in the hands to eat is harvesting and threshing. But their strict

interpretation of what constitutes work has made the Sabbath burdensome, whereas it was meant to be a joyous, spiritually upbuilding time. So Jesus counters with Scriptural examples to show that Jehovah God never purposed such an unduly strict application of His Sabbath law.

Jesus says that when David and his men were hungry, they stopped at the tabernacle and ate the loaves of presentation. Those loaves had already been removed from before Jehovah and replaced by fresh ones, and they were ordinarily reserved for the priests to eat. Yet, under the circumstances, David and his men were not condemned for eating them.

Providing another example, Jesus says: "Have you not read in the Law that on the sabbaths the priests in the temple treat the sabbath as not sacred and continue guiltless?" Yes, even on

the Sabbath the priests carry on butchering and other work at the temple in preparing animal sacrifices! "But I tell you," Jesus says, "that something greater than the temple is here."

Admonishing the Pharisees, Jesus continues: "If you had understood what this means, 'I want mercy, and not sacrifice,' you would not have condemned the guiltless ones." Then he concludes: "For Lord of the sabbath is what the Son of man is." What does Jesus mean by that? Jesus is referring to his peaceful Kingdom rule of a thousand years.

For 6,000 years now, humankind has been suffering laborious enslavement under Satan the Devil, with violence and war being the order of the day. On the other hand, the great Sabbath rule of Christ will be a time of rest from all such suffering and oppression. **Matthew 12:1-8; Leviticus 24:5-9; 1 Samuel 21:1-6; Numbers 28:9; Hosea 6:6.**

- What charge is made against Jesus' disciples, and how does Jesus answer it?
- What failing of the Pharisees does Jesus identify?
- In what way is Jesus "Lord of the sabbath"?

32

What Is Lawful on the Sabbath?

IT IS on another Sabbath that Jesus visits a synagogue near the Sea of Galilee. Present is a man with a withered right hand. The scribes and the Pharisees are watching closely to see whether Jesus will heal him. Finally they ask: "Is it lawful to cure on the sabbath?"

The Jewish religious leaders believe that healing is lawful on the Sabbath only if life is in danger. They teach, for example, that on the Sabbath it is unlawful to set a bone or bandage a sprain. So the scribes and the Pharisees are questioning Jesus in an effort to get an accusation against him.

Jesus, however, knows their reasonings. At the same time, he realizes they have adopted an extreme, unscriptural view as to what constitutes a violation of the Sabbath-day requirement prohibiting work. Thus Jesus sets the stage for a dramatic confrontation by telling the man with the withered hand: "Get up and come to the center."

Now, turning to the scribes and the Pharisees, Jesus says: "Who will be the man among you that has one sheep and, if this falls into a pit on the sabbath, will not get hold of it and lift it out?" Since a sheep represents a financial investment, they would not leave it in the pit until the next day, perhaps to sicken and cause them loss. Besides, the Scriptures say: "The righteous one is caring for the soul of his domestic animal."

Drawing a parallel, Jesus continues: "All considered, of how much more worth is a man than a sheep! So it is lawful to do a fine thing on the sabbath." The religious leaders are unable to refute such logical, compassionate reasoning, and they remain silent.

With indignation, as well as grief at their obstinate stupidity, Jesus looks around. Then he says to the man: "Stretch out your hand." And he stretches it out and the hand is healed.

Instead of being happy that the man's hand is restored, the Pharisees go out and immediately conspire with the party followers of Herod to kill Jesus. This political party evidently includes members of the religious Sadducees. Ordinarily, this political party and the Pharisees are openly opposed to each other, but they are solidly united in their opposition to Jesus.   Matthew 12:9-14; Mark 3:1-6; Luke 6:6-11; Proverbs 12:10; Exodus 20:8-10.

■ What is the setting for a dramatic confrontation between Jesus and Jewish religious leaders?

■ What do these Jewish religious leaders believe regarding healing on the Sabbath?

■ What illustration does Jesus use to refute their wrong views?

33

Fulfilling Isaiah's Prophecy

AFTER Jesus learns that the Pharisees and party followers of Herod plan to kill him, he and his disciples
withdraw to the Sea of Galilee. Here great crowds
from all over Palestine, and even from outside its borders,
flock to him. He cures many, with the result that all those
with grievous diseases press forward to touch him.

Because the crowds are so large, Jesus tells his disciples to
have a boat continually at his service. By pulling away from
shore, he can keep the crowds from pressing in upon him. He
can teach them from the boat or travel to another area along
the shore to help the people there.

The disciple Matthew notes that Jesus' activity fulfills
"what was spoken through Isaiah the prophet." Then Matthew quotes the prophecy that Jesus fulfills:

"Look! My servant whom I chose, my beloved, whom my
soul approved! I will put my spirit upon
him, and what justice is he will make
clear to the nations. He will not

wrangle, nor cry aloud, nor will anyone hear his voice in the broad ways. No bruised reed will he crush, and no smoldering flaxen wick will he extinguish, until he sends out justice with success. Indeed, in his name nations will hope."

Jesus, of course, is the beloved servant of whom God approves. And Jesus makes clear what is true justice, which is being obscured by false religious traditions. Because of their unjust application of God's law, the Pharisees will not even come to a sick person's aid on the Sabbath! Making clear God's justice, Jesus relieves people of the burden of unjust traditions, and for this, the religious leaders try to kill him.

What does it mean that 'he will not wrangle, nor raise his voice so as to be heard in the broad ways'? When curing people, Jesus 'strictly charges them not to make him manifest.' He does not want to have noisy advertising of himself in the streets or to have distorted reports excitedly passed from mouth to mouth.

Also, Jesus carries his comforting message to persons who are figuratively like a bruised reed, bent over and knocked underfoot. They are like a smoldering flaxen wick, whose last spark of life has nearly been smothered. Jesus does not crush the bruised reed or quench the flickering, smoking flax. But with tenderness and love, he skillfully lifts up the meek. Truly, Jesus is the one in whom the nations can hope! **Matthew 12: 15-21; Mark 3:7-12; Isaiah 42:1-4.**

■ How does Jesus make justice clear, not wrangling or raising his voice in the broad ways?
■ Who are like a bruised reed and a flaxen wick, and how does Jesus treat them?

34 Choosing His Apostles

IT HAS been about a year and a half since John the Baptizer introduced Jesus as the Lamb of God and Jesus began his public ministry. At that time Andrew, Simon Peter, John, and perhaps James (John's brother), as well as Philip and Nathanael (also called Bartholomew), had become his first disciples. In time, many others joined them in following Christ.

Now Jesus is ready to select his apostles. These will be his intimate associates who will be given special training. But before selecting them, Jesus goes into a mountain and spends the whole night in prayer, likely asking for wisdom and God's blessing. When it becomes day, he calls his disciples and from

among them chooses 12. However, since they continue to be Jesus' pupils, they are still called disciples as well.

Six that Jesus selects, named above, are those who became his first disciples. Matthew, whom Jesus called from his tax office, is also selected. The other five chosen are Judas (also called Thaddaeus), Judas Iscariot, Simon the Cananaean, Thomas, and James the son of Alphaeus. This James is also called James the Less, perhaps because of being either smaller in physical stature or younger in age than the other apostle James.

By now these 12 have been with Jesus for some time, and he knows them well. In fact, a number of them are his own relatives. James and his brother John evidently are Jesus' first cousins. And it is probable that Alphaeus was the brother of Joseph, Jesus' adoptive father. So Alphaeus' son, the apostle James, would also be a cousin of Jesus.

Jesus, of course, has no problem in remembering his apostles' names. But can you remember them? Well, just remember that there are two named Simon, two named James, and two named Judas, and that Simon has a brother Andrew, and that James has a brother John. That is the key to remembering eight apostles. The other four include a tax collector (Matthew), one who later doubted (Thomas), one called from under a tree (Nathanael), and his friend Philip.

Eleven of the apostles are from Galilee, Jesus' home territory. Nathanael is from Cana. Philip, Peter, and Andrew are originally from Bethsaida, Peter and Andrew later moving to Capernaum, where it appears that Matthew lived. James and John were in the fishing business and also likely lived in or near Capernaum. It seems that Judas Iscariot, who later betrayed Jesus, is the only apostle from Judea. **Mark 3:13-19; Luke 6:12-16.**

- What apostles may have been relatives of Jesus?
- Who are Jesus' apostles, and how can you remember their names?
- From which territories did the apostles come?

35 The Most Famous Sermon Ever Given

THE scene is one of the most memorable in Bible history: Jesus seated on a mountainside, delivering his famous Sermon on the Mount. The site is near the Sea of Galilee, probably close to Capernaum. After spending the whole night in prayer, Jesus has just chosen 12 of his disciples to be apostles. Then, along with all of them, he comes down to this level place on the mountain.

By now, you would think, Jesus would be very tired and would want some sleep. But great crowds have come, some all the way from Judea and Jerusalem, 60 to 70 miles away. Others have come from the seacoast of Tyre and Sidon located to the north. They have come to hear Jesus and to be healed of their sicknesses. There are even persons who are troubled by the demons, the wicked angels of Satan.

As Jesus comes down, sick people draw close to touch him, and he heals all of them. Afterward, Jesus apparently climbs to a higher place on the mountain. There he sits down and begins teaching the crowds spread out on the level place before him. And think of it! Now there is not even one person in the entire audience who is suffering from a serious infirmity!

The people are eager to hear the teacher who is able to perform these amazing miracles. Jesus, however, delivers his sermon mainly for the benefit of his disciples, who are probably gathered around closest to him. But so that we can benefit too, both Matthew and Luke have recorded it.

Matthew's account of the sermon is about four times as long as Luke's. Moreover, portions of what Matthew records, Luke presents as being said by Jesus at another time during his ministry, as can be noted by comparing Matthew 6:9-13 with Luke 11:1-4, and Matthew 6:25-34 with Luke 12:22-31. Yet this should not be surprising. Jesus obviously taught the same things more than once, and Luke chose to record some of these teachings in a different setting.

What makes Jesus' sermon so valuable is not only the depth of its spiritual contents but the simplicity and clarity with which he presents these truths. He draws on ordinary experiences and uses things familiar to people, thus making his ideas easily understood by all who are seeking a better life in God's way.

Who Are Truly Happy?

Everyone wants to be happy. Realizing this, Jesus begins his Sermon on the Mount by describing those who are truly happy. As we can imagine, this immediately captures the attention of his vast audience. And yet his opening words must seem contradictory to many.

Directing his comments to his disciples, Jesus begins: "Happy are you poor, because yours is the kingdom of God. Happy are you who hunger now, because you will be filled. Happy are you who weep now, because you will laugh. Happy are you whenever men hate you . . . Rejoice in that day and leap, for, look! your reward is great in heaven."

This is Luke's account of the introduction of Jesus' sermon. But according to Matthew's record, Jesus also says that the mild-tempered, the merciful, the pure in heart, and the peaceable are happy. These are happy, Jesus notes, because they will inherit the earth, they will be shown mercy, they will see God, and they will be called sons of God.

What Jesus means by being happy, however, is not simply being jovial or mirthful, as when one is having fun. True happiness is deeper, carrying the thought of contentment,

a sense of satisfaction and fulfillment in life.

So those who are truly happy, Jesus shows, are people who recognize their spiritual need, are saddened by their sinful condition, *and come to know and serve God.* Then, even if they are hated or persecuted for doing God's will, they are happy because they know they are pleasing God and will receive his reward of everlasting life.

However, many of Jesus' listeners, just like some people today, believe that being prosperous and enjoying pleasures is what makes a person happy. Jesus knows otherwise. Drawing a contrast that must surprise many of his listeners, he says:

"Woe to you rich persons, because you are having your consolation in full. Woe to you who are filled up now, because you will go hungry. Woe, you who are laughing now, because you will mourn and weep. Woe, whenever all men speak well of you, for things like these are what their forefathers did to the false prophets."

What does Jesus mean? Why do having riches, laughingly pursuing pleasures, and enjoying the plaudits of men bring woe? It is because when a person has and cherishes these things, then service to God, which alone brings true happiness, is excluded from his life. At the same time, Jesus did not mean that simply being poor, hungry, and mournful makes a person happy. Often, however, such disadvantaged persons may respond to Jesus' teachings, and they thereby are blessed with true happiness.

Next, addressing his disciples, Jesus says: "You are the salt of the earth." He does not mean, of course, that they literally are salt. Rather, salt is a preservative. A large heap of it lay near the altar at Jehovah's temple, and priests officiating there used it to salt the offerings.

The disciples of Jesus are "the salt of the earth" in that they have a preserving influence on people. Indeed, the message they bear will preserve the lives of all who respond to it! It will bring into the lives of such persons the qualities of permanence, loyalty, and faithfulness, preventing any spiritual and moral decay in them.

"You are the light of the world," Jesus tells his disciples. A lamp is not put under a basket but is set on a lampstand, so Jesus says: "Likewise let your light shine before men." Jesus' disciples do this by their public witnessing, as well as by serving as shining examples of conduct that accords with Bible principles.

A High Standard for His Followers

The religious leaders consider Jesus a transgressor of God's Law and recently have even conspired to kill him. So as Jesus continues his Sermon on the Mount, he explains: "Do not think I came to destroy the Law or the Prophets. I came, not to destroy, but to fulfill."

Jesus has the highest regard for God's Law and encourages others to have such also. In fact, he says: "Whoever, therefore, breaks one of these least commandments and teaches mankind to that effect, he will be called 'least' in relation to the kingdom of the heavens," meaning that such a person would not get into the Kingdom at all.

Far from disregarding God's Law, Jesus condemns even the attitudes that contribute to a person's breaking it. After noting that the Law says, "You must not murder," Jesus adds: "However, I say to you that everyone who continues wrathful with his brother will be accountable to the court of justice."

Since continuing wrathful with an associate is so serious, perhaps even leading to murder, Jesus illustrates the extent to which one should go to achieve peace. He instructs: "If, then, you are bringing your [sacrificial] gift to the altar and you there remember that your brother has something against you, leave your gift there in front of the altar, and go away; first make your peace with your brother, and then, when you have come back, offer up your gift."

Turning attention to the seventh of the Ten Commandments, Jesus continues: "You heard that it was said, 'You must not commit adultery.'" However, Jesus condemns even the steady attitude toward adultery. "I say to you that everyone that keeps on looking at a woman so as to have a passion for her has already committed adultery with her in his heart."

Jesus is not here speaking merely about a passing immoral thought but about *'keeping on looking.'* Such continued looking arouses passionate desire, which, if opportunity affords, can culminate in adultery. How can a person prevent this from happening? Jesus illustrates how extreme measures may be necessary, saying: "If, now, that right eye of yours is making you stumble, tear it out and throw it away from you. . . . Also, if your right hand is making you stumble, cut it off and throw it away from you."

People are often willing to sacrifice a literal limb that is diseased in order to save their lives. But according to Jesus, it is even more vital to 'throw away' *anything*, even something as precious as an eye or a hand, to avoid immoral thinking and actions. Otherwise, Jesus explains, such persons will be thrown into Gehenna (a burning rubbish heap near Jerusalem), which symbolizes eternal destruction.

Jesus also discusses how to deal with people who cause injury and offense. "Do not resist him that is wicked," is his counsel. "But whoever slaps you on your right cheek, turn the

other also to him." Jesus does not mean that a person should not defend himself or his family if attacked. A slap is not delivered to hurt another physically but, rather, to insult. So, what Jesus is saying is that if anyone tries to provoke a fight or an argument, either by literally slapping with an open hand or by stinging with insulting words, it would be wrong to retaliate.

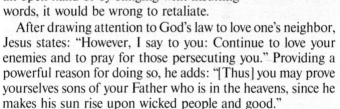

After drawing attention to God's law to love one's neighbor, Jesus states: "However, I say to you: Continue to love your enemies and to pray for those persecuting you." Providing a powerful reason for doing so, he adds: "[Thus] you may prove yourselves sons of your Father who is in the heavens, since he makes his sun rise upon wicked people and good."

Jesus concludes this portion of his sermon by admonishing: "You must accordingly be perfect, as your heavenly Father is perfect." Jesus does not mean that people can be perfect in the absolute sense. Rather, they can, by imitating God, expand their love to embrace even their enemies. Luke's parallel account records Jesus' words: "Continue becoming merciful, just as your Father is merciful."

Prayer, and Trust in God

As Jesus proceeds with his sermon, he condemns the hypocrisy of people who make a show of their supposed godliness. "When you go making gifts," he says, "do not blow a trumpet ahead of you, just as the hypocrites do."

"Also," Jesus continues, "when you pray, you must not be as the hypocrites; because they like to pray standing in the synagogues and on the corners of the broad ways to be visible to men." Rather, he instructs: "When you pray, go into your private room and, after shutting your door, pray to your Father who is in secret." Jesus himself said public prayers, so he is not condemning these. What he is denouncing are prayers that are said to impress listeners and draw their admiring compliments.

Jesus further counsels: "When praying, do not say the same things over and over again, just as the people of the nations do." Jesus does not mean that repetition in itself is wrong. Once, he himself repeatedly used "the same word" when praying. But what he disapproves of is the saying of memorized phrases "over and over again," the way those do who finger beads as they repeat their prayers by rote.

To help his listeners pray, Jesus provides a model prayer that includes seven petitions. The first three rightly give recognition to God's sovereignty and his purposes. They are requests for God's name to be sanctified, his Kingdom to come, and his will to be done. The remaining four are personal requests, namely, for daily food, for forgiveness of sins, not to be tempted beyond one's endurance, and to be delivered from the wicked one.

Going on, Jesus addresses the snare of putting undue emphasis on material possessions. He urges: "Stop storing up for yourselves treasures upon the earth, where moth and rust consume, and where thieves break in and steal." Not only are such treasures perishable but they build up no merit with God.

Hence, Jesus says: "Rather, store up for yourselves treasures in heaven." This is done by putting God's service first in

your life. Nobody can take away the merit thus accumulated with God or its grand reward. Then Jesus adds: "Where your treasure is, there your heart will be also."

Further addressing the snare of materialism, Jesus gives the illustration: "The lamp of the body is the eye. If, then, your eye is simple, your whole body will be bright; but if your eye is wicked, your whole body will be dark." The eye that functions properly is to the body like a lighted lamp in a dark place. But to see correctly, the eye must be simple, that is, it must focus on one thing. An out-of-focus eye leads to a mistaken estimate of things, to putting material pursuits ahead of service to God, with the result that the "whole body" becomes dark.

Jesus climaxes this matter with the powerful illustration: "No one can slave for two masters; for either he will hate the one and love the other, or he will stick to the one and despise the other. You cannot slave for God and for Riches."

After giving this counsel, Jesus assures his listeners that they need not be anxious about their material needs if they put God's service first.

"Observe intently the birds of heaven," he says, "because they do not sow seed or reap or gather into storehouses; still your heavenly Father feeds them." Then he asks: "Are you not worth more than they are?"

Next, Jesus points to the lilies of the field and notes that "not even Solomon in all his glory was arrayed as one of these. If, now," he continues, "God thus clothes the vegetation of the field, . . . will he not much rather clothe you, you with little faith?" Therefore Jesus concludes: "Never be anxious and say, 'What are we to eat?' or, 'What are we to drink?' or, 'What are we to put on?' . . . For your heavenly Father knows you need all these things. Keep on, then, seeking first the kingdom and his righteousness, and all these other things will be added to you."

The Way to Life

The way to life is that of abiding by Jesus' teachings. But this is not easy to do. The Pharisees, for example, tend to judge others harshly, and likely many imitate them. So as Jesus continues his Sermon on the Mount, he gives this admonition: "Stop judging that you may not be judged; for with what judgment you are judging, you will be judged."

It is dangerous to follow the lead of the overly critical Pharisees. According to Luke's account, Jesus illustrates this danger by saying: "A blind man cannot guide a blind man, can he? Both will tumble into a pit, will they not?"

Being too critical of others, magnifying their faults and picking on them, is a serious offense. So Jesus asks: "How can you say to your brother, 'Allow me to extract the straw from your eye'; when, look! a rafter is in your own eye? Hypocrite! First extract the rafter from your own eye, and then you will see clearly how to extract the straw from your brother's eye."

This does not mean that Jesus' disciples are to use no discernment in connection with other people, for he says: "Do not give what is holy to dogs, neither throw your pearls before swine." The truths from God's Word are holy. They are like figurative pearls. But if some individuals, who are like dogs or swine, show no appreciation for these precious truths, Jesus' disciples should leave those people and seek out those who are more receptive.

Although Jesus has discussed prayer earlier in his Sermon on the Mount, he now stresses the need to persist in it. "Keep on asking," he urges, "and it will be given you." To illustrate God's readiness to answer prayers, Jesus asks: "Who is the man among you whom his son asks for bread—he will not hand him a stone, will he? . . . Therefore, if you, although being wicked, know how to give good gifts to your children, how much more so will your Father who is in the heavens give good things to those asking him?"

Next Jesus provides what has become a famous rule of conduct, commonly called the Golden Rule. He says: "All things, therefore, that you want men to do to you, you also must likewise do to them." Living by this rule involves positive action in doing good to others, treating them as you want to be treated.

That the way to life is not easy is revealed by Jesus' instruction: "Go in through the narrow gate; because broad and spacious is the road leading off into destruction, and many are the ones going in through it; whereas narrow is the gate and cramped the road leading off into life, and few are the ones finding it."

The danger of being misled is great, so Jesus warns: "Be on the watch for the false prophets that come to you in sheep's covering, but inside they are ravenous wolves." Even as good trees and bad trees can be recognized by their fruits, Jesus notes, false prophets can be recognized by their conduct and teachings.

Going on, Jesus explains that it is not simply what a person *says* that makes him His disciple but what he *does*. Some people claim that Jesus is their Lord, but if they are not doing the will of his Father, he says: "I will confess to them: I never knew you! Get away from me, you workers of lawlessness."

Finally, Jesus gives the memorable conclusion to his sermon. He says: "Everyone that hears these sayings of mine and does them will be likened to a discreet man, who built his house upon the rock-mass. And the rain poured down and the floods came and the winds blew and lashed against that house, but it did not cave in, for it had been founded upon the rock-mass."

On the other hand, Jesus declares: "Everyone hearing these sayings of mine and not doing them will be likened to a foolish man, who built his house upon the sand. And the rain poured down and the floods came and the winds blew and struck

against that house and it caved in, and its collapse was great."

When Jesus finishes his sermon, the crowds are astounded at his way of teaching, for he teaches them as a person having authority and not as their religious leaders. Luke 6: 12-23; Matthew 5:1-12; Luke 6:24-26; Matthew 5:13-48; 6:1-34; 26:36-45; 7:1-29; Luke 6:27-49.

■ Where is Jesus when he gives his most memorable sermon, who are present, and what has occurred just prior to his giving it?

■ Why is it not surprising that Luke records some teachings of the sermon in another setting?

■ What makes Jesus' sermon so valuable?

■ Who are truly happy, and why?

■ Who receive woe, and why?

■ How are Jesus' disciples "the salt of the earth" and "the light of the world"?

■ How does Jesus show high regard for God's Law?

■ What instruction does Jesus provide to root out causes of murder and adultery?

■ What does Jesus mean when he speaks about turning the other cheek?

■ How can we be perfect as God is perfect?

■ What instructions on prayer does Jesus provide?

■ Why are heavenly treasures superior, and how are they obtained?

■ What illustrations are given to help one avoid materialism?

■ Why does Jesus say that there is no need to be anxious?

■ What does Jesus say about judging others; yet how does he show that his disciples need to use discernment regarding people?

■ What does Jesus further say regarding prayer, and what rule of conduct does he provide?

■ How does Jesus show that the way to life would not be easy and that there is a danger of being misled?

■ How does Jesus conclude his sermon, and what effect does it have?

An Army Officer's Great Faith

WHEN Jesus gives his Sermon on the Mount, he has reached about the halfway point in his public ministry. This means he has only a year and nine months or so left to complete his work on earth.

Jesus now enters the city of Capernaum, a kind of home base for his activities. Here older men of the Jews approach him with a request. They have been sent by an officer in the Roman army who is a Gentile, a man of a different race than the Jews.

The army officer's beloved servant is about to die from a serious illness, and he wants Jesus to heal his servant. The Jews earnestly plead in behalf of the officer: "He is worthy of your conferring this upon him," they say, "for he loves our nation and he himself built the synagogue for us."

Without hesitation, Jesus leaves with the men. However, when they get near, the army officer sends out friends to say: "Sir, do not bother, for I am not fit to have you come in under my roof. For that reason I did not consider myself worthy to come to you."

What a humble expression for an officer who is accustomed to ordering others! But he is also probably thinking of Jesus, realizing that custom prohibits a Jew from having social connections with non-Jews. Even Peter said: "You well know how unlawful it is for a Jew to join himself to or approach a man of another race."

Perhaps not wanting Jesus to suffer the consequences of violating this custom, the officer has his friends request of him: "Say the word, and let my servant be healed. For I too am a man placed under authority, having soldiers under me,

and I say to this one, 'Be on your way!' and he is on his way, and to another, 'Come!' and he comes, and to my slave, 'Do this!' and he does it."

Well, when Jesus hears this, he marvels. "I tell you the truth," he says, "with no one in Israel have I found so great a faith." After healing the officer's servant, Jesus uses the occasion to relate how non-Jews of faith will be favored with blessings that are rejected by faithless Jews.

"Many," Jesus says, "from eastern parts and western parts will come and recline at the table with Abraham and Isaac and Jacob in the kingdom of the heavens; whereas the sons of the kingdom will be thrown into the darkness outside. There is where their weeping and the gnashing of their teeth will be."

"The sons of the kingdom . . . thrown into the darkness outside" are natural Jews who do not accept the opportunity offered first to them of being rulers with Christ. Abraham, Isaac, and Jacob represent God's Kingdom arrangement. Thus Jesus is relating how Gentiles will be welcomed to recline at the heavenly table, as it were, "in the kingdom of the heavens." Luke 7:1-10; Matthew 8:5-13; Acts 10:28.

■ Why do Jews plead in behalf of a Gentile army officer?

■ What may explain why the officer has not invited Jesus to enter his house?

■ What does Jesus mean by his concluding remarks?

37 Jesus Dispels a Widow's Grief

SHORTLY after healing the army officer's servant, Jesus leaves for Nain, a city over 20 miles to the southwest of Capernaum. His disciples and a great crowd accompany him. It is probably toward evening when they approach the outskirts of Nain. Here they meet a funeral procession. The dead body of a young man is being carried out of the city for burial.

The mother's situation is especially tragic, since she is a widow and this is her only child. When her husband died, she could take comfort in the fact that she had her son. Her hopes, desires, and ambitions became wrapped up in his future. But now there is no one in whom to find consolation. Her grief is great as the townspeople accompany her to the place of burial.

When Jesus catches sight of the woman, his heart is touched by her extreme sadness. So with tenderness, and yet with a firmness that imparts confidence, he says to her: "Stop weeping." His manner and action arrest the crowd's attention. So when he approaches and touches the bier on which the body is being carried, the bearers stand still. All must wonder what he is going to do.

It is true that those accompanying Jesus have seen him miraculously heal many persons of diseases. But apparently they have never seen him raise anyone from the dead. Can he do such a thing? Addressing the body, Jesus commands: "Young man, I say to you, Get up!" And the man sits up! He starts to speak, and Jesus gives him to his mother.

When the people see that the young man truly is alive, they begin to say: "A great prophet has been raised up among us." Others say: "God has turned his attention to his people." Quickly the news concerning this amazing deed spreads out into all Judea and all the surrounding country.

John the Baptizer is still in prison, and he wants to learn more about the works that Jesus is able to perform. John's disciples tell him about these miracles. What is his response? **Luke 7:11-18.**

- What is happening as Jesus approaches Nain?
- How is Jesus affected by what he sees, and what does he do?
- How do the people respond to Jesus' miracle?

38 Did John Lack Faith?

JOHN the Baptizer, who has been in prison about a year now, receives the report about the resurrection of the widow's son at Nain. But John wants to hear directly from Jesus regarding the significance of this, so he sends two of his disciples to inquire: "Are you the Coming One or are we to expect a different one?"

That may seem a strange question, especially since John saw God's spirit descend upon Jesus and heard God's voice of approval when baptizing Jesus nearly two years before. John's question may cause some to conclude that his faith has grown weak. But this is not so. Jesus would not speak so highly of John, which he does on this occasion, if John has begun to doubt. Why, then, does John ask this question?

John may simply want a verification from Jesus that He is the Messiah. This would be very strengthening to John as he languishes in prison. But apparently there is more to John's question than that. He evidently wants to know if there is to be another one coming, a successor, as it were, who will complete the fulfillment of all the things that were foretold to be accomplished by the Messiah.

According to Bible prophecies with which John is acquainted, the Anointed One of God is to be a king, a deliverer. Yet, John is still being held as a prisoner, even many months after Jesus' baptism. So John evidently is asking Jesus: 'Are you really the one to establish the Kingdom of God in outward power, or is there a different one, a successor, for whom we

should wait to fulfill all the wonderful prophecies relating to the Messiah's glory?'

Instead of telling John's disciples, 'Of course I am the one who was to come!' Jesus in that very hour puts on a remarkable display by healing many people, curing them of all kinds of diseases and ailments. Then he tells the disciples: "Go your way, report to John what you saw and heard: the blind are receiving sight, the lame are walking, the lepers are being cleansed and the deaf are hearing, the dead are being raised up, the poor are being told the good news."

In other words, John's question may imply an expectation that Jesus will do more than he is doing and will perhaps free John himself. Jesus, however, is telling John not to expect more than the miracles Jesus is performing.

When John's disciples leave, Jesus turns to the crowds and tells them that John is the "messenger" of Jehovah foretold in Malachi 3:1 and is also the prophet Elijah foretold in Malachi 4:5, 6. He thus extols John as being the equal of any prophet who lived before him, explaining: "Truly I say to you people, Among those born of women there has not been raised up a greater than John the Baptist; but a person that is a lesser one in the kingdom of the heavens is greater than he is. But from the days of John the Baptist until now the kingdom of the heavens is the goal toward which men press."

Jesus is here showing that John will not be in the heavenly Kingdom, since a lesser one there is greater than John. John prepared the way for Jesus but dies before Christ seals the covenant, or agreement, with his disciples, for them to be corulers with him in his Kingdom. That is why Jesus says that John will not be in the heavenly Kingdom. John will instead be an earthly subject of God's Kingdom. Luke 7:18-30; Matthew 11:2-15.

- Why does John ask whether Jesus is the Coming One or whether a different one should be expected?
- What prophecies does Jesus say that John fulfilled?
- Why will John the Baptizer not be in heaven with Jesus?

The Proud and the Lowly

AFTER mentioning the virtues of John the Baptizer, Jesus turns attention to the proud, fickle people who are around him. "This generation," he declares, "is like young children sitting in the marketplaces who cry out to their playmates, saying, 'We played the flute for you, but you did not dance; we wailed, but you did not beat yourselves in grief.'"

What does Jesus mean? He explains: "John came neither eating nor drinking, yet people say, 'He has a demon'; the Son of man did come eating and drinking, still people say, 'Look! A man gluttonous and given to drinking wine, a friend of tax collectors and sinners.'"

It is impossible to satisfy the people. Nothing pleases them. John has lived an austere life of

self-denial as a Nazirite, in keeping with the angel's declaration that "he must drink no wine and strong drink at all." And yet the people say he is demonized. On the other hand, Jesus lives like other men, not practicing any austerity, and he is accused of excesses.

How hard to please the people are! They are like playmates, some of whom refuse to respond with dancing when other children play the flute or with grief when their fellows wail. Nevertheless, Jesus says: "Wisdom is proved righteous by its works." Yes, the evidence—the works—make clear that the accusations against both John and Jesus are false.

Jesus goes on to single out for reproach the three cities of Chorazin, Bethsaida, and Capernaum, where he has performed most of his powerful works. If he had done those works in the Phoenician cities of Tyre and Sidon, Jesus says, these cities would have repented in sackcloth and ashes. Condemning Capernaum, which apparently has been his home base during the period of his ministry, Jesus declares: "It will be more endurable for the land of Sodom on Judgment Day than for you."

Jesus next publicly praises his heavenly Father. He is moved to do so because God conceals precious spiritual truths from wise and intellectual ones but reveals these marvelous things to lowly ones, to babes, as it were.

Finally, Jesus gives the appealing invitation: "Come to me, all you who are toiling and loaded down, and I will refresh you. Take my yoke upon you and learn from me, for I am mild-tempered and lowly in heart, and you will find refreshment for your souls. For my yoke is kindly and my load is light."

How does Jesus offer refreshment? He does so by providing freedom from the enslaving traditions with which the religious leaders have burdened the people, including, for example, restrictive Sabbath-keeping regulations. He also shows the way of relief to those who feel the crushing weight of domination by the political authorities and to those who feel the weight of their sins through an afflicted conscience. He reveals to such afflicted ones how their sins can be forgiven and how they can enjoy a precious relationship with God.

The kindly yoke Jesus offers is one of complete dedication to God, being able to serve our compassionate, merciful heavenly Father. And the light load Jesus offers to those who come to him is that of obeying God's requirements for life, which are His commandments recorded in the Bible. And obeying these is not at all burdensome. **Matthew 11:16-30; Luke 1:15; 7:31-35; 1 John 5:3.**

- How are the proud, fickle people of Jesus' generation like children?

- Why is Jesus moved to praise his heavenly Father?

- In what ways are people burdened down, and what relief does Jesus offer?

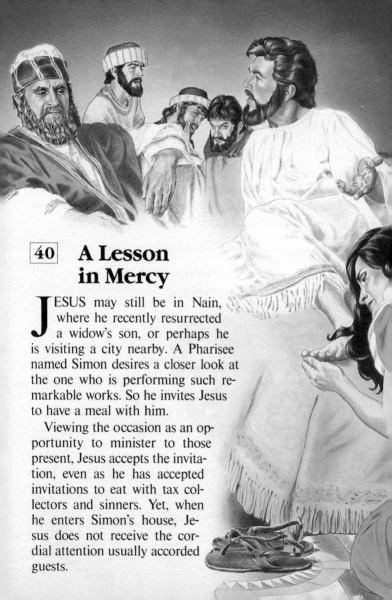

40 A Lesson in Mercy

JESUS may still be in Nain, where he recently resurrected a widow's son, or perhaps he is visiting a city nearby. A Pharisee named Simon desires a closer look at the one who is performing such remarkable works. So he invites Jesus to have a meal with him.

Viewing the occasion as an opportunity to minister to those present, Jesus accepts the invitation, even as he has accepted invitations to eat with tax collectors and sinners. Yet, when he enters Simon's house, Jesus does not receive the cordial attention usually accorded guests.

Sandal-clad feet become hot and dirty as a result of traveling dusty roads, and it is a customary act of hospitality to wash the feet of guests with cool water. But Jesus' feet are not washed when he arrives. Neither does he receive a welcoming kiss, which is common etiquette. And the customary oil of hospitality is not provided for his hair.

During the course of the meal, while the guests are reclining at the table, an uninvited woman quietly enters the room. She is known in the city to be living an immoral life. Likely she has heard Jesus' teachings, including his invitation for 'all those who are loaded down to come to him for refreshment.' And being deeply moved by what she has seen and heard, she has now sought out Jesus.

The woman comes up behind Jesus at the table and kneels at his feet. As her tears fall on his feet, she wipes them off with her hair. She also takes perfumed oil from her flask, and as she tenderly kisses his feet, she pours the oil on them. Simon watches with disapproval. "This man, if he were a prophet," he reasons, "would know who and what kind of woman it is that is touching him, that she is a sinner."

Perceiving his thinking, Jesus says: "Simon, I have something to say to you."

"Teacher, say it!" he responds.

"Two men were debtors to a certain lender," Jesus begins. "The one was in debt for five hundred denarii, but the other for fifty. When they did not have anything with which to pay back, he freely forgave them both. Therefore, which of them will love him the more?"

"I suppose," says Simon, perhaps with an air of indifference at the seeming irrelevance of the question, "it is the one to whom he freely forgave the more."

"You judged correctly," Jesus says. And then turning to the woman, he says to Simon: "Do you behold this woman? I entered into your house; you gave me no water for my feet. But this woman wet my feet with her tears and wiped them off with her hair. You gave me no kiss; but this woman, from the hour that I came in, did not leave off tenderly kissing my feet. You did not grease my head with oil; but this woman greased my feet with perfumed oil."

The woman has thus given evidence of heartfelt repentance for her immoral past. So Jesus concludes, saying: "By virtue of this, I tell you, her sins, many though they are, are forgiven, because she loved much; but he who is forgiven little, loves little."

Jesus is in no way excusing or condoning immorality. Rather, this incident reveals his compassionate understanding of people who make mistakes in life but who then manifest that they are sorry for these and so come to Christ for relief. Providing true refreshment to the woman, Jesus says: "Your sins are forgiven. . . . Your faith has saved you; go your way in peace."   **Luke 7:36-50; Matthew 11:28-30.**

- How is Jesus received by his host, Simon?
- Who seeks Jesus out, and why?
- What illustration does Jesus provide, and how does he apply it?

41

A Center of Controversy

SHORTLY after he is entertained at the home of Simon, Jesus begins a second preaching tour of Galilee. On his previous tour of the territory, he was accompanied by his first disciples, Peter, Andrew, James, and John. But now the 12 apostles, as well as certain women, accompany him. These include Mary Magdalene, Susanna, and Joanna, whose husband is an officer of King Herod.

As the pace of Jesus' ministry intensifies, so does the controversy regarding his activity. A demon-possessed man, who is also blind and unable to speak, is brought to Jesus. When Jesus cures him, so that he is free of demon control and can both speak and see, the crowds are simply carried away. They begin to say: "May this not perhaps be the Son of David?"

Crowds gather in such numbers around the house where Jesus is staying that he and his disciples cannot even eat a meal. In addition to those who think that he may be the promised "Son of David," there are scribes and Pharisees who have come all the way from Jerusalem to discredit him. When Jesus' relatives hear about the commotion revolving around Jesus, they come to lay hold of him. For what reason?

Well, even Jesus' own brothers do not as yet believe that he is God's Son. Also, the public uproar and strife that he has created is totally uncharacteristic of the Jesus that they knew while he was growing up in Nazareth. Therefore, they believe that something is seriously wrong with Jesus mentally. "He has gone out of his mind," they conclude, and they want to seize him and take him away.

Yet the evidence is clear that Jesus healed the demonized man. The scribes and Pharisees know that they cannot deny the actuality of this. So to discredit Jesus they tell the people: "This fellow does not expel the demons except by means of Beelzebub, the ruler of the demons."

Knowing their thinking, Jesus calls the scribes and Pharisees to him and says: "Every kingdom divided against itself comes to desolation, and every city or house divided against itself will not stand. In the same way, if Satan expels Satan, he has become divided against himself; how, then, will his kingdom stand?"

What devastating logic! Since the Pharisees claim that persons from their own ranks have cast out demons, Jesus also asks: "If I expel the demons by means of Beelzebub, by means of whom do your sons expel them?" In other words, their charge against Jesus should just as well be applied to them as to him. Jesus then warns: "But if it is by means of God's spirit that I expel the demons, the kingdom of God has really overtaken you."

To illustrate that his casting out of demons is evidence of his power over Satan, Jesus says: "How can anyone invade the house of a strong man and seize his movable goods, unless first he binds the strong man? And then he will plunder his house. He that is not on my side is against me, and he that does not gather with me scatters." The Pharisees clearly are against Jesus, demonstrating themselves to be Satan's agents. They are scattering Israelites away from him.

Consequently, Jesus warns these satanic opposers that "the blasphemy against the spirit will not be forgiven." He explains: "Whoever speaks a word against the Son of man, it will be forgiven him; but whoever speaks against the holy spirit, it will not be forgiven him, no, not in this system of things nor in that to come." Those scribes and Pharisees have committed that unforgivable sin by maliciously attributing to Satan what is plainly a miraculous operation of God's holy spirit. **Matthew 12:22-32; Mark 3:19-30; John 7:5.**

- How does Jesus' second tour of Galilee differ from the first?
- Why do Jesus' relatives attempt to lay hold of him?
- How do the Pharisees attempt to discredit Jesus' miracles, and how does Jesus refute them?
- Of what are those Pharisees guilty, and why?

42

Jesus Rebukes the Pharisees

IF IT is by Satan's power that he expels demons, Jesus argues, then Satan is divided against himself. "Either you people make the tree fine and its fruit fine," he continues, "or make the tree rotten and its fruit rotten; for by its fruit the tree is known."

It is foolish to charge that the good fruit of casting out demons is a result of Jesus' serving Satan. If the fruit is fine, the tree cannot be rotten. On the other hand, the Pharisees' rotten fruitage of absurd accusations and groundless opposition to Jesus is proof that they themselves are rotten. "Offspring of vipers," Jesus exclaims, "how can you speak good things, when you are wicked? For out of the abundance of the heart the mouth speaks."

Since our words reflect the condition of our hearts, what we say provides a basis for judgment. "I tell you," Jesus says, "that every unprofitable saying that men speak, they will render an account concerning it on Judgment Day; for by your words you will be declared righteous, and by your words you will be condemned."

Despite all of Jesus' powerful works, the scribes and Pharisees request: "Teacher, we want to see a sign from you." Although these particular men from Jerusalem may not personally have seen his miracles, irrefutable eyewitness evidence regarding them exists. So Jesus tells the Jewish leaders: "A wicked and adulterous generation keeps on seeking for a sign, but no sign will be given it except the sign of Jonah the prophet."

Explaining what he means, Jesus continues: "Just as Jonah was in the belly of the huge fish three days and three nights, so the Son of man will be in the heart of the earth three days and three nights." After being swallowed by the fish, Jonah came out as if resurrected, so Jesus is foretelling that he will die and on the third day will be raised alive. Yet, the Jewish leaders, even when Jesus later is resurrected, reject "the sign of Jonah."

Thus Jesus says that the men of Nineveh who repented at the preaching of Jonah will rise up in the judgment to condemn the Jews who reject Jesus. Similarly, he draws a parallel with the queen of Sheba, who came from the ends of the earth to hear Solomon's wisdom and marveled at what she saw and heard. "But, look!" Jesus notes, "something more than Solomon is here."

Jesus then gives the illustration of a man from whom an unclean spirit comes out. The man, however, does not fill the void with good things, so he becomes possessed by seven more wicked spirits. "That is how it will be also with this wicked generation," Jesus says. The Israelite nation had been cleansed and had experienced reformations—like the temporary departure of an unclean spirit. But the nation's rejection of God's prophets, culminating in its opposition to Christ himself, reveals its wicked condition to be much worse than at its beginning.

While Jesus is speaking, his mother and his brothers arrive and take a position at the edge of the crowd. So someone says: "Look! Your mother and your brothers are standing outside, seeking to speak to you."

"Who is my mother, and who are my brothers?" Jesus asks. Extending his hand toward his disciples, he says: "Look! My mother and my brothers! For whoever does the will of my Father who is in heaven, the same is my brother, and sister, and mother." In this way Jesus shows that regardless of how dear the ties are that bind him to his relatives, dearer still is his relationship with his disciples. **Matthew 12:33-50; Mark 3:31-35; Luke 8:19-21.**

▪ How do the Pharisees fail to make both the "tree" and the "fruit" fine?
▪ What is "the sign of Jonah," and how is it later rejected?
▪ How is the first-century Israelite nation like the man from whom an unclean spirit came out?
▪ How does Jesus emphasize his close relationship with his disciples?

43 | Teaching With Illustrations

JESUS is apparently in Capernaum when he rebukes the Pharisees. Later the same day, he leaves the house and walks to the nearby Sea of Galilee, where crowds of people gather. There he boards a boat, pulls away, and begins teaching the people on the shore about the Kingdom of the heavens. He does so by means of a series of parables, or illustrations, each with a setting familiar to the people.

First, Jesus tells of a sower who sows seed. Some seed falls on the roadside and is eaten by birds. Other seed falls on soil with an underlying rock-mass. Since the roots lack depth, the new plants wither under the scorching sun. Still other seed falls among thorns, which choke the plants when they come up. Finally, some seed falls on good soil and produces a hundredfold, some sixtyfold, and some thirtyfold.

In another illustration, Jesus compares the Kingdom of God to a man who sows seed. As the days go by, while the man sleeps and when he is awake, the seed grows. The man does not know how. It grows all by itself and produces grain. When the grain ripens, the man harvests it.

Jesus tells a third illustration about a man who sows the right kind of seed, but "while men were sleeping," an enemy comes and sows weeds in among the wheat. The man's servants ask if they should pull out the weeds. But he replies: 'No, you will uproot some of the wheat if you do. Let them both grow together until the harvest. Then I will tell the reapers to sort out the weeds and burn them and put the wheat in the barn.'

Continuing his speech to the crowds on the shore, Jesus provides two more illustrations. He explains that "the kingdom of the heavens" is like a mustard grain that a man plants. Though it is the tiniest of all seeds, he says, it grows into the largest of all vegetables. It becomes a tree to which birds come, finding shelter among its branches.

Some today object that there are tinier seeds than mustard seeds. But Jesus is not giving a lesson in botany. Of the seeds that Galileans of his day are familiar with, the mustard seed really is the tiniest. So they appreciate the matter of phenomenal growth that Jesus is illustrating.

Finally, Jesus compares "the kingdom of the heavens" to leaven that a woman takes and mixes into three large measures of flour. In time, he says, it permeates every part of the dough.

After giving these five illustrations, Jesus dismisses the crowds and returns to the house where he is staying. Soon his 12 apostles and others come to him there.

Benefiting From Jesus' Illustrations

When the disciples come to Jesus after his speech to the crowds on the beach, they are curious about his new method of teaching. Oh, they have heard him use illustrations before, but never so extensively. So they inquire: "Why is it you speak to them by the use of illustrations?"

One reason he does so is to fulfill the prophet's words: "I will open my mouth with illustrations, I will publish things hidden since the founding." But there is more to it than this. His use of illustrations serves the purpose of helping to reveal the heart attitude of people.

Actually, most people are interested in Jesus simply as a masterful storyteller and miracle worker, not as one to be served as Lord and to be unselfishly followed. They do not want to be disturbed in their view of things or their way of life. They do not want the message to penetrate to that extent.

So Jesus says: "This is why I speak to them by the use of illustrations, because, looking, they look in vain, and hearing, they hear in vain, neither do they get the sense of it; and toward them the prophecy of Isaiah is having fulfillment, which says, '... For the heart of this people has grown unreceptive.'"

"However," Jesus goes on to say, "happy are your

eyes because they behold, and your ears because they hear. For I truly say to you, Many prophets and righteous men desired to see the things you are beholding and did not see them, and to hear the things you are hearing and did not hear them."

Yes, the 12 apostles and those with them have receptive hearts. Therefore Jesus says: "To you it is granted to understand the sacred secrets of the kingdom of the heavens, but to those people it is not granted." Because of their desire for understanding, Jesus provides his disciples with an explanation of the illustration of the sower.

"The seed is the word of God," Jesus says, and the soil is the heart. Of the seed sown on the hard roadside surface, he explains: "The Devil comes and takes the word away from their hearts in order that they may not believe and be saved."

On the other hand, seed sown on soil with an underlying rock-mass refers to the hearts of people who receive the word with joy. However, because the word cannot take deep root in such hearts, these people fall away when a time of testing or persecution comes.

As for the seed that fell among the thorns, Jesus continues, this refers to people who have heard the word. These ones, however, are carried away by anxieties and riches and pleasures of this life, so they are completely choked and bring nothing to perfection.

Finally, as for the seed sown on fine soil, Jesus says, these are the ones who, after hearing the word with a fine and good heart, retain it and bear fruit with endurance.

How blessed are these disciples who have sought out Jesus to obtain an explanation of his teachings! Jesus intends that his illustrations be understood in order to impart truth to others. "A lamp is not brought to be put under a measuring basket or under a bed, is it?" he asks. No, "it is brought to be put upon a lampstand." Thus Jesus adds: "Therefore, pay attention to how you listen."

Blessed With More Instruction

After receiving Jesus' explanation of the illustration of the sower, the disciples want to learn more. "Explain to us," they request, "the illustration of the weeds in the field."

How different the attitude of the disciples from that of the rest of the crowd on the beach! Those people lack an earnest desire to learn the meaning behind the illustrations, being satisfied with merely the outline of things set out in them. Contrasting that seaside audience with his inquisitive disciples who have come to him in the house, Jesus says:

"With the measure that you are measuring out, you will have it measured out to you, yes, you will have more added to you." The disciples are measuring out to Jesus earnest interest and attention, and so they are blessed with receiving more instruction. Thus, in answer to his disciples' inquiry, Jesus explains:

"The sower of the fine seed is the Son of man; the field is the world; as for the fine seed, these are the sons of the kingdom; but the weeds are the sons of the wicked one, and the enemy that sowed them is the Devil. The harvest is a conclusion of a system of things, and the reapers are angels."

After identifying each feature of his illustration, Jesus describes the outcome. At the conclusion of the system of things, he says that the reapers, or angels, will separate weedlike imitation Christians from the true "sons of the kingdom." Then "the sons of the wicked one" will be marked for destruction, but the sons of God's Kingdom, "the righteous ones," will shine brilliantly in the Kingdom of their Father.

Jesus next blesses his inquisitive disciples with three more illustrations. First, he says: "The kingdom of the heavens is like a treasure hidden in the field, which a man found and hid; and for the joy he has he goes and sells what things he has and buys that field."

"Again," he continues, "the kingdom of the heavens is like a traveling merchant seeking fine pearls. Upon finding one pearl of high value, away he went and promptly sold all the things he had and bought it."

Jesus himself is like the man who discovers a hidden treasure and like the merchant who finds a pearl of high value. He sold everything, as it were, giving up an honored position in heaven to become a lowly human. Then, as a man on earth, he suffers reproach and hateful persecution, proving worthy of becoming the Ruler of God's Kingdom.

The challenge is placed before Jesus' followers also to sell everything in order to obtain the grand reward of being either a coruler with Christ or an earthly Kingdom subject. Will we consider having a share in God's Kingdom as something more valuable than anything else in life, as a priceless treasure or a precious pearl?

Finally, Jesus likens "the kingdom of the heavens" to a dragnet that gathers up fish of every kind. When the fish are separated, the unsuitable are thrown away but the good are kept. So, Jesus says, it will be in the conclusion of the system of things; the angels will separate the wicked from the righteous, reserving the wicked for annihilation.

Jesus himself begins this fishing project, calling his first disciples to be "fishers of men." Under angelic surveillance, the fishing work continues down through the centuries. At last the time comes to haul in the "dragnet," which symbolizes the organizations on earth professing to be Christian.

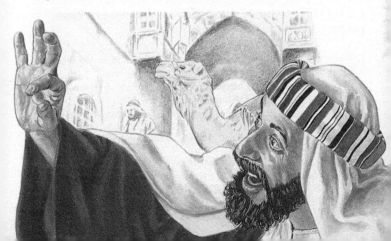

Although the unsuitable fish are cast into destruction, thankfully we can be counted among the 'good fish' that are kept. By exhibiting the same earnest desire as Jesus' disciples did for more knowledge and understanding, we will be blessed not only with more instruction but with God's blessing of eternal life. **Matthew 13:1-52; Mark 4:1-34; Luke 8:4-18; Psalm 78:2; Isaiah 6:9, 10.**

- When and where does Jesus speak with illustrations to the crowds?
- What five illustrations does Jesus now tell the crowds?
- Why does Jesus say the mustard seed is the tiniest of all seeds?
- Why does Jesus speak in illustrations?
- How do Jesus' disciples show themselves to be different from the crowds?
- What explanation does Jesus provide of the illustration of the sower?
- How do the disciples differ from the crowds on the beach?
- Who or what is represented by the sower, the field, the fine seed, the enemy, the harvest, and the reapers?
- What three additional illustrations does Jesus provide, and what can we learn from them?

44

Silencing a Terrifying Storm

J ESUS' day has been filled with activity, including teaching the crowds on the beach and afterward explaining the illustrations privately to his disciples. When evening comes, he says: "Let us cross to the other shore."

Over on the eastern shore of the Sea of Galilee is the region called the Decapolis, from the Greek *de'ka,* meaning "ten," and *po'lis,* meaning "city." The cities of the Decapolis are a center of Greek culture, although doubtless they are also the home of many Jews. Jesus' activity in the region, however, is very limited. Even on this visit, as we will see later, he is prevented from staying long.

When Jesus requests that they leave for the other shore, the disciples take him in the boat. Their departure, however, does not go unnoticed. Soon others board their boats to accompany them. It is not very far across. Actually, the Sea of Galilee is just a large lake about 13 miles long and a maximum of 7 1/2 miles wide.

Jesus is understandably tired. So, soon after they shove off, he lies down in the back of the boat, puts his head on a pillow, and falls fast asleep. Several of the apostles are experienced sailors, having fished extensively on the Sea of Galilee. So they take charge of sailing the boat.

But this is not to be an easy trip. Because of the warmer temperature at the lake's surface, which is about 700 feet below sea level, and the colder air in the nearby mountains, strong winds at times sweep down and create sudden violent windstorms on the lake. This is what now occurs. Soon the waves are dashing against the boat and splashing into it, so that it is close to being swamped. Yet, Jesus continues to sleep!

The experienced seamen work frantically to steer the boat. No doubt they have maneuvered through storms before. But this time they are at the end of their resources. Fearing for

their lives, they wake Jesus up. 'Master, do you not care? We are sinking!' they exclaim. 'Save us, we are going to drown!'

Rousing himself, Jesus commands the wind and the sea: "Hush! Be quiet!" And the raging wind stops and the sea becomes calm. Turning to his disciples, he asks: 'Why are you so fearful? Do you not yet have any faith?'

At that, an unusual fear grips the disciples. 'Who really is this man?' they ask one another, 'for he orders even the winds and the water, and they obey him.'

What power Jesus displays! How reassuring it is to know that our King has power over the natural elements and that when his full attention is directed toward our earth during his Kingdom rule, all people will dwell in security from terrifying natural calamities!

Sometime after the storm subsides, Jesus and his disciples arrive safely on the eastern shore. Perhaps the other boats were spared the intensity of the storm and safely returned home. **Mark 4:35–5:1; Matthew 8:18, 23-27; Luke 8:22-26.**

- What is the Decapolis, and where is it located?
- What physical features are responsible for violent storms on the Sea of Galilee?
- When their sailing skills cannot save them, what do the disciples do?

45

An Unlikely Disciple

WHAT a frightening sight as Jesus steps ashore! Two unusually fierce men come out from the nearby cemetery and run toward him. They are demon possessed. Since one of them is possibly more violent than the other and has suffered much longer under demon control, he becomes the focus of attention.

For a long time this pitiful man has been living naked among the tombs. Continually, day and night, he cries out and slashes himself with stones. He is so violent that nobody has the courage to pass that way on the road. Attempts have been made to bind him, but he tears the chains apart and breaks the irons off his feet. Nobody has the strength to subdue him.

As the man approaches Jesus and falls at his feet, the demons controlling him make him scream: "What have I to

do with you, Jesus, Son of the Most High God? I put you under oath by God not to torment me."

"Come out of the man, you unclean spirit," Jesus keeps saying. But then Jesus asks: "What is your name?"

"My name is Legion, because there are many of us," is the reply. The demons revel in seeing the sufferings of those they are able to possess, apparently taking delight in ganging up on them in a cowardly mob spirit. But confronted with Jesus, they beg not to be sent into the abyss. We again see that Jesus had great power; he was able to conquer even vicious demons. This also reveals that the demons are aware that their abyssing along with that of their leader, Satan the Devil, is God's eventual judgment for them.

A herd of about 2,000 swine are grazing nearby on the mountain. So the demons say: "Send us into the swine, that we may enter into them." Evidently the demons get some sort of unnatural, sadistic pleasure from invading the bodies of fleshly creatures. When Jesus permits them to enter the swine, all 2,000 of them stampede over the cliff and drown in the sea.

When those taking care of the swine see this, they rush to report the news in the city and in the countryside. At that, the people come out to see what has happened. When they arrive, they see the man from whom the demons came out. Why, he is clothed and in his sound mind, sitting at the feet of Jesus!

Eyewitnesses relate how the man was made well. They also tell the people about the bizarre death of the swine. When the people hear this, great fear grips them, and they earnestly urge Jesus to leave their territory. So he complies and boards the boat. The former demoniac begs Jesus to allow him to come along. But Jesus tells him: "Go home to your relatives, and report to them all the things Jehovah has done for you and the mercy he had on you."

Jesus usually instructs those whom he heals not to tell anyone, since he does not want to have people reach conclusions on the basis of sensational reports. But this exception is appropriate because the former demoniac will be witnessing among people that Jesus now will probably not have opportunity to reach. Moreover, the man's presence will provide testimony about Jesus' power to work good, counteracting any unfavorable report that might be circulated over the loss of the swine.

In keeping with Jesus' instruction, the former demoniac goes away. He starts proclaiming throughout the Decapolis all the things Jesus did for him, and the people are simply amazed. **Matthew 8:28-34; Mark 5:1-20; Luke 8:26-39; Revelation 20:1-3.**

- Why, perhaps, is attention focused on one demon-possessed man when two are present?

- What shows that the demons know about a future abyssing?

- Why, apparently, do demons like to possess humans and animals?

- Why does Jesus make an exception with the former demoniac, instructing him to tell others about what He did for him?

46

She Touched His Garment

NEWS of Jesus' return from the Decapolis reaches Capernaum, and a great crowd assembles by the sea to welcome him back. No doubt they have heard that he stilled the storm and cured the demon-possessed men. Now, as he steps ashore, they gather around him, eager and expectant.

One of those anxious to see Jesus is Jairus, a presiding officer of the synagogue. He falls at Jesus' feet and begs over and over: "My little daughter is in an extreme condition. Would you please come and put your hands upon her that she may get well and live." Since she is his only child and just 12 years old, she is especially precious to Jairus.

Jesus responds and, accompanied by the crowd, heads for the home of Jairus. We can imagine the excitement of the people as they anticipate another miracle. But the attention of one woman in the crowd is focused on her own severe problem.

For 12 long years, this woman has suffered from a flow of blood. She has been to one doctor after another, spending all her money on treatments. But she has not been helped; rather, her problem has become worse.

As you can probably appreciate, besides weakening her very much, her ailment is also embarrassing and humiliating.

One generally does not speak publicly about such an affliction. Moreover, under the Mosaic Law a running discharge of blood makes a woman unclean, and anyone touching her or her blood-stained garments is required to wash and be unclean until the evening.

The woman has heard of Jesus' miracles and has now sought him out. In view of her uncleanness, she makes her way through the crowd as inconspicuously as possible, saying to herself: "If I touch just his outer garments I shall get well." When she does so, immediately she senses that her flow of blood has dried up!

"Who was it that touched me?" How those words of Jesus must shock her! How could he know? 'Instructor,' Peter protests, 'the crowds are hemming you in and closely pressing you, and do you say, "Who touched me?"'

Looking around for the woman, Jesus explains: "Someone touched me, for I perceived that power went out of me." Indeed, it is no ordinary touch, for the healing that results draws on Jesus' vitality.

Seeing that she has not escaped notice, the woman comes and falls down before Jesus, frightened and trembling. In front of all the people, she tells the whole truth about her illness and how she has just now been cured.

Moved by her full confession, Jesus compassionately comforts her: "Daughter, your faith has made you well. Go in peace, and be in good health from your grievous sickness." How fine it is to know that the One whom God has chosen to rule the earth is such a warm, compassionate person, who both cares for people and has the power to help them! Matthew 9:18-22; Mark 5:21-34; Luke 8:40-48; Leviticus 15:25-27.

- Who is Jairus, and why does he come to Jesus?
- What problem does one woman have, and why is coming to Jesus for help so difficult for her?
- How is the woman healed, and how does Jesus comfort her?

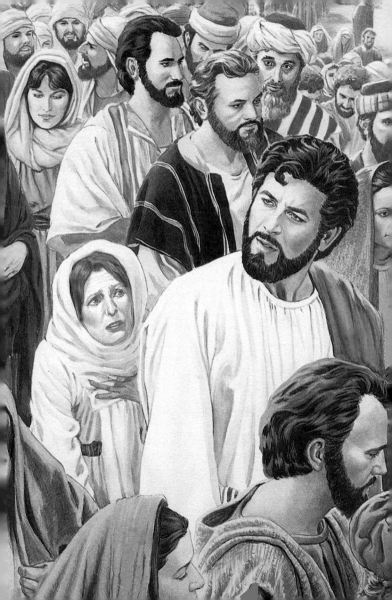

47

Tears Turned to Great Ecstasy

WHEN Jairus sees the woman with the flow of blood healed, his confidence in Jesus' miraculous powers no doubt increases. Earlier in the day, Jesus had been asked by Jairus to come and help his beloved 12-year-old daughter, who lay near death. Now, however, what Jairus fears most occurs. While Jesus is still speaking with the woman, some men arrive and quietly tell Jairus: "Your daughter died! Why bother the teacher any longer?"

How devastating the news is! Just think: This man, who commands great respect in the community, is now totally helpless as he learns of his daughter's death. Jesus, however,

overhears the conversation. So, turning to Jairus, he says encouragingly: "Have no fear, only exercise faith."

Jesus accompanies the grief-stricken man back to his home. When they arrive, they find a great commotion of weeping and wailing. A crowd of people have gathered, and they are beating themselves in grief. When Jesus steps inside, he asks: "Why are you causing noisy confusion and weeping? The young child has not died, but is sleeping."

On hearing this, the people begin to laugh scornfully at Jesus because they know that the girl is really dead. Jesus, however, says that she is only sleeping. By using his God-given powers, he will show that people can be brought back from death as easily as they can be awakened from a deep sleep.

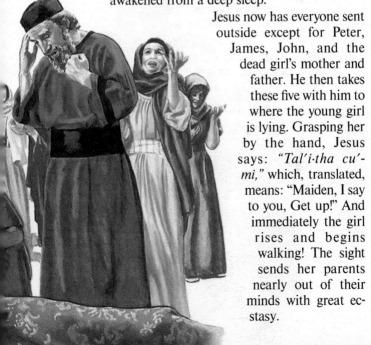

Jesus now has everyone sent outside except for Peter, James, John, and the dead girl's mother and father. He then takes these five with him to where the young girl is lying. Grasping her by the hand, Jesus says: *"Tal'i·tha cu'-mi,"* which, translated, means: "Maiden, I say to you, Get up!" And immediately the girl rises and begins walking! The sight sends her parents nearly out of their minds with great ecstasy.

After instructing that the child be given something to eat, Jesus orders Jairus and his wife not to tell anyone what has happened. But despite what Jesus says, talk about it spreads out into all that region. This is the second resurrection Jesus performs. **Matthew 9:18-26; Mark 5:35-43; Luke 8:41-56.**

- What news does Jairus receive, and how does Jesus encourage him?
- What is the situation when they arrive at Jairus' home?
- Why does Jesus say that the dead child is only sleeping?
- Who are the five with Jesus that witness the resurrection?

48

Leaving Jairus' Home and Revisiting Nazareth

THE day has been busy for Jesus—a sea voyage from the Decapolis, healing the woman with the flow of blood, and resurrecting Jairus' daughter. But the day is not over. Evidently as Jesus leaves the home of Jairus, two blind men follow behind, shouting: "Have mercy on us, Son of David."

By addressing Jesus as "Son of David," these men are hereby expressing belief that Jesus is heir to the throne of David, hence that he is the promised Messiah. Jesus, however, seemingly ignores their cries for help, perhaps to test their persistence. But the men do not give up. They follow Jesus to where he is staying, and when he enters the house, they follow him inside.

There Jesus asks: "Do you have faith that I can do this?"

"Yes, Lord," they answer confidently.

So, touching their eyes, Jesus says: "According to your faith let it happen to you." Suddenly they can see! Jesus then sternly charges them: "See that nobody gets to know it." But filled with gladness, they ignore Jesus' command and talk about him throughout the countryside.

Just as these men leave, people bring in a demon-possessed man whom the demon has robbed of his speech. Jesus expels the demon, and instantly the man begins to talk. The crowds marvel at these miracles, saying: "Never was anything like this seen in Israel."

Pharisees also are present. They cannot deny the miracles, but in their wicked unbelief they repeat their charge as to the source of Jesus' powerful works, saying: "It is by the ruler of the demons that he expels the demons."

Shortly after these events, Jesus returns to his hometown of Nazareth, this time accompanied by his disciples. About a year earlier, he had visited the synagogue and taught there. Although the people at first marveled at his pleasing words, they later took offense at his teaching and tried to kill him. Now, mercifully, Jesus makes another attempt to help his former neighbors.

While in other places people flock to Jesus, here they apparently do not. So, on the Sabbath, he goes to the synagogue to teach. Most of those hearing him are astounded. "Where did this man get this wisdom and these powerful works?" they ask. "Is this not the carpenter's son? Is not his

mother called Mary, and his brothers James and Joseph and Simon and Judas? And his sisters, are they not all with us? Where, then, did this man get all these things?"

'Jesus is just a local man like us,' they reason. 'We saw him grow up, and we know his family. How can he be the Messiah?' So despite all the evidence—his great wisdom and miracles—they reject him. Because of their intimate familiarity, even his own relatives stumble at him, causing Jesus to conclude: "A prophet is not unhonored except in his home territory and among his relatives and in his own house."

Indeed, Jesus wonders at their lack of faith. So he does not perform any miracles there apart from laying his hands on a few sick people and healing them.   **Matthew 9:27-34; 13:54-58; Mark 6:1-6; Isaiah 9:7.**

- ■ By addressing Jesus as "Son of David," what do the blind men show they believe?
- ■ What explanation for Jesus' miracles have the Pharisees settled upon?
- ■ Why is it merciful for Jesus to return to help those in Nazareth?
- ■ What reception does Jesus receive in Nazareth, and why?

49

Another Preaching Tour of Galilee

AFTER about two years of intensive preaching, will Jesus now begin to let up and take it easy? On the contrary, he expands his preaching activity by setting out on yet another tour, a third one of Galilee. He visits all the cities and villages in the territory, teaching in the synagogues and preaching the good news of the Kingdom. What he sees on this tour convinces him more than ever of the need to intensify the preaching work.

Wherever Jesus goes, he sees the crowds in need of spiritual healing and comfort. They are like sheep without a shepherd, skinned and thrown about, and he feels pity for them. He tells his disciples: "Yes, the harvest is great, but the workers are few. Therefore, beg the Master of the harvest to send out workers into his harvest."

Jesus has a plan of action. He summons the 12 apostles, whom he had chosen nearly a year earlier. He divides them into pairs, making six teams of preachers, and gives them instructions. He explains: "Do not go off into the road of the nations, and do not enter into a Samaritan city; but, instead, go continually to the lost sheep of the house of Israel. As you go, preach, saying, 'The kingdom of the heavens has drawn near.'"

This Kingdom that they are to preach about is the one Jesus taught them to pray for in the model prayer. The Kingdom has drawn near in the sense that God's designated King, Jesus Christ, is present. To establish his disciples' credentials as representatives of that superhuman government, Jesus empowers them to cure the sick and even raise the dead. He instructs them to perform these services free.

Next he tells his disciples not to make material preparations for their preaching tour. "Do not procure gold or silver or copper for your girdle purses, or a food pouch for the trip, or two undergarments, or sandals or a staff; for the worker deserves his food." Those who appreciate the message will respond and contribute food and housing. As Jesus says: "Into whatever city or village you enter, search out who in it is deserving, and stay there until you leave."

Jesus then gives instructions on how to approach householders with the Kingdom message. "When you are entering into the house," he instructs, "greet the household; and if the house is deserving, let the peace you wish it come upon it; but if it is not deserving, let the peace from you return upon you. Wherever anyone does not take you in or listen to your words, on going out of that house or that city shake the dust off your feet."

Of a city that rejects their message, Jesus reveals that the judgment upon it will indeed be severe. He explains: "Truly I say to you, It will be more endurable for the land of Sodom and Gomorrah on Judgment Day than for that city." **Matthew 9:35–10:15; Mark 6:6-12; Luke 9:1-5.**

- When does Jesus begin a third preaching tour of Galilee, and of what does it convince him?

- When sending his 12 apostles out to preach, what instructions does he give them?

- Why is it correct for the disciples to teach that the Kingdom has drawn near?

50

Preparation to Face Persecution

AFTER instructing his apostles in methods of carrying out the preaching work, Jesus warns them about opposers. He says: "Look! I am sending you forth as sheep amidst wolves . . . Be on your guard against men; for they will deliver you up to local courts, and they will scourge you in their synagogues. Why, you will be haled before governors and kings for my sake."

Despite the severe persecution his followers will face, Jesus reassuringly promises: "When they deliver you up, do not become anxious about how or what you are to speak; for what you are to speak will be given you in that hour; for the ones speaking are not just you, but it is the spirit of your Father that speaks by you."

"Further," Jesus continues, "brother will deliver up brother to death, and a father his child, and children will rise up against parents and will have them put to death." He adds: "You will be objects of hatred by all people on account of my name; but he that has endured to the end is the one that will be saved."

The preaching is of primary importance. For this reason Jesus emphasizes the need for discretion in order to remain free to carry out the work. "When they persecute you in one city, flee to another," he says, "for truly I say to you, You will by no means complete the circuit of the cities of Israel until the Son of man arrives."

It is true that Jesus gave this instruction, warning, and encouragement to his 12 apostles, but it was also meant for those who would share in the worldwide preaching after his death and resurrection. This is shown by his saying that his disciples would be *'hated by all people,'* not just by the Israelites to whom the apostles were sent to preach. Further, the apostles evidently were not haled before governors and kings when Jesus sent them out on their short preaching campaign. Moreover, believers were not then delivered up to death by family members.

So when saying that his disciples would not complete their circuit of preaching "until the Son of man arrives," Jesus was prophetically telling us that his disciples would not complete the circuit of the entire inhabited earth with the preaching about God's established Kingdom before the glorified King Jesus Christ would arrive as Jehovah's executional officer at Armageddon.

Continuing his preaching instructions, Jesus says: "A disciple is not above his teacher, nor a slave above his lord." So Jesus' followers must expect to receive the same ill-treatment and persecution as he did for preaching God's Kingdom. Yet he admonishes: "Do not become fearful of those who kill the body but cannot kill the soul; but rather be in fear of him that can destroy both soul and body in Gehenna."

Jesus was to set the example in this matter. He would fearlessly endure death rather than compromise his loyalty to the One with all power, Jehovah God. Yes, it is Jehovah who can destroy one's "soul" (meaning in this in-

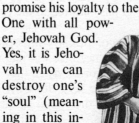

stance one's future prospects as a living soul) or can instead resurrect a person to enjoy everlasting life. What a loving, compassionate heavenly Father Jehovah is!

Jesus next encourages his disciples with an illustration that highlights Jehovah's loving care for them. "Do not two sparrows sell for a coin of small value?" he asks. "Yet not one of them will fall to the ground without your Father's knowledge. But the very hairs of your head are all numbered. Therefore have no fear: you are worth more than many sparrows."

The Kingdom message Jesus commissions his disciples to proclaim will divide households, as certain family members accept it and others reject it. "Do not think I came to put peace upon the earth," he explains. "I came to put, not peace, but a sword." Thus, for a family member to embrace Bible truth requires courage. "He that has greater affection for father or mother than for me is not worthy of me," Jesus observes, "and he that has greater affection for son or daughter than for me is not worthy of me."

Concluding his instructions, Jesus explains that those who receive his disciples receive him also. "And whoever gives one of these little ones only a cup of cold water to drink because he is a disciple, I tell you truly, he will by no means lose his reward." **Matthew 10:16-42.**

- What warnings does Jesus provide his disciples?
- What encouragement and comfort does he give them?
- Why do Jesus' instructions apply also to modern-day Christians?
    - In what way is a disciple of Jesus not above his teacher?

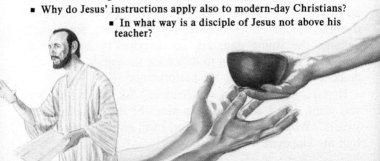

51

Murder During a Birthday Party

AFTER giving instructions to his apostles, Jesus sends them out into the territory in pairs. Probably the brothers Peter and Andrew go together, as do James and John, Philip and Bartholomew, Thomas and Matthew, James and Thaddaeus, and Simon and Judas Iscariot. The six pairs of evangelizers declare the good news of the Kingdom and perform miraculous cures everywhere they go.

Meanwhile, John the Baptizer is still in prison. He has been there almost two years now. You may recall that John had declared publicly that it was wrong for Herod Antipas to take Herodias, the wife of his brother Philip, as his own. Since Herod Antipas claimed to follow the Mosaic Law, John had properly exposed this adulterous union. So Herod had John thrown into prison, perhaps at the urging of Herodias.

Herod Antipas realizes that John is a righteous man and even listens to him with pleasure. Therefore, he is at a loss as to what to do with him. Herodias, on the other hand, hates John and keeps seeking to have him put to death. Finally, the opportunity she has been waiting for comes.

Shortly before the Passover of 32 C.E., Herod arranges a large celebration of his birthday. Assembled for the party are all Herod's top-ranking officials and army officers, as well as the leading citizens of Galilee. As the evening progresses, Salome, the young daughter of Herodias by her former husband Philip, is sent in to dance for the guests. The male audience is enthralled by her performance.

Herod is highly pleased with Salome. "Ask me for whatever you want, and I will give it to you," he declares. He even swears: "Whatever you ask me for, I will give it to you, up to half my kingdom."

Before answering, Salome goes out to consult with her mother. "What should I ask for?" she inquires.

The opportunity at last! "The head of John the baptizer," Herodias answers without hesitation.

Quickly Salome returns to Herod and makes the request: "I want you to give me right away on a platter the head of John the Baptist."

Herod is greatly distressed. Yet because his guests have heard his oath, he is embarrassed not to grant it, even though this means murdering an innocent man. An executioner is immediately dispatched to the prison with his grisly instructions. Shortly he returns with John's head on a platter, and he gives it to Salome. She, in turn, takes it to her mother. When John's disciples hear what has happened, they come and remove his body and bury it, and then they report the matter to Jesus.

Later, when Herod hears of Jesus' healing people and casting out demons, he is frightened, fearing that Jesus is actually John who has been raised from the dead. Thereafter, he greatly desires to see Jesus, not to hear his preaching, but to confirm whether his fears are well-founded or not. **Matthew 10:1-5; 11:1; 14:1-12; Mark 6:14-29; Luke 9:7-9.**

- Why is John in prison, and why does Herod not want to put him to death?
- How is Herodias finally able to have John killed?
- After John's death, why does Herod want to see Jesus?

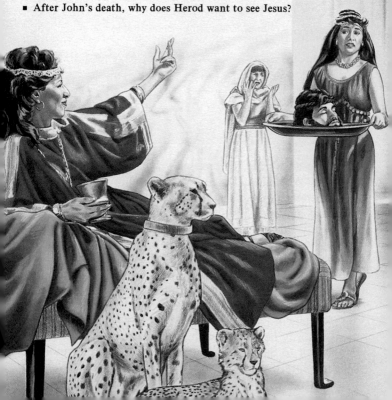

52

Jesus Miraculously Feeds Thousands

THE 12 apostles have enjoyed a remarkable preaching tour throughout Galilee. Now, shortly after John's execution, they return to Jesus and relate their wonderful experiences. Seeing that they are tired and that so many people are coming and going that they don't even have time to eat, Jesus says: 'Let us go off by ourselves to a lonely place where you can rest up.'

Boarding their boat, probably near Capernaum, they head for an out-of-the-way place, evidently east of the Jordan beyond Bethsaida. Many people, however, see them leave, and others learn about it. These all run ahead along the shore, and when the boat lands, the people are there to meet them.

Getting out of the boat and seeing the great crowd, Jesus is moved with pity because the people are as sheep without a shepherd. So he heals their sick and begins teaching them many things.

Time passes quickly, and Jesus' disciples come to him and say: "The place is isolated, and the hour is already late. Send them away, that they may go off into the countryside and villages round about and buy themselves something to eat."

However, in reply Jesus says: "You give them something to eat." Then, since Jesus already knows what he is going to do, he tests Philip by asking him: "Where shall we buy loaves for these to eat?"

From Philip's viewpoint the situation is impossible. Why, there are about 5,000 men, and probably well over 10,000 people counting also women and children! Philip responds that "two hundred denarii [a denarius was then a day's wage] worth of loaves is not enough for them, so that each one may get a little."

Perhaps to show the impossibility of feeding so many, Andrew volunteers: "Here is a little boy that has five barley loaves and two small fishes," adding, "but what are these among so many?"

Since it is springtime, just before Passover 32 C.E., there is a lot of green grass. So Jesus has his disciples tell the people to recline on the grass in groups of 50 and of 100. He takes the five loaves and two fishes, looks to heaven, and says a blessing. Then he begins breaking the loaves and dividing up

the fishes. He gives these to his disciples, who, in turn, distribute them to the people. Amazingly, all the people eat until they have had enough!

Afterward Jesus tells his disciples: "Gather together the fragments that remain over, so that nothing is wasted." When they do, they fill 12 baskets with the leftovers from what they have eaten! **Matthew 14:13-21; Mark 6:30-44; Luke 9:10-17; John 6:1-13.**

- Why does Jesus seek a place of privacy for his apostles?
- Where does Jesus take his disciples, and why does their need for rest go unfulfilled?
- When it becomes late, what do the disciples urge, but how does Jesus care for the people?

53

A Desired Superhuman Ruler

WHEN Jesus miraculously feeds the thousands, the people are amazed. "This is for a certainty the prophet that was to come into the world," they say. They conclude not only that Jesus must be that prophet greater than Moses but also that he would make a most desirable ruler. So they plan to seize him and make him king.

Jesus, however, is aware of what the people are planning. So he quickly moves to avoid being forcibly drafted by them. He dismisses the crowds and compels his disciples to get in their boat and head back toward Capernaum. He then withdraws into the mountain to pray. That night Jesus is there all alone.

Shortly before dawn Jesus looks out from his elevated vantage point and observes waves being whipped up on the sea by a strong wind. In the light of the almost full moon, since it is near Passover, Jesus sees the boat with his disciples struggling to make headway against the waves. The men are rowing with all their might.

At seeing this, Jesus descends from the mountain and begins walking toward the boat across the waves. The boat has gone about three or four miles when Jesus reaches it. However, he continues on as though he is going to pass by. When the disciples see him, they cry: "It is an apparition!"

Jesus comfortingly responds: "It is I; have no fear."

But Peter says: "Lord, if it is you, command me to come to you over the waters."

"Come!" Jesus answers.

Thereupon, Peter, getting out of the boat, walks over the waters toward Jesus. But looking at the windstorm, Peter becomes afraid, and starting to sink, he cries: "Lord, save me!"

Immediately stretching out his hand, Jesus catches him, saying: "You with little faith, why did you give way to doubt?"

After Peter and Jesus get back into the boat, the wind stops, and the disciples are amazed. But should they be? If they had grasped "the meaning of the loaves" by appreciating the great miracle Jesus performed a few hours earlier when he fed thousands with only five loaves and two little fishes, then it should not have seemed so amazing that he could walk on water and cause the wind to abate. Now, however, the disciples do obeisance to Jesus and say: "You are really God's Son."

In a short time, they reach Gennesaret, a beautiful, fruitful plain near Capernaum. There they anchor the boat. But when they go ashore, people recognize Jesus and go into the surrounding country, finding those who are sick. When these are brought on their cots and just touch the fringe of Jesus' outer garment, they are made completely well.

Meanwhile, the crowd that witnessed the miraculous feeding of the thousands discover that Jesus has left. So when little boats from Tiberias arrive, they board these and sail to Capernaum to look for Jesus. When they find him, they ask: "Rabbi, when did you get here?" Jesus rebukes them, as we soon will see. **John 6:14-25; Matthew 14:22-36; Mark 6:45-56.**

■ After Jesus miraculously feeds the thousands, what do the people want to do to him?

■ What does Jesus see from the mountain to which he has withdrawn, and what does he then do?

■ Why should the disciples not be so amazed by these things?

■ What happens after they reach the shore?

54

"True Bread From Heaven"

THE day before had truly been eventful. Jesus miraculously fed thousands and then escaped the attempt of the people to make him king. That night he walked on the stormy Sea of Galilee; rescued Peter, who began to sink when he walked on the storm-tossed water; and calmed the waves to save his disciples from shipwreck.

Now the people whom Jesus had miraculously fed northeast of the Sea of Galilee find him near Capernaum and inquire: "When did you get here?" Rebuking them, Jesus says that they have come looking for him only because they expect to get another free meal. He urges them to work, not for food that perishes, but for food that remains for everlasting life. So the people inquire: "What shall we do to work the works of God?"

Jesus names but one work of the highest value. "This is the work of God," he explains, "that you exercise faith in him whom that One sent forth."

The people, however, do not exercise faith in Jesus, despite all the miracles he has performed. Unbelievably, even after all the marvelous things that he has done, they ask: "What, then, are you performing as a sign, in order for us to see it and believe you? What work are you doing? Our forefathers ate the manna in the wilderness, just as it is written, 'He gave them bread from heaven to eat.'"

In response to their request for a sign, Jesus makes clear the Source of miraculous provisions, saying: "Moses did not give you the bread from heaven, but my Father does give you the true bread from heaven. For the bread of God is the one who comes down from heaven and gives life to the world."

"Lord," the people say, "always give us this bread."

"I am the bread of life," Jesus explains. "He that comes to me will not get hungry at all, and he that exercises faith in me will never get thirsty at all. But I have said to you, You have

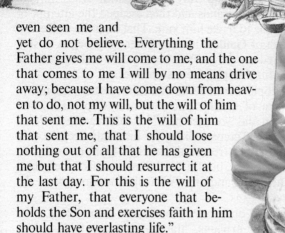

even seen me and yet do not believe. Everything the Father gives me will come to me, and the one that comes to me I will by no means drive away; because I have come down from heaven to do, not my will, but the will of him that sent me. This is the will of him that sent me, that I should lose nothing out of all that he has given me but that I should resurrect it at the last day. For this is the will of my Father, that everyone that beholds the Son and exercises faith in him should have everlasting life."

At this the Jews begin murmuring at Jesus because he said, "I am the bread that came down from heaven." They see in him nothing more than a son of human parents and so in the same manner as did the people of Nazareth, they object, saying: "Is this not Jesus the son of Joseph, whose father and mother we know? How is it that now he says, 'I have come down from heaven'?"

"Stop murmuring among yourselves," Jesus responds. "No man can come to me unless the Father, who sent me, draws him; and I will resurrect him in the last day. It is written in the Prophets, 'And they will all be taught by Jehovah.' Everyone that has heard from the Father and has learned comes to me. Not that any man has seen the Father, except he who is from God; this one has seen the Father. Most truly I say to you, He that believes has everlasting life."

Continuing, Jesus repeats: "I am the bread of life. Your forefathers ate the manna in the wilderness and yet died. This is the bread that comes down from heaven, so that anyone may eat of it and not die. I am the living bread that came down from heaven; if anyone eats of this bread he will live forever." Yes, by exercising faith in Jesus, the one sent forth by God, people can have everlasting life. No manna, or any other bread, can provide that!

The discussion regarding the bread from heaven apparently began shortly after the people found Jesus near Capernaum. But it continues, reaching a climax later while Jesus teaches in a synagogue in Capernaum. **John 6:25-51, 59; Psalm 78:24; Isaiah 54:13; Matthew 13:55-57.**

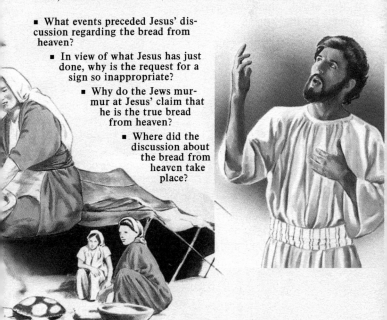

■ What events preceded Jesus' discussion regarding the bread from heaven?

   ■ In view of what Jesus has just done, why is the request for a sign so inappropriate?

      ■ Why do the Jews murmur at Jesus' claim that he is the true bread from heaven?

         ■ Where did the discussion about the bread from heaven take place?

55

Many Disciples Quit Following Jesus

JESUS is teaching in a synagogue in Capernaum concerning his part as the true bread from heaven. His talk is evidently an extension of the discussion that began with the people when they found him on their return from the eastern side of the Sea of Galilee, where they had eaten from the miraculously provided loaves and fishes.

Jesus continues his remarks, saying: "The bread that I shall give is my flesh in behalf of the life of the world." Just two years before, in the spring of 30 C.E., Jesus told Nicodemus that God loved the

world so much that he provided his Son as a Savior. Thus, Jesus is now showing that anyone of the world of mankind who eats symbolically of his flesh, by exercising faith in the sacrifice he is soon to make, may receive everlasting life.

The people, however, stumble over Jesus' words. "How can this man give us his flesh to eat?" they ask. Jesus wants his listeners to understand that the eating of his flesh would be done in a figurative way. So, to emphasize this, he says something still more objectionable if taken in a literal way.

"Unless you eat the flesh of the Son of man and drink his blood," Jesus declares, "you have no life in yourselves. He

that feeds on my flesh and drinks my blood has everlasting life, and I shall resurrect him at the last day; for my flesh is true food, and my blood is true drink. He that feeds on my flesh and drinks my blood remains in union with me, and I in union with him."

True, Jesus' teaching would sound most offensive if he were suggesting cannibalism. But, of course, Jesus is not advocating literally eating flesh or drinking blood. He is simply emphasizing that all who receive everlasting life must exercise faith in the sacrifice that he is to make when he offers up his perfect human body and pours out his lifeblood. Yet, even many of his disciples make no attempt to understand his teaching and so object: "This speech is shocking; who can listen to it?"

Knowing that many of his disciples are murmuring, Jesus says: "Does this stumble you? What, therefore, if you should behold the Son of man ascending to where he was before? . . . The sayings that I have spoken to you are spirit and are life. But there are some of you that do not believe."

Jesus continues: "This is why I have said to you, No one can come to me unless it is granted him by the Father." With that, many of his disciples leave and no longer follow him. So Jesus turns to his 12 apostles and asks: "You do not want to go also, do you?"

Peter responds: "Lord, whom shall we go away to? You have sayings of everlasting life; and we have believed and come to know that you are the Holy One of God." What a fine expression of loyalty, even though Peter and the other apostles may not have fully understood Jesus' teaching on this matter!

Although pleased by Peter's response, Jesus observes: "I chose you twelve, did I not? Yet one of you is a slanderer." He is speaking about Judas Iscariot. Possibly at this point Jesus detects in Judas a "beginning," or an outset, of a wrongful course.

Jesus has just disappointed the people by resisting their attempts to make him king, and they may be reasoning, 'How can this be the Messiah if he will not assume the Messiah's rightful position?' This, too, would be a matter fresh in the people's minds.   **John 6:51-71; 3:16.**

- For whom does Jesus give his flesh, and how do these 'eat his flesh'?
- What further words of Jesus shock the people, yet what is he emphasizing?
- When many quit following Jesus, what is Peter's response?

56

What Defiles a Man?

OPPOSITION to Jesus becomes stronger. Not only do many of his disciples leave but Jews in Judea are seeking to kill him, even as they did when he was in Jerusalem during the Passover of 31 C.E.

It is now the Passover of 32 C.E. Likely, in accordance with God's requirement to attend, Jesus goes up to the Passover in Jerusalem. However, he does so cautiously because his life is in danger. Afterward he returns to Galilee.

Jesus is perhaps in Capernaum when Pharisees and scribes from Jerusalem come to him. They are looking for grounds on which to accuse him of religious lawbreaking. "Why is it your disciples overstep the tradition of the men of former times?" they inquire. "For example, they do not wash their hands when about to eat a meal." This is not something required by God, yet the Pharisees consider it a serious offense not to perform this traditional ritual, which included washing up to the elbows.

Rather than answer them regarding their accusation, Jesus points to their wicked and willful breaking of God's Law. "Why is it you also overstep the commandment of God because of your tradition?" he wants to know. "For example, God said, 'Honor your father and your mother'; and, 'Let him that reviles father or mother end up in death.' But you say, 'Whoever says to his father or mother: "Whatever I have by which you might get benefit from me is a gift dedicated to God," he must not honor his father at all.'"

Indeed, the Pharisees teach that money, property, or anything dedicated as a gift to God belongs to the temple and cannot be used for some other purpose. Yet, actually, the dedicated gift is kept by the person who dedicated it. In this way a son, by simply saying that his money or property is "corban"—a gift dedicated to God or to the temple—evades his responsibility to help his aged parents, who may be in desperate straits.

Properly indignant at the Pharisees' wicked twisting of God's Law, Jesus says: "You have made the word of God invalid because of your tradition. You hypocrites, Isaiah aptly prophesied about you, when he said, 'This people honors me with their lips, yet their heart is far removed from me. It is in vain that they keep worshiping me, because they teach commands of men as doctrines.'"

Perhaps the crowd had backed away to allow the Pharisees to question Jesus. Now, when the Pharisees have no answer to Jesus' strong censure of them, he calls the crowd near. "Listen to me," he says, "and get the meaning. There is nothing from outside a man that passes into him that can defile him; but the things that issue forth out of a man are the things that defile a man."

Later, when they enter a house, his disciples ask: "Do you know that the Pharisees stumbled at hearing what you said?"

"Every plant that my heavenly Father did not plant will be uprooted," Jesus answers. "Let them be. Blind guides is what they are. If, then, a blind man guides a blind man, both will fall into a pit."

Jesus seems surprised when, in behalf of the disciples, Peter asks for clarification regarding what defiles a man. "Are you also yet without understanding?" Jesus responds. "Are you not aware that everything entering into the mouth passes along into the intestines and is discharged into the sewer? However, the things proceeding out of the mouth come out of the heart, and those things defile a man. For ex-

ample, out of the heart come wicked reasonings, murders, adulteries, fornications, thieveries, false testimonies, blasphemies. These are the things defiling a man; but to take a meal with unwashed hands does not defile a man."

Jesus is not here discouraging normal hygiene. He is not arguing that a person need not wash his hands before preparing food or eating a meal. Rather, Jesus is condemning the hypocrisy of religious leaders who deviously try to circumvent God's righteous laws by insisting on unscriptural traditions. Yes, it is wicked deeds that defile a man, and Jesus shows that these originate in a person's heart.   John 7:1; Deuteronomy 16:16; Matthew 15:1-20; Mark 7:1-23; Exodus 20:12; 21:17; Isaiah 29:13.

■ What opposition does Jesus now face?

■ What accusation do the Pharisees make, but according to Jesus, how do the Pharisees willfully break God's Law?

■ What does Jesus reveal are the things that defile a man?

AFTER denouncing the Pharisees for their self-serving traditions, Jesus leaves with his disciples. Not long before, you may recall, his attempt to get away with them to rest up a bit was interrupted when crowds found them. Now, with his disciples, he departs for the regions of Tyre and Sidon, many miles to the north. This apparently is the only trip Jesus makes with his disciples beyond the borders of Israel.

After finding a house to stay in, Jesus lets it be known that he does not want anyone to learn of their whereabouts. Yet, even in this non-Israelite territory, he cannot escape notice. A Greek woman, born here in Phoenicia of Syria, finds him and begins begging: "Have mercy on me, Lord, Son of David. My daughter is badly demonized." Jesus, however, does not say a word in reply.

Eventually, his disciples tell Jesus: "Send her away; because she keeps crying out after us." Explaining his reason for ignoring her, Jesus says: "I was not sent forth to any but to the lost sheep of the house of Israel."

However, the woman does not give up. She approaches Jesus and prostrates herself before him. She pleads, "Lord, help me!"

How Jesus' heart must be moved by the woman's earnest appeal! Yet, he again points to his first responsibility, to minister to God's people of Israel. At the same time, apparently to test her faith, he draws on the Jews' prejudiced view of those of other nationalities, arguing: "It is not right to take the bread of the children and throw it to little dogs."

By his compassionate tone of voice and facial expression, Jesus surely reveals his own tender feelings toward non-Jews. He even softens the comparison of Gentiles to dogs by referring to them as *"little* dogs," or puppies. Rather than take

offense, the woman picks up on Jesus' reference to Jewish prejudices and makes the humble observation: "Yes, Lord; but really the little dogs do eat of the crumbs falling from the table of their masters."

"O woman, great is your faith," Jesus replies. "Let it happen to you as you wish." And it does! When she returns to her home, she finds her daughter on the bed, completely healed.

From the coastal region of Sidon, Jesus and his disciples head across the country, toward the headwaters of the Jordan River. They apparently ford the Jordan somewhere above the

Sea of Galilee and enter the region of the Decapolis east of the sea. There they climb a mountain, but the crowds find them and bring to Jesus their lame, crippled, blind, and dumb, and many that are otherwise sick and deformed. They fairly throw them at Jesus' feet, and he cures them. The people are amazed, as they see the mute speaking, the lame walking, and the blind seeing; and they praise the God of Israel.

Jesus gives special attention to one man who is deaf and hardly able to talk. The deaf are often easily embarrassed, especially in a crowd. Jesus may note this man's particular nervousness. So Jesus compassionately takes him away from the crowd privately. When they are alone, Jesus indicates what he is going to do for him. He puts his fingers into the man's ears and, after spitting, touches his tongue. Then, looking toward heaven, Jesus sighs deeply and says: "Be opened." At that, the man's hearing powers are restored, and he is able to speak normally.

When Jesus has performed these many cures, the crowds respond with appreciation. They say: "He has done all things well. He even makes the deaf hear and the speechless speak." Matthew 15:21-31; Mark 7:24-37.

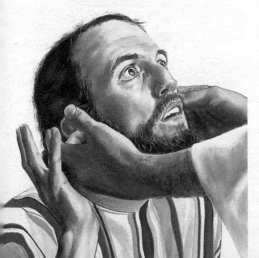

■ Why does Jesus not immediately heal the Greek woman's child?

■ Afterward, where does Jesus take his disciples?

■ How does Jesus compassionately treat the deaf man who can hardly speak?

58 The Loaves and the Leaven

GREAT crowds have flocked to Jesus in the Decapolis. Many came a long way to this largely Gentile-populated region to listen to him and to be healed of their infirmities. They have brought with them large baskets, or hampers, that they customarily use to carry provisions when traveling through Gentile areas.

Eventually, however, Jesus calls his disciples and says: "I feel pity for the crowd, because it is already three days that they have remained near me and they have nothing to eat; and if I should send them off to their homes fasting, they will give out on the road. Indeed, some of them are from far away."

"From where will anybody here in an isolated place be able to satisfy these people with loaves?" the disciples ask.

Jesus inquires: "How many loaves have you?"

"Seven," they answer, "and a few little fishes."

Instructing the people to recline on the ground, Jesus takes the loaves and the fishes, prays to God, breaks them, and begins giving them to his disciples. They, in turn, serve the people, who all eat to satisfaction. Afterward, when the leftovers are picked up, there are seven provision baskets full, even though about 4,000 men, as well as women and children, have eaten!

Jesus sends the crowds away, boards a boat with his disciples, and crosses to the western shore of the Sea of Galilee. Here the Pharisees, this time accompanied by members of the religious sect of the Sadducees, try to tempt Jesus by asking him to display a sign from heaven.

Aware of their efforts to tempt him, Jesus replies: "When evening falls you are accustomed to say, 'It will be fair weather, for the sky is fire-red'; and at morning, 'It will be wintry, rainy weather today, for the sky is fire-red, but gloomy-looking.' You know how to interpret the appearance of the sky, but the signs of the times you cannot interpret."

With that, Jesus calls them a wicked and adulterous generation and warns them that, as he told the Pharisees earlier, no sign will be given them except the sign of Jonah. Departing, he and his disciples get in a boat and head toward Bethsaida on the northeast shore of the Sea of Galilee. En route the disciples discover that they have forgotten to bring bread, there being but one loaf among them.

Having in mind his recent encounter with the Pharisees and the Sadducean supporters of Herod, Jesus admonishes: "Keep your eyes open, look out for the leaven of the Pharisees and the leaven of Herod." Evidently the mention of leaven makes the disciples think that Jesus is referring to their forgetting to bring bread, so they begin to argue about the matter. Noting their misunderstanding, Jesus says: "Why do you argue over your having no loaves?"

Recently, Jesus had miraculously provided bread for thousands of people, performing this last miracle perhaps only a day or two before. They should know that he is not concerned about a lack of literal loaves. "Do you not remember," he reminds them, "when I broke the five loaves for the five thousand men, how many baskets full of fragments you took up?"

"Twelve," they reply.

"When I broke the seven for the four thousand men, how many provision baskets full of fragments did you take up?"

"Seven," they answer.

"Do you not yet get the meaning?" Jesus asks. "How is it you do not discern that I did not talk to you about loaves? But watch out for the leaven of the Pharisees and Sadducees."

The disciples finally get the point. Leaven, a substance to cause fermentation and make bread rise, was a word used to denote corruption. So now the disciples understand that Jesus is using a symbolism, that he is warning them to be on guard against "the *teaching* of the Pharisees and Sadducees," which teaching has a corrupting effect. Mark 8:1-21; Matthew 15:32–16:12.

- Why do people have large provision baskets with them?

- After leaving the Decapolis, what boat trips does Jesus take?

- What misunderstanding do the disciples have regarding Jesus' comment about leaven?

- What does Jesus mean by the expression "the leaven of the Pharisees and Sadducees"?

59

Who Really Is Jesus?

WHEN the boat carrying Jesus and his disciples puts in at Bethsaida, the people bring a blind man to him and beg that he touch the man and heal him. Jesus leads the man by the hand outside the village and, after spitting on his eyes, asks: "Do you see anything?"

"I see men," the man answers, "because I observe what seem to be trees, but they are walking about." Laying his hands on the man's eyes, Jesus restores his sight so that he sees clearly. Jesus then sends the man home with the instruction not to enter into the city.

Jesus now leaves with his disciples for the villages of Caesarea Philippi, in the extreme north of Palestine. It is a long ascent, covering about 30 miles, to the beautiful location of Caesarea Philippi, some 1,150 feet above sea level. The trip probably takes a couple of days.

On the way, Jesus goes off by himself to pray. Only about nine or ten months remain before his death, and he is concerned about his disciples. Many have already left off following him. Others are apparently confused and disappointed because he rejected the people's efforts to make him king and because he did not, when challenged by his enemies, provide a sign from heaven to prove his kingship. What do his apostles believe about his identity? When they come over to where he is praying, Jesus inquires: "Who are the crowds saying that I am?"

"Some say John the Baptist," they answer, "others Elijah, still others Jeremiah or one of the prophets." Yes, the people think Jesus is one of these men raised from the dead!

"You, though, who do you say I am?" Jesus asks.

Peter quickly responds: "You are the Christ, the Son of the living God."

After expressing approval of Peter's response, Jesus says: "I say to you, You are Peter, and on this rock-mass I will build

my congregation, and the gates of Hades will not overpower it." Here Jesus first announces that he will build a congregation and that even death will not hold its members captive after their faithful course on earth. Then he tells Peter: "I will give you the keys of the kingdom of the heavens."

Jesus thus reveals that Peter is to receive special privileges. No, Peter is not given first place among the apostles, nor is he made the foundation of the congregation. Jesus himself is the Rock-Mass upon which his congregation will be built. But Peter is to be given three keys with which to open, as it were, the opportunity for groups of people to enter the Kingdom of the heavens.

Peter would use the first key at Pentecost 33 C.E. to show repentant Jews what they must do to be saved. He would use the second shortly afterward to open to believing Samaritans the opportunity to enter God's Kingdom. Then, in 36 C.E. he would use the third key to open to uncircumcised Gentiles, Cornelius and his friends, the same opportunity.

Jesus continues his discussion with his apostles. He disappoints them by telling of the sufferings and death that he will soon face in Jerusalem. Failing to understand that Jesus will be resurrected to heavenly life, Peter takes Jesus aside. "Be kind to yourself, Lord," he says. "You will not have this destiny at all." Turning his back, Jesus answers: "Get behind me, Satan! You are a stumbling block to me, because you think, not God's thoughts, but those of men."

Evidently, others besides the apostles are traveling with Jesus, so he now calls them to him and explains that it will not be easy to be his follower. "If anyone wants to come after me," he says, "let him disown himself and pick up his torture stake and follow me continually. For whoever wants to save his soul will lose it; but whoever loses his soul for the sake of me and the good news will save it."

Yes, if they would prove worthy of his favor, Jesus' followers must be courageous and self-sacrificing. He relates: "For whoever becomes ashamed of me and my words in this adulterous and sinful generation, the Son of man will also be ashamed of him when he arrives in the glory of his Father with the holy angels." Mark 8:22-38; Matthew 16:13-28; Luke 9:18-27.

■ Why is Jesus concerned about his disciples?

■ What views as to Jesus' identity do people have?

■ What keys are given to Peter, and how are they to be used?

■ What correction does Peter receive, and why?

60

A Preview
of Christ's Kingdom Glory

JESUS has come into the parts of Caesarea Philippi, and he is teaching a crowd that includes his apostles. He makes this startling announcement to them: "Truly I say to you that there are some of those standing here that will not taste death at all until first they see the Son of man coming in his kingdom."

'What could Jesus mean?' the disciples must wonder. About a week later, Jesus takes Peter, James, and John along with him, and they climb a lofty mountain. Possibly it is at night, since the disciples are sleepy. While Jesus is praying, he is transfigured before them. His face begins to shine as the sun, and his garments become brilliant as light.

Then, two figures, identified as "Moses and Elijah," appear and start talking to Jesus about his 'departure that is to occur at Jerusalem.' The departure evidently refers to Jesus' death and subsequent resurrection. Thus, this conversation proves that his humiliating death is not something to be avoided, as Peter had desired.

Fully awake now, the disciples watch and listen with amazement. Although this is a vision, it appears so real that Peter begins to participate in the scene, saying: "Lord, it is fine for us to be here. If you wish, I will erect three tents here, one for you and one for Moses and one for Elijah."

While Peter is speaking, a bright cloud covers them, and a voice from the cloud says: "This is my Son, the beloved, whom I have approved; listen to him." At hearing the voice, the disciples fall on their faces. But Jesus says: "Get up and have no fear." When they do, they see no one except Jesus.

On their way down the mountain the next day, Jesus commands: "Tell the vision to no one until the Son of man is raised up from the dead." Elijah's appearance in the vision raises a question in the disciples' minds. "Why," they ask, "do the scribes say that Elijah must come first?"

"Elijah has already come," says Jesus, "and they did not recognize him." Jesus, however, is speaking about John the Baptizer, who fulfilled a role similar to Elijah's. John prepared the way for Christ, as Elijah did for Elisha.

How strengthening this vision proves to be, both to Jesus and to the disciples! The vision is, as it were, a preview of Christ's Kingdom glory. The disciples saw, in effect, "the Son of man coming in his kingdom," just as Jesus had promised a week earlier. After Jesus' death, Peter wrote about their having 'become eyewitnesses of Christ's magnificence while they were with him in the holy mountain.'

The Pharisees had demanded from Jesus a sign to prove that he was the one promised in the Scriptures to be God's chosen King. They were given no such sign. On the other hand, Jesus' intimate disciples are permitted to see Jesus' transfiguration as confirmation of the Kingdom prophecies. Thus, Peter later wrote: "Consequently we have the prophetic word made more sure." Matthew 16:13, 28–17: 13; Mark 9:1-13; Luke 9:27-37; 2 Peter 1:16-19.

■ Before tasting death, how do some see Christ coming in his Kingdom?

■ In the vision, what do Moses and Elijah talk about with Jesus?

■ Why is this vision such a strengthening aid to the disciples?

WHILE Jesus, Peter, James, and John are away, likely on a spur of Mount Hermon, the other disciples run into a problem. On his return, Jesus immediately sees that something is wrong. There is a crowd gathered around his disciples, and the scribes are arguing with them. On seeing Jesus, the people are greatly surprised and run to greet him. "What are you disputing with them?" he asks.

Coming forward from the crowd, a man kneels before Jesus and explains: "Teacher, I brought my son to you because he has a speechless spirit; and wherever it seizes him it dashes him to the ground, and he foams and grinds his teeth and loses his strength. And I told your disciples to expel it, but they were not capable."

The scribes are apparently making the most of the disciples' failure to heal the boy, perhaps ridiculing their efforts. At just this critical moment, Jesus arrives. "O faithless generation," he says, "how long must I continue with you? How long must I put up with you?"

Jesus seems to address his remarks to everyone present, but no doubt they are directed particularly to the scribes, who have been making trouble for his disciples. Next, Jesus says of the boy: "Bring him to me." But as the boy comes to Jesus, the demon that possesses him knocks him to the ground and throws him into violent convulsions. The boy rolls on the ground and foams at the mouth.

"How long has this been happening to him?" Jesus asks.

"From childhood on," the father answers. "Time and again [the demon] would throw him both into the fire and into the water to destroy him." Then the father pleads: "If you can do anything, have pity on us and help us."

Perhaps for years, the father has been seeking help. And now, with the failure of Jesus' disciples, his despair is great. Picking up on the man's desperate appeal, Jesus encouraging-

ly says: "That expression, 'If you can'! Why, all things can be to one if one has faith."

"I have faith!" the father immediately cries out, but he begs: "Help me out where I need faith!"

Noticing that the crowd is running together upon them, Jesus rebukes the demon: "You speechless and deaf spirit, I order you, get out of him and enter into him no more." As the demon departs, it again causes the boy to cry out and drives him into many convulsions. Then the boy lies motionless on the ground, so that most of the people begin saying: "He is dead!" But Jesus takes the boy by the hand, and he rises.

Earlier, when the disciples had been sent forth to preach, they had expelled demons. So now, when they enter a house, they ask Jesus privately: "Why could we not expel it?"

Indicating that it was because of their lack of faith, Jesus answers: "This kind cannot get out by anything except by prayer." Evidently preparation was called for to expel the especially powerful demon involved in this case. Strong faith along with prayer requesting God's empowering help was needed.

And then Jesus adds: "Truly I say to you, If you have faith the size of a mustard grain, you will say to this mountain, 'Transfer from here to there,' and it will transfer, and nothing will be impossible for you." How powerful faith can be!

Obstacles and difficulties that block progress in Jehovah's service may seem to be as insurmountable and irremovable as a great literal mountain. Yet, Jesus is showing that if we cultivate faith in our hearts, watering it and encouraging it to grow, it will expand to maturity and will enable us to overcome such mountainlike obstacles and difficulties. Mark 9:14-29; Matthew 17:19, 20; Luke 9:37-43.

- What situation does Jesus encounter when he returns from Mount Hermon?

- What encouragement does Jesus give the father of the demon-possessed boy?

- Why were the disciples not able to expel the demon?

- How powerful does Jesus show that faith can become?

62

A Lesson in Humility

AFTER healing the demonized boy in the region near Caesarea Philippi, Jesus wishes to return home to Capernaum. However, he wants to be alone with his disciples on the trip so that he can further prepare them for his death and their responsibilities afterward. "The Son of man is to be delivered into men's hands," he explains to them, "and they will kill him, but, despite being killed, he will rise three days later."

Even though Jesus spoke earlier about this, and three apostles actually saw the transfiguration during which his "departure" was discussed, his followers are still without understanding regarding the matter. Although none of them try to deny that he will be killed, as Peter did earlier, they are afraid to question him further about it.

Eventually they come into Capernaum, which has been a kind of home base during Jesus' ministry. It is also the home-town of Peter and a number of other apostles. There, men who collect the temple tax approach Peter. Perhaps attempting to involve Jesus in some breach of accepted custom, they ask: "Does your teacher not pay the two drachmas [temple] tax?"

"Yes," Peter responds.

Jesus, who may have arrived at the house shortly afterward, is aware of what has occurred. So even before Peter can bring the matter up, Jesus asks: "What do you think, Simon? From whom do the kings of the earth receive duties or head tax? From their sons or from the strangers?"

"From the strangers," Peter answers.

"Really, then, the sons are tax-free," Jesus observes. Since Jesus' Father is the King of the universe, the One who is worshiped at the temple, it is not really a legal requirement for God's Son to pay the temple tax. "But that we do not cause them to stumble," Jesus says, "you go to the sea, cast a fishhook, and take the first fish coming up and, when you open its mouth, you will find a stater [four drachmas] coin. Take that and give it to them for me and you."

When the disciples get together after their return to Capernaum, perhaps at Peter's house, they ask: "Who really is greatest in the kingdom of the heavens?" Jesus knows what it is that prompts their question, being aware of what was going on among them as they trailed behind him on their return from Caesarea Philippi. So he asks: "What were you arguing over on the road?" Embarrassed, the disciples keep silent, for they had argued among themselves over who would be the greatest.

After nearly three years of Jesus' teaching, does it seem incredible that the disciples would have such an argument? Well, it reveals the strong influence of human imperfection, as well as of religious background. The Jewish religion in which the disciples had been reared stressed position or rank in all dealings. Furthermore, perhaps Peter, because of Jesus' promise of receiving certain "keys" to the Kingdom, felt superior. James and John may have had similar ideas because of being favored with witnessing Jesus' transfiguration.

Whatever the case, Jesus stages a moving demonstration in an effort to correct their attitudes. He calls a child, stands it in their midst, puts his arms around it, and says: "Unless you turn around and become as young children, you will by no means enter into the kingdom of the heavens. Therefore, whoever will humble himself like this young child is the one that is the greatest in the kingdom of the heavens; and whoever receives one such young child on the basis of my name receives me also."

What a marvelous way to correct his disciples! Jesus does not become angry with them and call them haughty, greedy, or ambitious. No, but he illustrates his corrective teaching by using the example of young children, who are characteristically modest and free from ambition and who generally have no thought of rank among themselves. Thus Jesus shows that his disciples need to develop these qualities that characterize humble children. As Jesus concludes: "He that conducts himself as a lesser one among all of you is the one that is great." Matthew 17:22-27; 18:1-5; Mark 9:30-37; Luke 9:43-48.

■ On the return to Capernaum, what teaching does Jesus repeat, and how is it received?
■ Why is Jesus not under obligation to pay the temple tax, but why does he pay it?
■ What perhaps contributed to the disciples' argument, and how does Jesus correct them?

63

Further Corrective Counsel

WHILE Jesus and his apostles are still in the house in Capernaum, something besides the apostles' argument over who is the greatest is discussed. This is an incident that may also have occurred on their return to Capernaum, when Jesus was not personally present. The apostle John reports: "We saw a certain man expelling demons by the use of your name and we tried to prevent him, because he was not accompanying us."

Evidently John views the apostles as an exclusive, title-holding team of healers. So he feels that the man was performing powerful works improperly because he was not part of their group.

However, Jesus counsels: "Do not try to prevent him, for there is no one that will do a powerful work on the basis of my name that will quickly be able to revile me; for he that is not against us is for us. For whoever gives you a cup of water to drink on the ground that you belong to Christ, I truly tell you, he will by no means lose his reward."

It was not necessary for this man bodily to follow Jesus to be on his side. The Christian congregation had not yet been set up, so his not being part of their group did not mean that he was of a separate congregation. The man really had faith in Jesus'

name and thus succeeded in expelling demons. He was doing something that compared favorably with what Jesus said was deserving of a reward. Jesus shows that for doing this, he will not lose his reward.

But what if the man was stumbled by the words and actions of the apostles? This would be very serious! Jesus observes: "Whoever stumbles one of these little ones that believe, it would be finer for him if a millstone such as is turned by an ass were put around his neck and he were actually pitched into the sea."

Jesus says that his followers should remove from their lives anything as dear to them as a hand, a foot, or an eye that may cause them to stumble. Better to be without this cherished thing and enter into God's Kingdom than to hold on to it and be pitched into Gehenna (a burning rubbish heap near Jerusalem), which symbolizes eternal destruction.

Jesus also warns: "See to it that you men do not despise one of these little ones; for I tell you that their angels in heaven always behold the face of my Father who is in heaven." He then illustrates the preciousness of "little ones" when he tells about a man who possesses a hundred sheep but loses one. The man will leave the 99 to search for the lost one, Jesus explains, and on finding it will rejoice more over it than over the 99. "Likewise,"

Jesus then concludes, "it is not a desirable thing with my Father who is in heaven for one of these little ones to perish."

Possibly having in mind his apostles' argument among themselves, Jesus urges: "Have salt in yourselves, and keep peace between one another." Tasteless foods are made more palatable by salt. Thus, figurative salt makes what one says easier to accept. Having such salt will help preserve the peace.

But because of human imperfection, at times serious disputes will occur. Jesus also provides guidelines for handling them. "If your brother commits a sin," Jesus says, "go lay bare his fault between you and him alone. If he listens to you, you have gained your brother." If he does not listen, Jesus advises, "take along with you one or two more, in order that at the mouth of two or three witnesses every matter may be established."

Only as a last resort, Jesus says, take the matter to "the congregation," that is, to responsible overseers of the congregation who can render a judicial decision. If the sinner will not abide by their decision, Jesus concludes, "let him be to you just as a man of the nations and as a tax collector."

In making such a decision, overseers need to adhere closely to instructions in Jehovah's Word. Thus, when they find an individual guilty and worthy of punishment, the judgment 'will already have been bound in heaven.' And when they "loose on earth," that is, find one innocent, it will already have been "loosed in heaven." In such judicial deliberations, Jesus says, "where there are two or three gathered together in my name, there I am in their midst." **Matthew 18:6-20; Mark 9:38-50; Luke 9:49, 50.**

- Why was it not necessary in Jesus' day to accompany him?
- How serious is the matter of stumbling a little one, and how does Jesus illustrate the importance of such little ones?
- What probably prompts Jesus' encouragement for the apostles to have salt among themselves?
- What significance is there to 'binding' and 'loosing'?

64

A Lesson in Forgiveness

JESUS is apparently still in the house in Capernaum with his disciples. He has been discussing with them how to handle difficulties between brothers, so Peter asks: "Lord, how many times is my brother to sin against me and am I to forgive him?" Since Jewish religious teachers propose granting forgiveness up to three times, Peter probably considers it very generous to suggest "up to seven times?"

But the whole idea of keeping such a record is wrong. Jesus corrects Peter: "I say to you, not, Up to seven times, but, Up to seventy-seven times." He is showing that no limit should be put on the number of times Peter forgives his brother.

To impress on the disciples their obligation to be forgiving, Jesus tells them an illustration. It is about a king who wants to settle accounts with his slaves. One slave is brought to him who owes the enormous debt of 60,000,000 denarii. There is no way that he can possibly pay it. So, as Jesus explains, the king orders that he and his wife and his children be sold and payment be made.

At that the slave falls down at his master's feet and begs: "Be patient with me and I will pay back everything to you."

Moved with pity for him, the master mercifully cancels the slave's enormous debt. But no sooner has he done so, Jesus continues, than this slave goes and finds a fellow slave who owes him only 100 denarii. The man grabs his fellow slave by the throat and begins choking him, saying: "Pay back whatever you owe."

But the fellow slave does not have the money. So he falls at the feet of the slave to whom he is in debt, begging: "Be patient with me and I will pay you back." Unlike his master, the slave is not merciful, and he has his fellow slave thrown into prison.

Well, Jesus continues, the other slaves who saw what had happened go and tell the master. He angrily summons the

slave. "Wicked slave," he says, "I canceled all that debt for you, when you entreated me. Ought you not, in turn, to have had mercy on your fellow slave, as I also had mercy on you?" Provoked to wrath, the master delivers the unmerciful slave over to the jailers until he should pay back all that he owes.

Then Jesus concludes: "In like manner my heavenly Father will also deal with you if you do not forgive each one his brother from your hearts."

What a fine lesson in forgiveness! Compared with the large debt of sin that God has forgiven us, whatever transgression may be committed against us by a Christian brother is small indeed. Furthermore, Jehovah God has forgiven us thousands of times. Often, we are not even aware of our sins against him. Therefore, can we not forgive our brother a few times, even if we have a legitimate cause for complaint? Remember, as Jesus taught in the Sermon on the Mount, God will "forgive us our debts, as we also have forgiven our debtors." **Matthew 18:21-35; 6:12; Colossians 3:13.**

■ What prompts Peter's question about forgiving his brother, and why may he consider his suggestion of forgiving someone seven times to be generous?

■ How does the response of the king to his slave's plea for mercy differ from the response of the slave to a fellow slave's plea?

■ What do we learn from Jesus' illustration?

I T IS the autumn of 32 C.E., and the Festival of Tabernacles is near. Jesus has confined his activity mostly to Galilee since the Passover of 31 C.E., when the Jews tried to kill him. Likely, since then Jesus has only visited Jerusalem to attend the three annual festivals of the Jews.

Jesus' brothers now urge him: "Pass on over from here and go into Judea." Jerusalem is Judea's main city and the religious center of the whole country. His brothers reason: "Nobody does anything in secret while himself seeking to be known publicly."

Although James, Simon, Joseph, and Judas do not believe that their elder brother, Jesus, is really the Messiah, they want him to show his miraculous powers to all those gathered at the festival. Jesus, however, is aware of the danger. "The world has no reason to hate you," he says, "but it hates me, because I bear witness concerning it that its works are wicked." So Jesus tells his brothers: "You go up to the festival; I am not yet going up to this festival."

The Festival of Tabernacles is a seven-day celebration. On the

eighth day it is brought to a close with solemn activities. The festival marks the end of the agricultural year and is a time of great rejoicing and thanksgiving. Several days after Jesus' brothers leave to attend along with the main body of travelers, he and his disciples go secretly, staying out of the public eye. They take the route through Samaria, rather than the one that most people take near the Jordan River.

Since Jesus and his company will need accommodations in a Samaritan village, he sends messengers ahead to make preparations. The people, however, refuse to do anything for Jesus after learning that he is heading for Jerusalem. Indignantly, James and John ask: "Lord, do you want us to tell fire to come down from heaven and annihilate them?" Jesus rebukes them for suggesting such a thing, and they travel on to another village.

As they are walking along the road, a scribe says to Jesus: "Teacher, I will follow you wherever you are about to go."

"Foxes have dens and birds of heaven have roosts," Jesus responds, "but the Son of man has nowhere to lay down his head." Jesus is explaining that the scribe will experience hardship if he becomes His follower. And the implication

seems to be that the scribe is too proud to accept this mode of life.

To another man, Jesus says: "Be my follower."

"Permit me first to leave and bury my father," the man answers.

"Let the dead bury their dead," Jesus replies, "but you go away and declare abroad the kingdom of God." The man's father evidently had not yet died, for if he had, it would be unlikely that his son would be here listening to Jesus. The son apparently is asking for time to await his father's death. He is not prepared to put the Kingdom of God first in his life.

As they proceed on the road toward Jerusalem, another man tells Jesus: "I will follow you, Lord; but first permit me to say good-bye to those in my household."

In answer Jesus says: "No man that has put his hand to a plow and looks at the things behind is well fitted for the kingdom of God." Those who will be Jesus' disciples must have their eyes focused on Kingdom service. Just as a furrow likely will become crooked if the plowman does not keep looking straight ahead, so anyone who looks behind at this old system of things may well stumble off the road leading to eternal life.   John 7:2-10; Luke 9:51-62; Matthew 8:19-22.

- Who are Jesus' brothers, and how do they feel about him?
- Why are the Samaritans so rude, and what do James and John want to do?
- What three conversations does Jesus have on the road, and how does he emphasize the need for self-sacrificing service?

66

At the Festival of Tabernacles

JESUS has become famous during the nearly three years since his baptism. Many thousands have seen his miracles, and reports about his activities have spread throughout the country. Now, as the people gather for the Festival of Tabernacles in Jerusalem, they look for him there. "Where is that man?" they want to know.

Jesus has become a subject of controversy. "He is a good man," some say. "He is not, but he misleads the crowd," others assert. There is a lot of subdued talk of this sort during the opening days of the festival. Yet no one has the courage to speak out publicly in Jesus' behalf. This is because the people fear reprisal from the Jewish leaders.

When the festival is half over, Jesus arrives. He goes up to the temple, where the people are amazed at his marvelous teaching ability. Since Jesus never attended the rabbinical schools, the Jews fall to wondering: "How does this man have a knowledge of letters, when he has not studied at the schools?"

"What I teach is not mine," Jesus explains, "but belongs to him that sent me. If anyone desires to do His will, he will know concerning the teaching whether it is from God or I speak of my own originality." Jesus' teaching holds closely to God's law. Thus, it should be obvious that he is seeking God's glory, not his own. "Moses gave you the Law, did he not?" Jesus asks. By way of rebuke, he says: "Not one of you obeys the Law."

"Why are you seeking to kill me?" Jesus then asks.

The people in the crowd, probably visitors to the festival, are unaware of such efforts. They consider it inconceivable that anyone would want to kill such a wonderful teacher. So they believe that something must be wrong with Jesus for him to think this. "You have a demon," they say. "Who is seeking to kill you?"

The Jewish leaders want Jesus killed, even though the crowd may not realize it. When Jesus healed a man on the Sabbath a year and a half before, the leaders tried to kill him. So Jesus now points up their unreasonableness by asking them: "If a man receives circumcision on a sabbath in order that the law of Moses may not be broken, are you violently angry at me because I made a man completely sound in health on a sabbath? Stop judging from the outward appearance, but judge with righteous judgment."

Inhabitants of Jerusalem, who are aware of the situation, now say: "This is the man they are seeking to kill, is it not? And yet, see! he is speaking in public, and they say nothing to him. The rulers have not come to know for a certainty that this is the Christ, have they?" These residents of Jerusalem explain why they do not believe that Jesus is the Christ: "We know where this man is from; yet when the Christ comes, no one is to know where he is from."

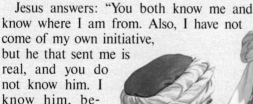

Jesus answers: "You both know me and know where I am from. Also, I have not come of my own initiative, but he that sent me is real, and you do not know him. I know him, because I am a rep-

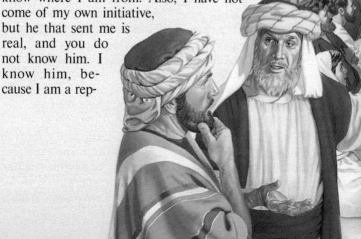

resentative from him, and that One sent me forth." At this they try to lay hold on him, perhaps to put him in prison or to have him killed. Yet they do not succeed because it is not time for Jesus to die.

Still, many put faith in Jesus, as indeed they should. Why, he has walked on water, calmed the winds, quieted stormy seas, miraculously fed thousands on a few loaves and fishes, cured the sick, made the lame walk, opened the eyes of the blind, cured lepers, and even raised the dead. So they ask: "When the Christ arrives, he will not perform more signs than this man has performed, will he?"

When the Pharisees hear the crowd murmuring these things, they and the chief priests send out officers to arrest Jesus. John 7:11-32.

■ When does Jesus arrive at the festival, and what are people saying about him?

■ Why may it be that some say Jesus has a demon?

■ What view of Jesus do inhabitants of Jerusalem have?

■ Why do many put faith in Jesus?

67

They Fail to Arrest Him

WHILE the Festival of Tabernacles is still in progress, the religious leaders send out police officers to arrest Jesus. He does not attempt to hide. Instead, Jesus keeps on teaching publicly, saying: "I continue a little while longer with you before I go to him that sent me. You will look for me, but you will not find me, and where I am you cannot come."

The Jews do not understand, and so they inquire among themselves: "Where does this man intend going, so that we shall not find him? He does not intend to go to the Jews dispersed among the Greeks and teach the Greeks, does he? What does this saying mean that he said, 'You will look for me, but you will not find me, and where I am you cannot come'?" Jesus, of course, is talking about his approaching death and resurrection to life in heaven, where his enemies cannot follow.

The seventh and last day of the festival arrives. Each morning of the festival, a priest has poured out water, which he took from the Pool of Siloam, so that it flowed to the base of the altar. Likely reminding the people of this daily ceremony, Jesus cries out: "If anyone is thirsty, let him come to me and drink. He that puts faith in me, just as the Scripture has said, 'Out from his inmost part streams of living water will flow.'"

Actually, Jesus is here speaking about the grand consequences when the holy spirit would be poured out. The following year this pouring out of holy spirit occurs at Pentecost. There, streams of living water flow forth when the 120 disciples begin ministering to the people. But until then, there is no spirit in the sense that none of Christ's disciples are anointed with holy spirit and called to heavenly life.

In response to Jesus' teaching, some begin saying: "This is for a certainty The Prophet," evidently referring to the prophet greater than Moses who was promised to come. Others say: "This is the Christ." But others protest: "The Christ is not actually coming out of Galilee, is he? Has not the Scripture said that the Christ is coming from the offspring of David, and from Bethlehem the village where David used to be?"

So a division develops among the crowd. Some want Jesus arrested, but no one lays a hand on him. When the police officers return without Jesus, the chief priests and Pharisees ask: "Why is it you did not bring him in?"

"Never has another man spoken like this," the officers reply.

Filled with anger, the religious leaders stoop to ridicule, misrepresentation, and name-calling. They sneer: "You have not been misled also, have you? Not one of the rulers or of the Pharisees has put faith in him, has he? But this crowd that does not know the Law are accursed people."

At this, Nicodemus, a Pharisee and a ruler of the Jews (that is, a member of the Sanhedrin), dares speak in Jesus' behalf. You may recall that two and a half years previously, Nicodemus came to Jesus at night and expressed faith in him. Now Nicodemus says: "Our law does not judge a man unless first it has heard from him and come to know what he is doing, does it?"

The Pharisees are angered even more that one of their own should defend Jesus. "You are not also out of Galilee, are you?" they caustically remark. "Search and see that no prophet is to be raised up out of Galilee."

Although the Scriptures do not directly say that a prophet would come out of Galilee, they do point to the Christ as coming from there, saying that "a great light" would be seen in this region. Furthermore, Jesus was born in Bethlehem, and he was an offspring of David. While the Pharisees are probably aware of this, they are likely responsible for spreading the misconceptions that people have about Jesus. **John 7:32-52; Isaiah 9:1, 2; Matthew 4:13-17.**

- What happens every morning of the festival, and how may Jesus be drawing attention to this?
- Why do the officers fail to arrest Jesus, and how do the religious leaders respond?
- Who is Nicodemus, what is his attitude toward Jesus, and how is he treated by his fellow Pharisees?
- What evidence is there that the Christ would come out of Galilee?

68

Further Teaching on the Seventh Day

THE last day of the Festival of Tabernacles, the seventh day, is still in progress. Jesus is teaching in the portion of the temple termed "the treasury." This is apparently in the area called the Court of Women where there are chests in which people deposit their contributions.

Every night during the festival, there is a special illumination display in this area of the temple. Four giant lampstands are installed here, each with four large basins filled with oil. The light from these lamps, burning oil from the 16 basins, is strong enough to illuminate the surroundings to a great distance at night. What Jesus now says may remind his listeners of this display. "I am the light of the world," Jesus proclaims. "He that follows me will by no means walk in darkness, but will possess the light of life."

The Pharisees object: "You bear witness about yourself; your witness is not true."

In answer Jesus replies: "Even if I do bear witness about myself, my witness is true, because I know where I came from and where I am going. But you do not know where I came from and where I am going." He adds: "I am one that bears witness about myself, and the Father who sent me bears witness about me."

"Where is your Father?" the Pharisees want to know.

"You know neither me nor my Father," Jesus answers. "If you did know me, you would know my Father also." Even though the Pharisees still want Jesus arrested, no one touches him.

"I am going away," Jesus again says. "Where I am going you cannot come."

At this the Jews begin to wonder: "He will not kill himself, will he? Because he says, 'Where I am going you cannot come.'"

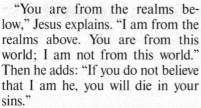

"You are from the realms below," Jesus explains. "I am from the realms above. You are from this world; I am not from this world." Then he adds: "If you do not believe that I am he, you will die in your sins."

Jesus, of course, is referring to his prehuman existence and his being the promised Messiah, or Christ. Nevertheless, they ask, no doubt with great contempt: "Who are you?"

In the face of their rejection, Jesus answers: "Why am I even speaking to you at all?" Yet he goes on to say: "He that sent me is true, and the very things I heard from him I am

speaking in the world." Jesus continues: "When once you have lifted up the Son of man, then you will know that I am he, and that I do nothing of my own initiative; but just as the Father taught me I speak these things. And he that sent me is with me; he did not abandon me to myself, because I always do the things pleasing to him."

When Jesus says these things, many put faith in him. To these he says: "If you remain in my word, you are really my disciples, and you will know the truth, and the truth will set you free."

"We are Abraham's offspring," his opposers chime in, "and never have we been slaves to anybody. How is it you say, 'You will become free'?"

Although the Jews have often been under foreign domination, they do not acknowledge any oppressor as master. They refuse to be called slaves. But Jesus points out that they are indeed slaves. In what way? "Most truly I say to you," Jesus says, "every doer of sin is a slave of sin."

Refusing to admit their slavery to sin puts the Jews in a dangerous position. "The slave does not remain in the household forever," Jesus explains. "The son remains forever." Since a slave has no inheritance rights, he may be in danger of dismissal at any time. Only the son actually born or adopted into the household remains "forever," that is, as long as he lives.

"Therefore if the Son sets you free," Jesus continues, "you will be actually free." Thus, the truth that sets people free is the truth regarding the Son, Jesus Christ. It is only by means of the sacrifice of his perfect human life that anyone can be freed from death-dealing sin.   **John 8:12-36.**

■ Where does Jesus teach on the seventh day? What occurs at night there, and how does this relate to Jesus' teaching?

■ What does Jesus say about his origin, and what should this reveal about his identity?

■ In what way are the Jews slaves, but what truth will set them free?

69

The Question of Fatherhood

DURING the festival, Jesus' discussion with the Jewish leaders grows more intense. "I know that you are Abraham's offspring," Jesus acknowledges, "but you are seeking to kill me, because my word makes no progress among you. What things I have seen with my Father I speak; and you, therefore, do the things you have heard from your father."

Although not identifying their father, Jesus makes clear that their father is different from his. Unaware of whom Jesus has in mind, the Jewish leaders respond: "Our father is Abraham." They feel that they have the same faith as Abraham, who was God's friend.

However, Jesus shocks them with the reply: "If you are Abraham's children, do the works of Abraham." Indeed, a real son imitates his father. "But now you are seeking to kill me," Jesus says, "a man that has told you the truth that I heard from God. Abraham did not do this." So Jesus again says: "You do the works of your father."

Still they do not comprehend whom Jesus is talking about. They maintain that they are legitimate sons of Abraham, saying: "We were not born from fornication." Hence, claiming to be true worshipers like Abraham, they assert: "We have one Father, God."

But is God really their Father? "If God were your Father," Jesus responds, "you would love me, for from God I came forth and am here. Neither have I come of my own initiative at all, but that One sent me forth. Why is it you do not know what I am speaking?"

Jesus has tried to show these religious leaders the consequences of their rejection of him. But now he pointedly says: "You are from your father the Devil, and you wish to do the desires of your father." What kind of father is the Devil? Jesus identified him as a manslayer and also said: "He is a liar and the father of the lie." So Jesus concludes: "He that is from God listens to the sayings of God. This is why you do not listen, because you are not from God."

Angered by Jesus' condemnation, the Jews answer: "Do we not rightly say, You are a Samaritan and have a demon?" The term "Samaritan" is used as an expression of contempt and reproach, the Samaritans being a people hated by the Jews.

Ignoring the contemptuous slur about being a Samaritan, Jesus responds: "I do not have a demon, but I honor my Father, and you dishonor me." Going on, Jesus makes the startling promise: "If anyone observes my word, he will never see death at all." Of course, Jesus does not mean that all those who follow him will literally never see death. Rather, he means that they will never see eternal destruction, or "second death," from which there is no resurrection.

However, the Jews take Jesus' words literally. Hence, they say: "Now we do know you have a demon. Abraham died, also the prophets; but you say, 'If anyone observes my word, he will never taste death at all.' You are not greater than our father Abraham, who died, are you? Also, the prophets died. Who do you claim to be?"

In this whole discussion, it is obvious that Jesus is pointing these men to the fact that he is the promised Messiah. But rather than directly answer their question as to his identity, Jesus says: "If I glorify myself, my glory is nothing. It is my Father that glorifies me, he who you say is your God; and yet you have not known him. But I know him. And if I said I do not know him I should be like you, a liar."

Going on, Jesus refers again to faithful Abraham, saying: "Abraham your father rejoiced greatly in the prospect of seeing my day, and he saw it and rejoiced." Yes, with eyes of faith, Abraham looked forward to the arrival of the promised Messiah. In disbelief, the Jews respond: "You are not yet fifty years old, and still you have seen Abraham?"

"Most truly I say to you," Jesus answers, "before Abraham came into existence, I have been." Jesus is, of course, referring to his prehuman existence as a mighty spirit person in heaven.

Enraged by Jesus' claim to have existed before Abraham, the Jews pick up stones to hurl at him. But he hides and goes out of the temple unharmed. **John 8:37-59; Revelation 3:14; 21:8.**

■ How does Jesus show that he and his enemies have different fathers?

■ What is the significance of the Jews' calling Jesus a Samaritan?

■ In what sense does Jesus mean that his followers will never see death?

70

Healing a Man Born Blind

WHEN the Jews try to stone Jesus, he does not leave Jerusalem. Later, on the Sabbath, he and his disciples are walking in the city when they see a man who has been blind from birth. The disciples ask Jesus: "Rabbi, who sinned, this man or his parents, so that he was born blind?"

Perhaps the disciples believe, as some rabbis do, that a person can sin in his mother's womb. But Jesus answers: "Neither this man sinned nor his parents, but it was in order that the works of God might be made manifest in his case." The man's blindness is not the consequence of a specific error or sin committed by either the man or his parents. The sin of the first man Adam resulted in all humans' being imperfect, and thus subject to defects such as being born blind. This defect in the man now furnishes an opportunity for Jesus to make manifest the works of God.

Jesus stresses an urgency in doing these works. "We must work the works of him that sent me while it is day," he says. "The night is coming when no man can work. As long as I am in the world, I am the world's light." Soon Jesus' death will plunge him into the darkness of the grave where he can no longer do anything. In the meantime, he is a source of enlightenment to the world.

After saying these things, Jesus spits on the ground and with the saliva makes some clay. He puts this on the blind man's eyes and says: "Go wash in the pool of Siloam." The man obeys. And when he does, he can see! How he rejoices on his return, seeing for the first time in his life!

Neighbors and others who know him are amazed. "This is the man that used to sit and beg, is it not?" they ask. "This is he," some answer. But others cannot believe it: "Not at all, but he is like him." Yet the man says: "I am he."

"How, then, were your eyes opened?" the people want to know.

"The man called Jesus made a clay and smeared it on my eyes and said to me, 'Go to Siloam and wash.' I therefore went and washed and gained sight."

"Where is that man?" they ask.

"I do not know," he answers.

The people now lead the once blind man to their religious leaders, the Pharisees. These also take up asking him how he gained sight. "He put a clay upon my eyes, and I washed and have sight," the man explains.

Surely, the Pharisees should rejoice with the healed beggar! But instead, they denounce Jesus. "This is not a man from God," they claim. Why do they say this? "Because he does not observe the Sabbath." And yet other Pharisees wonder: "How can a man that is a sinner perform signs of that sort?" So there is a division among them.

Hence, they ask the man: "What do you say about him, seeing that he opened your eyes?"

"He is a prophet," he answers.

The Pharisees refuse to believe this. They are convinced that there must be some secret agreement between Jesus and this man to fool the people. So to resolve the matter, they call the beggar's parents in order to question them. **John 8:59; 9:1-18.**

- What is responsible for the man's blindness, and what is not?
- What is the night when no man can work?
- When the man is healed, what is the reaction of those who know him?
- How are the Pharisees divided over the man's being healed?

71

Pharisees' Willful Unbelief

THE parents of the once blind beggar are afraid when they are called before the Pharisees. They know that it has been determined that anyone who expresses faith in Jesus will be expelled from the synagogue. Such cutting off of fellowship with others in the community can work a tremendous hardship, especially on a poor family. So the parents are cautious.

"Is this your son who you say was born blind?" the Pharisees ask. "How, then, is it he sees at present?"

"We know that this is our son and that he was born blind," the parents confirm. "But how it is he now sees we do not know, or who opened his eyes we do not know." Surely their son must have told them all that has occurred, but discreetly the parents say: "Ask him. He is of age. He must speak for himself."

Therefore, the Pharisees again call the man. This time they try to intimidate him by indicating that they have gathered incriminating evidence against Jesus. "Give glory to God," they demand. "We know that this man is a sinner."

The once blind man does not deny their charge, observing: "Whether he is a sinner I do not know." But he adds: "One thing I do know, that, whereas I was blind, I see at present."

Trying to find a flaw in his testimony, the Pharisees again ask: "What did he do to you? How did he open your eyes?"

"I told you already," the man complains, "and yet you did not listen. Why do you want to hear it again?" Sarcastically, he asks: "You do not want to become his disciples also, do you?"

This reply enrages the Pharisees. "You are a disciple of that man," they charge, "but we are disciples of Moses. We know that God has spoken to Moses; but as for this man, we do not know where he is from."

Expressing surprise, the humble beggar responds: "This certainly is a marvel, that you do not know where he is from, and yet he opened my eyes." What conclusion should be drawn from this? The beggar points to the accepted premise: "We know that God does not listen to sinners, but if anyone is God-fearing and does his will, he listens to this one. From of old it has never been heard that anyone opened the eyes of one born blind." Thus, the conclusion should be obvious: "If this man were not from God, he could do nothing at all."

The Pharisees have no answer for such straightforward, clear logic. They cannot face up to the truth, and so they revile the man: "You were altogether born in sins, and yet are you teaching us?" At this, they throw the man out, apparently expelling him from the synagogue.

When Jesus learns about what they have done, he finds the man and says: "Are you putting faith in the Son of man?"

In reply, the once blind beggar asks: "Who is he, sir, that I may put faith in him?"

"He that is speaking with you is that one," Jesus replies.

Immediately, the man bows before Jesus and says: "I do put faith in him, Lord."

Jesus then explains: "For this judgment I came into this world: that those not seeing might see and those seeing might become blind."

At that, Pharisees who are listening ask: "We are not blind also, are we?" If they would acknowledge that they are mentally blind, there would be an excuse for their opposition to Jesus. As Jesus tells them: "If you were blind, you would have no sin." Yet, they hardheartedly insist that they are not blind and need no spiritual enlightenment. So Jesus observes: "Now you say, 'We see.' Your sin remains."　　　**John 9:19-41.**

■ Why are the parents of the once blind beggar afraid when they are called before the Pharisees, and so how do they answer cautiously?

■ How do the Pharisees try to intimidate the once blind man?

■ What logical argument of the man infuriates the Pharisees?

■ Why are the Pharisees without excuse for their opposition to Jesus?

72

Jesus Sends Out the 70

IT IS the fall of 32 C.E., a full three years since Jesus' baptism. He and his disciples have recently attended the Festival of Tabernacles in Jerusalem, and apparently they are still nearby. In fact, Jesus spends most of the remaining six months of his ministry either in Judea or just across the Jordan River in the district of Perea. This territory needs to be covered too.

True, after the Passover of 30 C.E., Jesus spent about eight months preaching in Judea. But after the Jews tried to kill him there on the Passover of 31 C.E., he spent the next year and a half teaching almost exclusively in Galilee. During that time, he developed a large, well-trained organization of preachers, something he did not have earlier. So he now launches a final intensive witnessing campaign in Judea.

Jesus gets this campaign under way by choosing 70 disciples and sending them out by twos. Thus, there are altogether 35 teams of Kingdom preachers to work the territory. These go in advance into every city and place to which Jesus, evidently accompanied by his apostles, is planning to go.

Instead of directing the 70 to go to synagogues, Jesus tells them to enter private homes, explaining: "Wherever you enter into a house say first, 'May this house have peace.' And if a friend of peace is there, your peace will rest upon him." What is to be their message? "Go on telling them," Jesus says, "the kingdom of God has come near to you." Regarding the activity of the 70, *Matthew Henry's Commentary* reports: "Like their Master, wherever they *visited,* they *preached from house to house.*"

Jesus' instructions to the 70 are similar to those given to the 12 when he sent these out on a preaching campaign in Galilee about a year earlier. Not only does he warn the 70 of the opposition they will face, preparing them to present the message to householders, but he empowers them to cure the sick. Thus, when Jesus arrives shortly afterward, many will be eager to meet the Master whose disciples are able to do such marvelous things.

The preaching by the 70 and Jesus' follow-up work last a relatively short time. Soon the 35 teams of Kingdom preachers begin returning to Jesus. "Lord," they say joyfully, "even the demons are made subject to us by the use of your name." Such a fine service report surely thrills Jesus, for he responds: "I began to behold Satan already fallen like lightning from heaven. Look! I have given you the authority to trample underfoot serpents and scorpions."

Jesus knows that after the birth of God's Kingdom at the time of the end, Satan and his demons are to be cast out of heaven. But now this casting out of unseen demons by mere humans serves as

added assurance of that coming event. Therefore, Jesus speaks of the future fall of Satan from heaven as an absolute certainty. Hence, it is in a symbolic sense that the 70 are given authority to trample serpents and scorpions. Yet, Jesus says: "Do not rejoice over this, that the spirits are made subject to you, but rejoice because your names have been inscribed in the heavens."

Jesus is overjoyed and publicly praises his Father for using these humble servants of his in such a powerful way. Turning to his disciples, he says: "Happy are the eyes that behold the things you are beholding. For I say to you, Many prophets and kings desired to see the things you are beholding but did not see them, and to hear the things you are hearing but did not hear them." **Luke 10:1-24; Matthew 10:1-42; Revelation 12:7-12.**

■ Where did Jesus preach during the first three years of his ministry, and what territory does he cover in his final six months?

■ Where does Jesus direct the 70 to find people?

■ Why does Jesus say he beheld Satan already fallen from heaven?

■ In what sense can the 70 trample serpents and scorpions?

73

A Neighborly Samaritan

JESUS is perhaps near Bethany, a village about two miles from Jerusalem. A man who is an expert on the Law of Moses approaches him with a question, asking: "Teacher, by doing what shall I inherit everlasting life?"

Jesus detects that the man, a lawyer, is asking not simply for information but, rather, because he desires to test him. The lawyer's aim may be to get Jesus to answer in a way that will offend the sensibilities of the Jews. So Jesus gets the lawyer to commit himself, asking: "What is written in the Law? How do you read?"

In reply, the lawyer, exercising unusual insight, quotes from God's laws at Deuteronomy 6:5 and Leviticus 19:18, saying: "'You must love Jehovah your God with your whole heart and with your whole soul and with your whole strength and with your whole mind,' and, 'your neighbor as yourself.'"

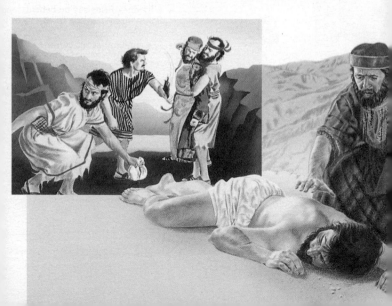

"You answered correctly," Jesus responds. "Keep on doing this and you will get life."

The lawyer, however, is not satisfied. Jesus' answer is not specific enough for him. He wants confirmation from Jesus that his own views are correct and hence that he is righteous in his treatment of others. Therefore, he asks: "Who really is my neighbor?"

The Jews believe that the term "neighbor" applies only to fellow Jews, as the context of Leviticus 19:18 seems to indicate. In fact, later even the apostle Peter said: "You well know how unlawful it is for a Jew to join himself to or approach a man of another race." So the lawyer, and perhaps Jesus' disciples too, believe that they are righteous if they treat only fellow Jews kindly, since, in their view, non-Jews are not really their neighbors.

Without offending his listeners, how can Jesus correct their view? He tells a story, possibly based on an actual happening. "A certain [Jew]," Jesus explains, "was going down from Jerusalem to Jericho and fell among robbers, who both stripped him and inflicted blows, and went off, leaving him half-dead."

"Now, by coincidence," Jesus continues, "a certain priest was going down over that road, but, when he saw him, he went by on the opposite side. Likewise, a Levite also, when he got down to the place and saw him, went by on the opposite side. But a certain Samaritan traveling the road came upon him and, at seeing him, he was moved with pity."

Many priests and their Levite temple assistants live in Jericho, a distance of 14 miles on a dangerous road that descends 3,000 feet from where they serve at the temple in Jerusalem. The priest and the Levite would be expected to help a fellow Jew in distress. But they do not. Instead, a Samaritan does. The Jews hate Samaritans so much that recently they insulted Jesus in the strongest terms by calling him "a Samaritan."

What does the Samaritan do to help the Jew? "He approached him," Jesus says, "and bound up his wounds, pouring oil and wine upon them. Then he mounted him upon his own beast and brought him to an inn and took care of him. And the next day he took out two denarii [about two days' wages], gave them to the innkeeper, and said, 'Take care of him, and whatever you spend besides this, I will repay you when I come back here.'"

After telling the story, Jesus asks the lawyer: "Who of these three seems to you to have made himself neighbor to the man that fell among the robbers?"

Feeling uncomfortable about attributing any merit to a Samaritan, the lawyer answers simply: "The one that acted mercifully toward him."

"Go your way and be doing the same yourself," Jesus concludes.

Had Jesus told the lawyer directly that non-Jews also were his neighbors, not only would the man not have accepted this but most of the audience would probably have taken his side in the discussion with Jesus. This true-to-life story, however, made it obvious in an irrefutable way that our neighbors include people besides those of our own race and nationality. What a marvelous way Jesus has of teaching! **Luke 10:25-37; Acts 10:28; John 4:9; 8:48.**

■ What questions does the lawyer ask Jesus, and what evidently is his purpose in asking?

■ Who do the Jews believe are their neighbors, and what reason is there to believe that even the disciples share this view?

■ How does Jesus get across the correct view so that the lawyer cannot refute it?

74

Counsel to Martha, and Instruction on Prayer

DURING the course of Jesus' Judean ministry, he enters the village of Bethany. This is where Martha, Mary, and their brother Lazarus live. Perhaps Jesus met these three earlier in his ministry and so is already a close friend of theirs. In any event, Jesus now goes to the home of Martha and is welcomed by her.

Martha is eager to provide Jesus with the very best that she has. Indeed, it is a great honor to have the promised Messiah visit one's home! So Martha becomes involved in preparing an elaborate meal and seeing to many other details designed to make Jesus' stay more enjoyable and comfortable.

On the other hand, Martha's sister Mary sits down at Jesus' feet and listens to him. After a while, Martha approaches and says to Jesus: "Lord, does it not matter to you that my sister has left me alone to attend to things? Tell her, therefore, to join in helping me."

But Jesus refuses to say anything to Mary. Rather, he counsels Martha for being overly concerned with material things. "Martha, Martha," he kindly reproves, "you are anxious and disturbed about many things. A few things, though, are needed, or just one." Jesus is saying that it is not necessary to spend a lot of time preparing many dishes for a meal. Only a few or even just one dish is sufficient.

Martha's intentions are good; she wants to be a hospitable hostess. Yet, by her anxious attention to material provisions, she is missing out on the opportunity to receive personal instruction from God's own Son! So Jesus concludes: "For her part, Mary chose the good portion, and it will not be taken away from her."

Later, on another occasion, a disciple asks Jesus: "Lord, teach us how to pray, just as John also taught his disciples." Possibly this disciple was not present about a year and a half earlier when Jesus provided the model prayer in his Sermon on the Mount. So Jesus repeats his instructions but then goes on to give an illustration to emphasize the need to be persistent in prayer.

"Who of you will have a friend," Jesus begins, "and will go to him at midnight and say to him, 'Friend, loan me three loaves, because a friend of mine has just come to me on a journey and I have nothing to set before him'? And that one from inside says in reply, 'Quit making me trouble. The door is already locked, and my young children are with me in bed; I cannot rise up and give you anything.' I tell you, Although he will not rise up and give him anything because of being his friend, certainly because of his bold persistence he will get up and give him what things he needs."

By this comparison Jesus does not mean to imply that Jehovah God is unwilling to respond to petitions, as was the friend in his story. No, but he is illustrating that if an unwilling friend will respond to persistent requests, how much more so will our loving heavenly Father! So Jesus continues: "Accordingly I say to you, Keep on asking, and it will be given you; keep on seeking, and you will find; keep on knocking, and it will be opened to you. For everyone asking receives, and everyone seeking finds, and to everyone knocking it will be opened."

Jesus then makes a reference to imperfect, sinful human fathers, saying: "Indeed, which father is there among you who, if his son asks for a fish, will perhaps hand him a serpent instead of a fish? Or if he also asks for an egg, will hand him a scorpion? Therefore, if you, although being wicked, know how to give good gifts to your children, how much more so will the Father in heaven give holy spirit to those asking him!" Indeed, what motivating encouragement Jesus provides to be persistent in prayer. Luke 10: 38–11:13.

■ Why does Martha go to such extensive preparations for Jesus?

■ What does Mary do, and why does Jesus commend her instead of Martha?

■ What prompts Jesus to repeat his instructions on prayer?

■ How does Jesus illustrate the need to be persistent in prayer?

75

The Source of Happiness

DURING his ministry in Galilee, Jesus performed miracles, and he now repeats these in Judea. For instance, he casts out of a man a demon that has prevented him from speaking. The crowds are amazed, but critics raise the same objection as was raised in Galilee. "He expels the demons by means of Beelzebub the ruler of the demons," they claim. Others want greater evidence from Jesus as to his identity, and they try to tempt him by asking for a sign from heaven.

Knowing what they are thinking, Jesus gives the same answer to his critics in Judea as he gave to those in Galilee. He observes that every kingdom divided against itself will fall. "So," he asks, "if Satan is also divided against himself, how will his kingdom stand?" He shows the dangerous position of his critics by saying: "If it is by means of God's finger I expel the demons, the kingdom of God has really overtaken you."

Those observing Jesus' miracles should respond to them in the same way as those did who centuries before saw Moses perform a miracle. They exclaimed: "It is the finger of God!" It was also "God's finger" that carved the Ten Commandments on stone tablets. And "God's finger"—his holy spirit, or active force—is what enables Jesus to cast out demons and to cure the sick. So the Kingdom of God has indeed overtaken these critics, since Jesus, the designated King of the Kingdom, is right there in their midst.

Jesus then illustrates that his ability to expel demons is evidence of his power over Satan, even as when a stronger man comes along and overpowers a well-armed man guarding his palace. He also repeats the illustration he told in Galilee regarding an unclean spirit. The spirit leaves a man, but when the man does not fill the void with good things,

the spirit returns with seven others, and the condition of the man becomes worse than at the first.

While listening to these teachings, a woman from the crowd is moved to exclaim loudly: "Happy is the womb that carried you and the breasts that you sucked!" Since the desire of every Jewish woman is to be the mother of a prophet and particularly the Messiah, it is understandable that this woman would say this. Apparently she thought Mary could especially be happy because of being Jesus' mother.

However, Jesus quickly corrects the woman regarding the true source of happiness. "No," he responds, "rather, Happy are those hearing the word of God and keeping it!" Never did Jesus imply that his mother, Mary, should be given special honor. Instead, he showed that true happiness is found in being a faithful servant of God, not in any physical ties or accomplishments.

As he did in Galilee, Jesus also goes on to rebuke the people in Judea for requesting a sign from heaven. He tells them that no sign will be given except the sign of Jonah. Jonah became a sign both by his three days in the fish and by his bold preaching, which resulted in the Ninevites' being moved to repent. "But, look!" Jesus says, "something more than Jonah is here." Similarly, the queen of Sheba marveled at Solomon's wisdom. "But, look!" Jesus also says, "something more than Solomon is here."

Jesus explains that when a person lights a lamp, he does not put it in a vault or under a basket but upon a lampstand so that people can see the light. Perhaps he is intimating that teaching and performing miracles before these obstinate persons in his audience is comparable to hiding the light of a lamp. The eyes of such observers are not simple, or in focus, so the intended purpose of his miracles is not accomplished.

Jesus has just expelled a demon and has caused a mute man to speak. This should motivate people with simple, or focused, eyes to praise this glorious feat and proclaim the good news! Yet, with these critics, this is not what occurs. So Jesus concludes: "Be alert, therefore. Perhaps the light that is in you is darkness. Therefore, if your whole body is bright with no part at all dark, it will all be as bright as when a lamp gives you light by its rays." Luke 11:14-36; Exodus 8:18, 19; 31:18; Matthew 12:22, 28.

- What is the response to Jesus' healing the man?
- What is "God's finger," and how had God's Kingdom overtaken Jesus' listeners?
- What is the source of true happiness?
- How can a person have a simple eye?

76

Dining With a Pharisee

AFTER Jesus answers critics who question the source of his power to heal a man who could not talk, a Pharisee invites him to dinner. Before they eat, the Pharisees engage in the ritual of washing their hands up to the elbow. They do this before and after a meal and even between courses. Although the tradition does not violate God's written law, it goes beyond what God requires in the matter of ceremonial cleanness.

When Jesus fails to observe the tradition, his host is surprised. Even though his surprise may not be expressed verbally, Jesus detects it and says: "Now you Pharisees, you cleanse the outside of the cup and dish, but the inside of you is full of plunder and wickedness. Unreasonable

persons! He that made the outside made also the inside, did he not?"

Jesus thus exposes the hypocrisy of the Pharisees who ritualistically wash their hands but fail to wash their hearts from wickedness. He counsels: "Give as gifts of mercy the things that are inside, and, look! all other things are clean about you." Their giving should be motivated by a loving heart, not by a desire to impress others with their pretense of righteousness.

"Woe to you Pharisees," Jesus continues, "because you give the tenth of the mint and the rue and of every other vegetable, but you pass by the justice and the love of God! These things you were under obligation to do, but those other things not to omit." God's Law to Israel requires the paying of tithes, or a tenth part, of the produce from the fields. The mint and the rue are small plants or herbs used in flavoring food. The Pharisees carefully pay a tenth of even these insignificant herbs, but Jesus condemns them for ignoring the more important requirement to show love, exercise kindness, and be modest.

Condemning them further, Jesus says: "Woe to you Pharisees, because you love the front seats in the synagogues and the greetings in the marketplaces! Woe to you, because you are as those memorial tombs which are not in evidence, so that men walk upon them and do not know it!" Their uncleanness is not apparent. The religion of the Pharisees has outward show but no inner worth! It is based on hypocrisy.

Listening to such condemnation, a lawyer, one of those versed in God's Law, complains: "Teacher, in saying these things you also insult us."

Jesus holds these experts on the Law responsible too, saying: "Woe also to you who are versed in the Law, because you load men with loads hard to be borne, but you yourselves do not touch the loads with one of your fingers! Woe to you, because you build the memorial tombs of the prophets, but your forefathers killed them!"

The loads Jesus mentions are the oral traditions, but these lawyers would not so much as lift one little regulation to make it easier for the people. Jesus reveals that they even consent to the murder of the prophets, and he warns: "'The blood of all the prophets spilled from the founding of the world [will] be required from this generation, from the blood of Abel down to the blood of Zechariah, who was slain between the altar and the house.' Yes, I tell you, it will be required from this generation."

The world of redeemable mankind had its start with the birth of children to Adam and Eve; thus, Abel lived at "the founding of the world." Following the vicious murder of Zechariah, a Syrian force despoiled Judah. But Jesus foretells a worse despoiling of his own generation because of its greater wickedness. This despoiling occurs about 38 years later, in 70 C.E.

Continuing his condemnation, Jesus says: "Woe to you who are versed in the Law, because you took away the key of knowledge; you yourselves did not go in, and those going in you hindered!" The experts on the Law are duty-bound to explain God's Word to the people, unlocking its meaning. But they fail to do this and even take away from the people the opportunity to understand.

The Pharisees and the legal experts are furious at Jesus for exposing them. When he leaves the house, they begin to oppose him fiercely and besiege him with questions. They try to trap him into saying something for which they can have him arrested.   Luke 11:37-54; Deuteronomy 14:22; Micah 6:8; 2 Chronicles 24:20-25.

- Why does Jesus condemn the Pharisees and the experts on the Law?
- What loads do the lawyers place on the people?
- When was "the founding of the world?"

77

The Question of Inheritance

THE people evidently know that Jesus has been dining at the Pharisee's house. So they gather outside by the thousands and are waiting when Jesus comes out. Unlike the Pharisees who oppose Jesus and try to catch him in saying something wrong, the people eagerly listen to him with appreciation.

Turning first to his disciples, Jesus says: "Watch out for the leaven of the Pharisees, which is hypocrisy." As demonstrated during the meal, the whole religious system of the Pharisees is filled with hypocrisy. But even though the wickedness of the Pharisees may be concealed by a show of piety, eventually

it will be exposed. "There is nothing carefully concealed," Jesus says, "that will not be revealed, and secret that will not become known."

Jesus goes on to repeat the encouragement that he had given to the 12 when he sent them forth on a preaching tour of Galilee. He says: "Do not fear those who kill the body and after this are not able to do anything more." Since God does not forget even a single sparrow, Jesus assures his followers that God will not forget them. He states: "When they bring you in before public assemblies and government officials and authorities, . . . the holy spirit will teach you in that very hour the things you ought to say."

A man from the crowd speaks up. "Teacher," he petitions, "tell my brother to divide the inheritance with me." The Law of Moses stipulates that the firstborn son is to receive two parts of the inheritance, so there should be no reason for a dispute. But the man apparently wants more than his legal share of the inheritance.

Jesus properly refuses to get involved. "Man, who appointed me judge or apportioner over you persons?" he asks. He then gives this vital admonition to the crowd: "Keep your eyes open and guard against every sort of covetousness, because even when a person has an abundance his life does not result from the things he possesses." Yes, no matter how much a man may come to have, normally he will die and leave it all behind. To emphasize this fact, as well as to show the folly of failing to build up a good reputation with God, Jesus uses an illustration. He explains:

"The land of a certain rich man produced well. Consequently he began reasoning within himself, saying, 'What shall I do, now that I have nowhere to gather my crops?' So he said, 'I will do this: I will tear down my storehouses and build bigger ones, and there I will gather all my grain and all my good things; and I will say to my soul: "Soul, you have many good things laid up for many years; take your ease, eat, drink, enjoy yourself.'" But God said to him, 'Unreasonable one, this night they are demanding your soul from you. Who, then, is to have the things you stored up?'"

In conclusion, Jesus observes: "So it goes with the man that lays up treasure for himself but is not rich toward God." While the disciples may not be ensnared by the folly of piling up wealth, because of the daily cares of life they could easily be distracted from whole-souled service to Jehovah. So Jesus uses the occasion to repeat the fine counsel he had given about a year and a half earlier in the Sermon on the Mount. Turning to his disciples, he says:

"On this account I say to you, Quit being anxious about your souls as to what you will eat or about your bodies as to what you will wear. . . . Mark well that the ravens neither sow seed nor reap, and they have neither barn nor storehouse, and yet God feeds them. . . . Mark well how the lilies grow; they neither toil nor spin; but I tell you, Not even Solomon in all his glory was arrayed as one of these. . . .

"So quit seeking what you might eat and what you might drink, and quit being in anxious suspense; for all these are the things the nations of the world are eagerly pursuing, but your Father knows you need these things. Nevertheless, seek continually his kingdom, and these things will be added to you."

Especially during times of economic hardship do Jesus' words bear close consideration. The person who becomes overanxious about his material needs and begins to slack off in spiritual pursuits is, in fact, demonstrating a lack of faith in God's ability to provide for His servants. Luke 12:1-31; Deuteronomy 21:17.

- Why, perhaps, does the man ask about inheritance, and what admonition does Jesus give?

- What illustration does Jesus use, and what is its point?

- What counsel does Jesus repeat, and why is it appropriate?

78

Keep Ready!

AFTER warning the crowds about covetousness, and cautioning his disciples about giving undue attention to material things, Jesus encourages: "Have no fear, little flock, because your Father has approved of giving you the kingdom." He thus reveals that only a relatively small number (later identified as 144,000) will be in the heavenly Kingdom. The majority of the ones who receive eternal life will be earthly subjects of the Kingdom.

What a marvelous gift, "the kingdom"! Describing the proper response the disciples should have upon receiving it, Jesus urges them: "Sell the things belonging to you and give gifts of mercy." Yes, they should use their assets to

benefit others spiritually and thus build up "a never-failing treasure in the heavens."

Jesus next admonishes his disciples to keep ready for his return. He says: "Let your loins be girded and your lamps be burning, and you yourselves be like men waiting for their master when he returns from the marriage, so that at his arriving and knocking they may at once open to him. Happy are those slaves whom the master on arriving finds watching! Truly I say to you, He will gird himself and make them recline at the table and will come alongside and minister to them."

In this illustration, the readiness of the servants at their master's return is shown by their pulling up their long robes and fastening these under their girdles and their continuing to care for their duties on into the night by the light of well-fueled lamps. Jesus explains: 'If the master arrives in the second watch [from about nine in the evening to midnight], even if in the third [from midnight to about three in the morning], and finds them ready, happy are they!'

The master rewards his servants in an unusual way. He has them recline at the table and begins serving them. He treats them, not as slaves, but as loyal friends. What a fine reward for their continuing to work for their master throughout the night while waiting for his return! Jesus concludes: "You also, *keep ready,* because at an hour that you do not think likely the Son of man is coming."

Peter now asks: "Lord, are you saying this illustration to us or also to all?"

Rather than answer directly, Jesus gives another illustration. "Who really is the faithful steward," he asks, "whom his master will appoint over his body of attendants to keep giving them their measure of food supplies at the proper time? Happy is that slave, if his master on arriving finds him doing so! I tell you truthfully, He will appoint him over all his belongings."

The "master" obviously is Jesus Christ. The "steward" pictures the "little flock" of disciples as a collective body, and the "body of attendants" refers to this same group of 144,000 who receive the heavenly Kingdom, but this expression highlights their work as individuals. The "belongings" that the faithful steward is appointed to care for are the master's royal interests on earth, which include the Kingdom's earthly subjects.

Continuing the illustration, Jesus points to the possibility that not all members of that steward, or slave, class will be loyal, explaining: "If ever that slave should say in his heart, 'My master delays coming,' and should start to beat the menservants and the maidservants, and to eat and drink and get drunk, the master of that slave will come on a day that he is not expecting him . . . , and he will punish him with the greatest severity."

Jesus notes that his coming has brought a fiery time for the Jews, as some accept and others reject his teachings. Over three years earlier, he was baptized in water, but now his baptism into death is drawing ever closer to a conclusion, and as he says: "I am being distressed until it is finished!"

After directing these remarks to his disciples, Jesus again addresses the crowds. He laments their stubborn refusal to accept the clear evidence of his identity and its significance. "When you see a cloud rising in western parts," he observes, "at once you say, 'A storm is coming,' and it turns out so. And when you see that a south wind is blowing, you say, 'There will be a heat wave,' and it occurs. Hypocrites, you know how to examine the outward appearance of earth and sky, but how is it you do not know how to examine this particular time?"   Luke 12:32-59.

- How many make up the "little flock," and what do they receive?
- How does Jesus emphasize the need for his servants to be ready?
- In Jesus' illustration, who are the "master," the "steward," the "body of attendants," and the "belongings"?

79

A Nation Lost, but Not All

SHORTLY after Jesus' discussion with those who had gathered outside the house of a Pharisee, certain ones tell him "about the Galileans whose blood [the Roman governor Pontius] Pilate had mixed with their sacrifices." These Galileans are perhaps the ones who were killed when thousands of Jews protested Pilate's use of money from the temple treasury to build an aqueduct to bring water into Jerusalem. Those relating this matter to Jesus may be suggesting that the Galileans suffered the calamity because of their own wicked deeds.

Jesus, however, sets them straight, asking: "Do you imagine that these Galileans were proved worse sinners than all other Galileans because they have suffered these things? No, indeed," Jesus answers. Then he uses the incident to warn the Jews: "Unless you repent, you will all likewise be destroyed."

Continuing, Jesus recalls another local tragedy, perhaps also associated with the aqueduct construction. He asks: "Or those eighteen upon whom the tower in Siloam fell, thereby killing them, do you imagine that they were proved greater debtors than all other men inhabiting Jerusalem?" No, it was not because of the badness of these persons that they happened to die, Jesus says. Rather, "time and unforeseen occurrence" are generally responsible for such tragedies. Jesus, however, once again uses the occasion to warn: "But, unless you repent, you will all be destroyed in the same way."

Jesus then goes on to give a fitting illustration, explaining: "A certain man had a fig tree planted in his vineyard, and he came looking for fruit on it, but found none. Then he said to the vinedresser, 'Here it is three years that I have come looking for fruit on this fig tree, but have found none. Cut it down! Why really should it keep the ground useless?' In reply he said to him, 'Master, let it alone also this year, until I dig around it and put on manure; and if then it produces fruit in

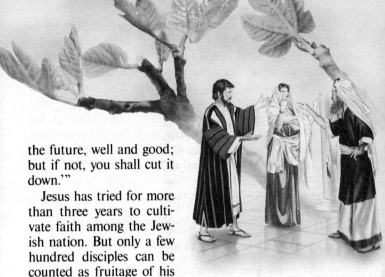

the future, well and good; but if not, you shall cut it down.'"

Jesus has tried for more than three years to cultivate faith among the Jewish nation. But only a few hundred disciples can be counted as fruitage of his labors. Now, during this fourth year of his ministry, he is intensifying his efforts, symbolically digging and putting manure around the Jewish fig tree by zealously preaching and teaching in Judea and Perea. Yet to no avail! The nation refuses to repent and so is in line for destruction. Only a remnant of the nation respond.

Shortly afterward Jesus is teaching in a synagogue on a Sabbath. There he sees a woman who, because of a demon afflicting her, has been bent double for 18 years. Compassionately, Jesus addresses her: "Woman, you are released from your weakness." At that he lays his hands on her, and instantly she straightens up and begins glorifying God.

The presiding officer of the synagogue, however, is angry. "There are six days on which work ought to be done," he protests. "On them, therefore, come and be cured, and not on the sabbath day." The officer thus acknowledges Jesus' power to heal but condemns the people for coming to be healed on the Sabbath!

"Hypocrites," Jesus answers, "does not each one of you on the sabbath untie his bull or his ass from the stall and lead it away to give it drink? Was it not due, then, for this woman who is a daughter of Abraham, and whom Satan held bound, look! eighteen years, to be loosed from this bond on the sabbath day?"

Well, on hearing this, those opposing Jesus begin to feel shame. The crowd, however, rejoice at all the glorious things they see Jesus do. In response Jesus repeats two prophetic illustrations regarding the Kingdom of God, ones that he told from a boat on the Sea of Galilee about a year earlier. **Luke 13:1-21; Ecclesiastes 9:11; Matthew 13:31-33.**

- What tragedies are here mentioned, and what lesson does Jesus draw from them?
- What application can be made regarding the unfruitful fig tree, as well as the attempts to make it productive?
- How does the presiding officer acknowledge Jesus' healing ability, yet how does Jesus expose the man's hypocrisy?

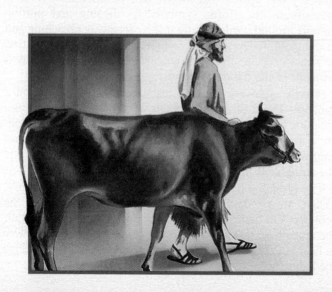

80

The Sheepfolds and the Shepherd

JESUS has come to Jerusalem for the Festival of Dedication, or Hanukkah, a festival that celebrates the rededication to Jehovah of the temple. In 168 B.C.E., about 200 years earlier, Antiochus IV Epiphanes captured Jerusalem and desecrated the temple and its altar. However, three years later Jerusalem was recaptured and the temple was rededicated. Afterward, an annual rededication celebration was held.

This Festival of Dedication takes place on Chislev 25, the Jewish month that corresponds to the last part of November and first part of December on our modern calendar. Thus, only a little over a hundred days remain until the momentous Passover of 33 C.E. Because it is the season of cold weather, the apostle John calls it "wintertime."

Jesus now uses an illustration in which he mentions three sheepfolds and his role as the Fine Shepherd. The first sheepfold he speaks of is identified with the Mosaic Law covenant arrangement. The Law served as a fence, separating the Jews from the corrupting practices of those people not in this special covenant with God. Jesus explains: "Most truly I say to you, He that does not enter into the sheepfold through the door but climbs up some other place, that one is a thief and a plunderer. But he that enters through the door is shepherd of the sheep."

Others had come and claimed to be the Messiah, or Christ, but they were not the true shepherd of whom Jesus goes on to speak: "The doorkeeper opens to this one, and the sheep listen to his voice, and he calls his own sheep by name and leads them out. . . . A stranger they will by no means follow but will flee from him, because they do not know the voice of strangers."

The "doorkeeper" of the first sheepfold was John the Baptizer. As the doorkeeper, John 'opened to' Jesus by identifying him to those symbolic sheep that he would lead out to pasture. These sheep that Jesus calls by name and leads out are eventually admitted to another sheepfold, as he explains: "Most truly I say to you, I am the door of the sheep," that is, the door of a new sheepfold. When Jesus institutes the new covenant with his disciples and from heaven pours holy spirit upon them the following Pentecost, they are admitted to this new sheepfold.

Further explaining his role, Jesus says: "I am the door; whoever enters through me will be saved, and he will go in and out and find pasturage. . . . I have come that they might have life and might have it in abundance. . . . I am the fine shepherd, and I know my sheep and my sheep know me, just as the Father knows me and I know the Father; and I surrender my soul in behalf of the sheep."

Recently, Jesus had comforted his followers, saying: "Have no fear, little flock, because your Father has approved of giving you the kingdom." This little flock, which eventually numbers 144,000, comes into this new, or second, sheepfold. But Jesus goes on to observe: "I have other sheep, which are not of this fold; those also I must bring, and they will listen to my voice, and they will become one flock, one shepherd."

Since the "other sheep" are "not of this fold," they must be of another fold, a third one. These last two folds, or pens of sheep, have different destinies. The "little flock" in one fold

will rule with Christ in heaven, and the "other sheep" in the other fold will live on the Paradise earth. Yet, despite being in two folds, the sheep have no jealousy, nor do they feel segregated, for as Jesus says, they "become one flock" under "one shepherd."

The Fine Shepherd, Jesus Christ, willingly gives his life for both folds of sheep. "I surrender it of my own initiative," he says. "I have authority to surrender it, and I have authority to receive it again. The commandment on this I received from my Father." When Jesus says this, a division results among the Jews.

Many of the crowd say: "He has a demon and is mad. Why do you listen to him?" But others respond: "These are not the sayings of a demonized man." Then, evidently referring back a couple of months to his curing of the man born blind, they add: "A demon cannot open blind people's eyes, can it?" John 10:1-22; 9:1-7; Luke 12:32; Revelation 14:1, 3; 21:3, 4; Psalm 37:29.

- What is the Festival of Dedication, and when is it celebrated?
- What is the first sheepfold, and who is its doorkeeper?
- How does the doorkeeper open to the Shepherd, and to what are the sheep thereafter admitted?
- Who make up the Fine Shepherd's two folds, and how many flocks do they become?

81

Further Attempts to Kill Jesus

SINCE it is wintertime, Jesus is walking in the sheltered area known as the colonnade of Solomon. It is alongside the temple. Here Jews encircle him and begin to say: "How long are you to keep our souls in suspense? If you are the Christ, tell us outspokenly."

"I told you," Jesus replies, "and yet you do not believe." Jesus had not *directly* told them that he was the Christ, as he had told the Samaritan woman at the well. Yet he had, in effect, revealed his identity when he explained to them that he was from the realms above and had existed before Abraham.

Jesus, however, wants people to reach the conclusion themselves that he is the Christ by comparing his activities with what the Bible foretold that the Christ would accomplish. That is why earlier he charged his disciples not to tell anyone that he was the Christ. And that is why he now goes on to say to these hostile Jews: "The works that I am doing in the name of my Father, these bear witness about me. But you do not believe."

Why do they not believe? Because of lack of evidence that Jesus is the Christ? No, but for the reason Jesus gives when he tells them: "You are none of my sheep. My sheep listen to my voice, and I know them, and they follow me. And I give them everlasting life, and they will by no means ever be destroyed, and no one will snatch them out of my hand. What my Father has given me is something greater than all other things, and no one can snatch them out of the hand of the Father."

Jesus then describes his close relationship with his Father, explaining: "I and the Father are one." Since Jesus is on earth and his Father is in heaven, clearly he is not saying that he and his Father are literally, or physically, one. Rather, he means that they are one in purpose, that they are at unity.

Angered by Jesus' words, the Jews pick up stones to kill him, even as they had earlier, during the Festival of Tabernacles, or Booths. Courageously facing his would-be murderers, Jesus says: "I displayed to you many fine works from the Father. For which of those works are you stoning me?"

"We are stoning you, not for a fine work," they answer, "but for blasphemy, even because you, although being a man, make yourself a god." Since Jesus never claimed to be a god, why do the Jews say this?

Evidently it is because Jesus attributes to himself powers that they believe belong exclusively to God. For example, he just said of the "sheep," "I give them everlasting life," which is something no human can do. The Jews, however, overlook the fact that Jesus acknowledges receiving authority from his Father.

That Jesus claims to be less than God, he next shows by asking: "Is it not written in your Law [at Psalm 82:6], 'I said: "You are gods"'? If he called 'gods' those against whom the word of God came, . . . do you say to me whom the Father sanctified and dispatched into the world, 'You blaspheme,' because I said, I am God's Son?"

Since the Scriptures call even unjust human judges "gods," what fault can these Jews find with Jesus for saying, "I am God's Son"? Jesus adds: "If I am not doing the works of my Father, do not believe me. But if I am doing them, even though you do not believe me, believe the works, in order that you may come to know and may continue knowing that the Father is in union with me and I am in union with the Father."

When Jesus says this, the Jews try to seize him. But he escapes, as he did earlier at the Festival of Tabernacles. He leaves Jerusalem and travels across the Jordan River to where John began baptizing nearly four years earlier. This location apparently is not far from the southern shore of the Sea of Galilee, a two-day journey or so from Jerusalem.

Many people come to Jesus at this place and begin to say: "John, indeed, did not perform a single sign, but as many things as John said about this man were all true." Thus many put faith in Jesus here. **John 10:22-42; 4:26; 8:23, 58; Matthew 16:20.**

■ By what means does Jesus want people to identify him as the Christ?

■ How are Jesus and his Father one?

■ Why, evidently, do the Jews say that Jesus is making himself a god?

■ How does Jesus' quotation from the Psalms show that he is not claiming to be equal to God?

82

Jesus Again Heads for Jerusalem

SOON Jesus is on the road again, teaching from city to city and from village to village. Evidently he is in the district of Perea, across the Jordan River from Judea. But his destination is Jerusalem.

The Jewish philosophy that only a limited number will merit salvation is what perhaps prompts a man to ask: "Lord, are those who are being saved few?" With his answer, Jesus forces the people to think of what is needed for salvation: "Exert yourselves vigorously [that is, struggle, or agonize] to get in through the narrow door."

Such vigorous effort is urgent "because many," Jesus continues, "will seek to get in but will not be able." Why will they not be able? He explains that 'once the householder has got up and locked the door and people stand outside and knock, saying, "Sir, open to us," he will say: "I do not know where you are from. Get away from me, all you workers of unrighteousness!"'

The ones locked out apparently come at a time convenient only to themselves. But by then the door of opportunity is shut and bolted. To get in, they should have come earlier, even though it may then have been inconvenient to do so. Indeed, a sad outcome awaits those who put off making the worship of Jehovah their chief purpose in life!

The Jews to whom Jesus is sent to minister have, for the most part, failed to seize their marvelous opportunity of accepting God's provision for salvation. So Jesus says they will weep and gnash their teeth when they are thrown outside. On the other hand, people from "eastern parts and western, and from north and south," yes, from all nations, "will recline at the table in the kingdom of God."

Jesus continues: "There are those last [despised non-Jews, as well as downtrodden Jews] who will be first, and there are those first [the materially and religiously favored Jews] who will be last." Their being last means that such slothful, ungrateful ones will not be in the Kingdom of God at all.

Pharisees now come to Jesus and say: "Get out and be on your way from here, because Herod [Antipas] wants to kill you." It may be that Herod himself started this rumor to cause Jesus to flee from the territory. Herod may have been afraid of becoming involved in the death of another prophet of God as he was in the killing of John the Baptizer. But Jesus tells the Pharisees: "Go and tell that fox, 'Look! I am casting out demons and accomplishing healing today and tomorrow, and the third day I shall be finished.'"

After finishing his work there, Jesus continues his journey toward Jerusalem because, as he explains, "it is not admissible for a prophet to be destroyed outside of Jerusalem." Why is it to be expected that Jesus would be killed at Jerusalem? Because Jerusalem is the capital city, where the 71-member Sanhedrin high court is located and where the animal sacrifices are offered. Therefore, it would be inadmissible for "the Lamb of God" to be killed anywhere but Jerusalem.

"Jerusalem, Jerusalem, the killer of the prophets and stoner of those sent forth to her,"

Jesus laments, "how often I wanted to gather your children together in the manner that a hen gathers her brood of chicks under her wings, but you people did not want it! Look! Your house is abandoned to you." For rejecting the Son of God, the nation is doomed!

As Jesus continues toward Jerusalem, he is invited to the house of a ruler of the Pharisees. It is a Sabbath, and the people are closely watching him, since there is a man present who is suffering from dropsy, an accumulation of water probably in his arms and legs. Jesus addresses the Pharisees and the experts in the Law who are present, asking: "Is it lawful on the sabbath to cure or not?"

Nobody says a word. So Jesus heals the man and sends him away. Then he asks: "Who of you, if his son or bull falls into a well, will not immediately pull him out on the sabbath day?" Again, nobody says a word in reply. Luke 13:22–14:6; John 1:29.

- What does Jesus show is needed for salvation, and why are many locked outside?
- Who are the "last" that become first, and the "first" that become last?
- Why possibly was it said that Herod wanted to kill Jesus?
- Why is it not admissible for a prophet to be destroyed outside Jerusalem?

83

Entertained by a Pharisee

JESUS is still in the home of a prominent Pharisee and has just healed a man suffering from dropsy. As he observes fellow guests choosing prominent places at the meal, he teaches a lesson in humility.

"When you are invited by someone to a marriage feast," Jesus then explains, "do not lie down in the most prominent place. Perhaps someone more distinguished than you may at the time have been invited by him, and he that invited you and him will come and say to you, 'Let this man have the place.' And then you will start off with shame to occupy the lowest place."

So Jesus advises: "When you are invited, go and recline in the lowest place, that when the man that has invited you comes he will say to you, 'Friend, go on up higher.' Then you will have honor in front of all your fellow guests." Concluding, Jesus says: *"For everyone that exalts himself will be humbled and he that humbles himself will be exalted."*

Next, Jesus addresses the Pharisee who invited him and describes how to provide a dinner having real merit with God. "When you spread a dinner or evening meal, do not call your friends or your brothers or your relatives or rich neighbors. Perhaps sometime they might also invite you in return and it would become a repayment to you. But when you spread a feast, invite poor people, crippled, lame, blind; and you will be happy, because they have nothing with which to repay you."

Providing such a meal for the unfortunate will bring happiness to the provider of it because, as Jesus explains to his host, "You will be repaid in the resurrection of the righteous ones." Jesus' description of this meritorious meal calls to the mind of a fellow guest another kind of meal. "Happy is he who eats bread in the kingdom of God," this guest says. Yet, not all properly prize that happy prospect, as Jesus goes on to show by an illustration.

"A certain man was spreading a grand evening meal, and he invited many. And he sent his slave out . . . to say to the invited ones, 'Come, because things are now ready.' But they all in common started to beg off. The first said to him, 'I bought a field and need to go out and see it; I ask you, Have me excused.' And another said, 'I bought five yoke of cattle and am going to examine them; I ask you, Have me excused.' Still another said, 'I just married a wife and for this reason I cannot come.'"

What lame excuses! A field or livestock are normally examined before they are bought, so no real urgency exists to look at them afterward. Similarly, a person's marriage should not prevent him from accepting such an important invitation. So on hearing about these excuses, the master becomes angry and commands his slave:

"'Go out quickly into the broad ways and the lanes of the city, and bring in here the poor and crippled and blind and lame.' In time the slave said, 'Master, what you ordered has been done, and yet there is room.' And the master said to the slave, 'Go out into the roads and the fenced-in places, and compel them to come in, that my house may be filled. . . . None of those men that were invited shall have a taste of my evening meal.'"

What situation is described by the illustration? Well, "the master" providing the meal represents Jehovah God; "the slave" extending the invitation, Jesus Christ; and the "grand evening meal," the opportunities to be in line for the Kingdom of the heavens.

Those first to receive the invitation to come in line for the Kingdom were, above all others, the Jewish religious leaders of Jesus' day. However, they rejected the invitation. Thus, beginning particularly at Pentecost 33 C.E., a second invitation was extended to the despised and lowly ones of the Jewish nation. But not enough responded to fill the 144,000 places in God's heavenly Kingdom. So in 36 C.E., three and a half years later, the third and final invitation was extended to uncircumcised non-Jews, and the gathering of such ones has continued into our day.   Luke 14:1-24.

▪ What lesson in humility does Jesus teach?
▪ How can a host provide a meal having merit with God, and why will it bring him happiness?
▪ Why are the excuses of the invited guests lame?
▪ What is represented by Jesus' illustration of the "grand evening meal"?

84

The Responsibility of Discipleship

AFTER leaving the house of the prominent Pharisee, who apparently is a member of the Sanhedrin, Jesus continues on toward Jerusalem. Great crowds follow him. But what are their motives? What is really involved in being his true follower?

As they travel along, Jesus turns to the crowds and perhaps shocks them when he says: "If anyone comes to me and does not hate his father and mother and wife and children and brothers and sisters, yes, and even his own soul, he cannot be my disciple."

What does Jesus mean? Jesus is not here saying that his followers should literally hate their relatives. Rather, they must hate them in the sense of loving them less than they love him. Jesus' forefather Jacob is said to have "hated" Leah and loved Rachel, which meant that Leah was loved less than her sister Rachel.

Consider, too, that Jesus said a disciple should hate "even his own soul," or life. Again what Jesus means is that a true disciple must love Him even more than he loves his own life. Jesus is thus emphasizing that becoming his disciple is a serious responsibility. It is not something to be undertaken without careful consideration.

Hardship and persecution are involved in being Jesus' disciple, as he goes on to indicate: "Whoever is not carrying his torture stake and coming after me cannot be my disciple." Thus, a true disciple must be willing to undergo the same burden of reproach that Jesus endured, even including, if necessary, dying at the hands of God's enemies, which Jesus is soon to do.

Being a disciple of Christ, therefore, is a matter that the crowds following him need to analyze very carefully. Jesus emphasizes this fact by means of an illustration. "For example," he says, "who of you that wants to build a tower does not first sit down and calculate the expense, to see if he has enough to complete it? Otherwise, he might lay its foundation but not be able to finish it, and all the onlookers might start to ridicule him, saying, 'This man started to build but was not able to finish.'"

So Jesus is illustrating to the crowds who are following him that before becoming his disciples, they should be firmly decided that they can fulfill what is involved, even as a man who wants to build a tower makes sure before he begins that he has the resources to complete it. Providing another illustration, Jesus continues:

"Or what king, marching to meet another king in war, does not first sit down and take counsel whether he is able with ten thousand troops to cope with the one that comes against him with twenty thousand? If, in fact, he cannot do so, then while that one is yet far away he sends out a body of ambassadors and sues for peace."

Jesus then emphasizes the point of his illustrations, saying: "Thus, you may be sure, none of you that does not say good-bye to all his belongings can be my disciple." That is what the crowds following him, and, yes, everyone else who learns of Christ, must be willing to do. They must be ready to sacrifice everything that they have—all their belongings, including

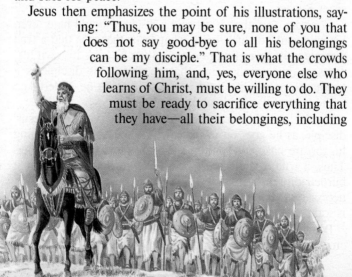

life itself—if they would be his disciples. Are you willing to do this?

"Salt, to be sure, is fine," Jesus continues. In his Sermon on the Mount, he said that his disciples are "the salt of the earth," meaning that they have a preserving influence on people, even as literal salt is a preservative. "But if even the salt loses its strength, with what will it be seasoned? It is suitable neither for soil nor for manure," Jesus concludes. "People throw it outside. Let him that has ears to listen, listen."

So Jesus shows that even those who have been his disciples for some time must not weaken in their determination to continue. If they do, they will become useless, an object of ridicule to this world and unfit before God, in fact, a reproach upon God. Hence, like strengthless, contaminated salt, they will be thrown outside, yes, destroyed. Luke 14:25-35; Genesis 29:30-33; Matthew 5:13.

- What does it mean to "hate" one's relatives and oneself?
- What two illustrations does Jesus give, and what do they mean?
- What is the point of Jesus' concluding comments about salt?

85

Searching for the Lost

JESUS is eager to seek and find those who will humbly serve God. So he searches out and talks to everyone about the Kingdom, including notorious sinners. Such persons now draw near to listen to him.

Observing this, the Pharisees and scribes criticize Jesus for keeping company with people whom they consider unworthy. They mutter: "This man welcomes sinners and eats with them." How far beneath their dignity that is! The Pharisees and scribes treat common people like dirt under their feet. In fact, they use the Hebrew expression *'am ha·'a'rets,* "people of the land [earth]," to show the disdain they have for such ones.

On the other hand, Jesus treats everyone with dignity, kindness, and compassion. As a result, many of these lowly ones, including persons who are well-known for practicing wrongdoing, are eager to listen to him. But what of the Pharisees' criticism of Jesus for expending efforts in behalf of those they consider unworthy?

Jesus answers their objection by using an illustration. He speaks from the Pharisees' own viewpoint, as though they are righteous and are safe in the fold of God, while the despicable 'am ha·'a'rets have gone astray and are in a lost state. Listen as he asks:

"What man of you with a hundred sheep, on losing one of them, will not leave the ninety-nine behind in the wilderness and go for the lost one until he finds it? And when he has found it he puts it upon his shoulders and rejoices. And when he gets home he calls his friends and his neighbors together, saying to them, 'Rejoice with me, because I have found my sheep that was lost.'"

Jesus then makes the application of his story, explaining: "I tell you that thus there will be more joy in heaven over one sinner that repents than over ninety-nine righteous ones who have no need of repentance."

The Pharisees consider themselves to be righteous and thus to have no need of repentance. When some of them criticized Jesus a couple of years earlier for eating with tax collectors and sinners, he told them: "I came to call, not righteous people, but sinners." The self-righteous Pharisees, who fail to see their need to repent, bring no joy in heaven. But truly repentant sinners do.

To make doubly strong the point that the restoration of lost sinners is a cause for great rejoicing, Jesus relates another illustration. He says: "What woman with ten drachma coins, if she loses one drachma coin, does not light a lamp and sweep her house and search carefully until she finds it? And when she has found it she calls the women who are her friends and neighbors together, saying, 'Rejoice with me, because I have found the drachma coin that I lost.'"

Jesus then gives a similar application. He goes on to say: "Thus, I tell you, joy arises among the angels of God over one sinner that repents."

How remarkable this loving concern of God's angels for the restoration of lost sinners! Especially is this so since these once lowly, despised 'am ha·'a'rets eventually come into line for membership in God's heavenly Kingdom. As a result, they attain a position in heaven higher than that of the angels themselves! But rather than feel jealous or slighted, the an-

gels humbly appreciate that these sinful humans have faced and overcome situations in life that will equip them to serve as sympathetic and merciful heavenly kings and priests. **Luke 15: 1-10; Matthew 9:13; 1 Corinthians 6:2, 3; Revelation 20:6.**

■ Why does Jesus associate with known sinners, and what criticism does he draw from the Pharisees?

■ How do the Pharisees view the common people?

■ What illustrations does Jesus use, and what can we learn from them?

■ Why is the rejoicing of the angels remarkable?

86

The Story of a Lost Son

HAVING just finished relating illustrations to the Pharisees about regaining a lost sheep and a lost drachma coin, Jesus continues now with another illustration. This one is about a loving father and his treatment of his two sons, each of whom has serious faults.

First, there is the younger son, the principal character of the illustration. He collects his inheritance, which is unhesitatingly given to him by his father. He then leaves home and becomes involved in a very immoral way of life. But listen as Jesus tells the story, and see if you can determine who the characters are meant to represent.

"A certain man," Jesus begins, "had two sons. And the younger of them said to his father, 'Father, give me the part of the property that falls to my share.' Then [the father] divided his means of living to them." What does this younger one do with what he receives?

"Later," Jesus explains, "after not many days, the younger son gathered all things together and traveled abroad into

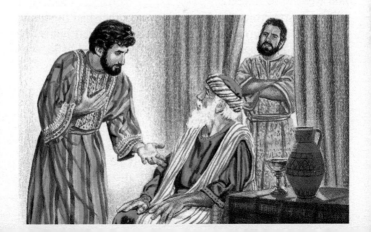

a distant country, and there squandered his property by living a debauched life." Actually, he spends his money living with prostitutes. Afterward hard times come, as Jesus goes on to relate:

"When he had spent everything, a severe famine occurred throughout that country, and he started to be in need. He even went and attached himself to one of the citizens of that country, and he sent him into his fields to herd swine. And he used to desire to be filled with the carob pods which the swine were eating, and no one would give him anything."

How degrading to be forced to take up swineherding, since these animals were unclean according to the Law! But what pained the son the most was the gnawing hunger that even caused him to desire the food that was fed to the pigs. Because of his terrible calamity, Jesus said, "he came to his senses."

Continuing his story, Jesus explains: "He said [to himself], 'How many hired men of my father are abounding with bread, while I am perishing here from famine! I will rise and journey to my father and say to him: "Father, I have sinned against heaven and against you. I am no longer worthy of being called your son. Make me as one of your hired men."' So he rose and went to his father."

Here is something to consider: If his father had turned on him and had angrily shouted at him when he left home, the son would not likely have been so single-minded as to what he should do. He may have decided to return and try to find work elsewhere in his home country so that he would not have to face his father. However, no such thought was on his mind. Home was where he wanted to be!

Clearly, the father in Jesus' illustration represents our loving, merciful heavenly Father, Jehovah God. And you perhaps also recognize that the lost, or prodigal, son represents

known sinners. The Pharisees, to whom Jesus is speaking, have previously criticized Jesus for eating with these very ones. But whom does the older son represent?

When the Lost Son Is Found

When the lost, or prodigal, son in Jesus' illustration returns to his father's house, what kind of reception does he receive? Listen as Jesus describes it:

"While he was yet a long way off, his father caught sight of him and was moved with pity, and he ran and fell upon his neck and tenderly kissed him." What a merciful, warmhearted father, so well representing our heavenly Father, Jehovah!

Likely the father had heard of his son's debauched living. Yet he welcomes him home without waiting for a detailed explanation. Jesus also has such a welcoming spirit, taking the initiative in approaching sinners and tax collectors, who are represented in the illustration by the prodigal son.

True, the discerning father of Jesus' illustration no doubt has some idea of his son's repentance by observing his sad, downcast countenance as he returns. But the father's loving initiative makes it easier for the son to confess his sins, as Jesus relates: "Then the son said to him, 'Father, I have sinned against heaven and against you. I am no longer worthy of being called your son. Make me as one of your hired men.'"

Yet, the words are hardly off the son's lips when his father goes into action, ordering his slaves: "Quick! bring out a robe, the best one, and clothe him with it, and put a ring on his hand and sandals on his feet. And bring the fattened young bull, slaughter it and let us eat and enjoy ourselves, because this my son was dead and came to life again; he was lost and was found." Then they start "to enjoy themselves."

In the meantime, the father's "older son was in the field." See if you can identify whom he represents by listening to the rest of the story. Jesus says of the older son: "As he came and got near the house he heard a music concert and dancing. So he called one of the servants to him and inquired what these things meant. He said to him, 'Your brother has come, and your father slaughtered the fattened young bull, because he got him back in good health.' But he became wrathful and was unwilling to go in. Then his father came out and began to entreat him. In reply he said to his father, 'Here it is so many years I have slaved for you and never once did I transgress your commandment, and yet to me you never once gave a kid for me to enjoy myself with my friends. But as soon as this your son who ate up your means of living with harlots arrived, you slaughtered the fattened young bull for him.'"

Who, like the older son, has been critical of the mercy and attention accorded sinners? Is it not the scribes and the Pharisees? Since it is their criticism of Jesus because he welcomes sinners that prompted this illustration, they clearly must be the ones represented by the older son.

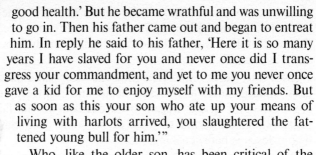

Jesus concludes his story with the father's appeal to his older son: "Child, you have

always been with me, and all the things that are mine are yours; but we just had to enjoy ourselves and rejoice, because this your brother was dead and came to life, and he was lost and was found."

Jesus thus leaves unresolved what the older son eventually does. Indeed, later, after Jesus' death and resurrection, "a great crowd of priests began to be obedient to the faith," possibly including some of these of the "older son" class to whom Jesus is here speaking.

But who in modern times are represented by the two sons? It must be those who have come to know enough about Jehovah's purposes to have a basis for their entering into a relationship with him. The older son represents some members of the "little flock," or "congregation of the firstborn who have been enrolled in the heavens." These adopted an attitude similar to that of the older son. They had no desire to welcome an earthly class, the "other sheep," who they felt were stealing the limelight.

The prodigal son, on the other hand, represents those of God's people who leave to enjoy the pleasures that the world offers. In time, however, these repentantly return and again become active servants of God. Indeed, how loving and merciful the Father is toward those who recognize their need of forgiveness and return to him! Luke 15:11-32; Leviticus 11: 7, 8; Acts 6:7; Luke 12:32; Hebrews 12:23; John 10:16.

- To whom does Jesus tell this illustration, or story, and why?
- Who is the principal character in the story, and what happens to him?
- Whom of Jesus' day do the father and the younger son represent?
- How does Jesus imitate the example of the compassionate father of his illustration?
- What is the older son's view of his brother's welcome, and how do the Pharisees behave like the older son?
- What application does Jesus' illustration have in our day?

87

Provide for the Future With Practical Wisdom

JESUS has just finished telling the story of the prodigal son to a crowd that includes his disciples, dishonest tax collectors and other recognized sinners, and scribes and Pharisees. Now, addressing his disciples, he relates an illustration regarding a rich man who has received an unfavorable report about his house manager, or steward.

According to Jesus, the rich man calls his steward and tells him that he is going to dismiss him. "What am I to do, seeing that my master will take the stewardship away from me?" the steward wonders. "I am not strong enough to dig, I am ashamed to beg. Ah! I know what I shall do, so that, when I am put out of the stewardship, people will receive me into their homes."

What is the steward's plan? He calls those who are in debt to his master. "How much are you owing?" he asks.

The first one answers, '580 gallons of olive oil.'

'Take your written agreement back and sit down and quickly write 290,' he tells him.

He asks another one: 'Now you, how much are you owing?'

He says, '630 bushels of wheat.'

'Take your written agreement back and write 504.'

The steward is within his rights in reducing the bills owed to his master, since he is still in charge of his master's financial affairs. By reducing the amounts, he is making friends with those who can return him favors when he does lose his job.

When the master hears what has happened, he is impressed. In fact, he "commended the steward, though unrighteous, because he acted with *practical wisdom.*" Indeed, Jesus adds: "The sons of this system of things are wiser in a practical way toward their own generation than the sons of the light are."

Now, drawing the lesson for his disciples, Jesus encourages: "Make friends for yourselves by means of the unrighteous riches, so that, when such fail, they may receive you into the everlasting dwelling places."

Jesus is not commending the steward for his unrighteousness but for his farsighted, *practical wisdom.* Often "the sons of this system of things" shrewdly use their money or position to make friends with those who can return them favors. So God's servants, "the sons of the light," also need to use their material assets, their "unrighteous riches," in a wise way to benefit themselves.

But as Jesus says, they should make friends by means of these riches with those who may receive them "into the everlasting dwelling places." For members of the little flock, these places are in heaven; for the "other sheep," they are in the Paradise earth. Since only Jehovah God and his Son can receive persons into these places, we should be diligent to cultivate friendship with them by using any "unrighteous riches" we may have in support of Kingdom interests. Then, when material riches fail or perish, as they surely will, our everlasting future will be assured.

Jesus goes on to say that persons faithful in caring for even these material, or least, things will also be faithful in caring for matters of greater importance. "Therefore," he continued, "if you have not proved yourselves faithful in connection with the unrighteous riches, who will entrust you with what is true [that is, spiritual, or Kingdom, interests]? And if you have not proved yourselves faithful in connection with what is another's [the Kingdom interests with which God entrusts his servants], who will give you what is for yourselves [the reward of life in everlasting dwelling places]?"

We simply cannot be true servants of God and at the same time be slaves to unrighteous riches, material riches, as Jesus concludes: "No house servant can be a slave to two masters; for, either he will hate the one and love the other, or he will stick to the one and despise the other. You cannot be slaves to God and to riches."   **Luke 15:1, 2; 16:1-13; John 10:16.**

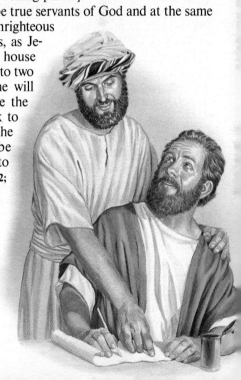

■ How does the steward in Jesus' illustration make friends with those who can help him later?

■ What are "unrighteous riches," and how can we make friends by means of them?

■ Who can receive us into "the everlasting dwelling places," and what places are these?

JESUS has been talking to his disciples about the proper use of material riches, explaining that we cannot be slaves to these and at the same time be slaves to God. The Pharisees are also listening, and they begin to sneer at Jesus because they are money lovers. So he says to them: "You are those who declare yourselves righteous before men, but God knows your hearts; because what is lofty among men is a disgusting thing in God's sight."

The time has come for the tables to be turned on people who are rich in worldly goods, political power, and religious control and influence. They are to be put down. However, the people who recognize their spiritual need are to be lifted up. Jesus points to such a change when he goes on to say to the Pharisees:

"The Law and the Prophets were until John [the Baptizer]. From then on the kingdom of God is being declared as good news, and every sort of person is pressing forward toward it. Indeed, it is easier for heaven and earth to pass away than for one particle of a letter of the Law to go unfulfilled."

The scribes and the Pharisees are proud of their professed adherence to the Law of Moses. Recall that when Jesus miraculously gave sight to a certain man in Jerusalem, they boasted: "We are disciples of Moses. We know that God has spoken to Moses." But now the Law of Moses has fulfilled its intended purpose of leading humble ones to God's designated King, Jesus Christ. So with the beginning of John's ministry, all kinds of persons, especially the humble and the poor, are exerting themselves to become subjects of God's Kingdom.

Since the Mosaic Law is now being fulfilled, the obligation to keep it is to be removed. The Law permits divorce on various grounds, but Jesus now says: "Everyone that divorces his wife and marries another commits adultery, and he that marries a woman divorced from a husband commits adultery." How such pronouncements must irritate the Pharisees, especially since they permit divorce on many grounds!

Continuing his remarks to the Pharisees, Jesus relates an illustration that features two men whose status, or situation, is eventually changed dramatically. Can you determine who are represented by the men and what the reversal of their situations means?

"But a certain man was rich," Jesus explains, "and he used to deck himself with purple and linen, enjoying himself from day to day with magnificence. But a certain beggar named Lazarus used to be put at his gate, full of ulcers and desiring to be filled with the things dropping from the table of the rich man. Yes, too, the dogs would come and lick his ulcers."

Jesus here uses the rich man to represent the Jewish religious leaders, including not only the Pharisees and the scribes but the Sadducees and the chief priests as well. They are rich in spiritual privileges and opportunities, and they conduct themselves as the rich man did. Their clothing of royal purple represents their favored position, and the white linen pictures their self-righteousness.

This proud rich-man class views the poor, common people with utter contempt, calling them 'am ha·'a'rets, or people of the earth. The beggar Lazarus thus represents these people to whom the religious leaders deny proper spiritual nourishment and privileges. Hence, like Lazarus covered with ulcers, the common people are looked down upon as spiritually diseased and fit only to associate with dogs. Yet, those of the Lazarus class hunger and thirst for spiritual nourishment and so are at the gate, seeking to receive whatever meager morsels of spiritual food may drop from the rich man's table.

Jesus now goes on to describe changes in the condition of the rich man and Lazarus. What are these changes, and what do they represent?

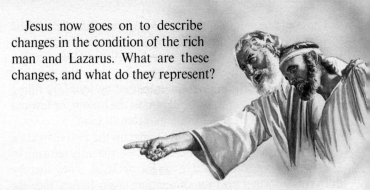

Rich Man and Lazarus Experience a Change

The rich man represents the religious leaders who are favored with spiritual privileges and opportunities, and Lazarus pictures the common people who hunger for spiritual nourishment. Jesus continues his story, describing a dramatic change in the men's circumstances.

"Now in course of time," Jesus says, "the beggar died and he was carried off by the angels to the bosom position of Abraham. Also, the rich man died and was buried. And in Hades he lifted up his eyes, he existing in torments, and he saw Abraham afar off and Lazarus in the bosom position with him."

Since the rich man and Lazarus are not literal persons but symbolize classes of people, logically their deaths are also symbolic. What do their deaths symbolize, or represent?

Jesus has just finished pointing to a change in circumstances by saying that 'the Law and the Prophets were until John the Baptizer, but from then on the kingdom of God is being declared.' Hence, it is with the preaching of John and Jesus Christ that both the rich man and Lazarus die to their former circumstances, or condition.

Those of the humble, repentant Lazarus class die to their former spiritually deprived condition and come into a position of divine favor. Whereas they had earlier looked to the religious leaders for what little dropped from the spiritual table, now the Scriptural truths imparted by Jesus are filling their needs. They are thus brought into the bosom, or favored position, of the Greater Abraham, Jehovah God.

On the other hand, those who make up the rich-man class come under divine disfavor because of persistently refusing to accept the Kingdom message taught by Jesus. They thereby die to their former position of seeming favor. In fact, they are spoken of as being in figurative torment. Listen now, as the rich man speaks:

"Father Abraham, have mercy on me and send Lazarus to dip the tip of his finger in water and cool my tongue, because I am in anguish in this blazing fire." God's fiery judgment messages proclaimed by Jesus' disciples are what torment individuals of the rich-man class. They want the disciples to let up on declaring these messages, thus providing them some measure of relief from their torments.

"But Abraham said, 'Child, remember that you received in full your good things in your lifetime, but Lazarus correspondingly the injurious things. Now, however, he is having comfort here but you are in anguish. And besides all these things, a great chasm has been fixed between us and you people, so that those wanting to go over from here to you people cannot, neither may people cross over from there to us.'"

How just and appropriate that such a dramatic reversal take place between the Lazarus class and the rich-man class! The change in conditions is accomplished a few months later at Pentecost 33 C.E., when the old Law covenant is replaced by the new covenant. It then becomes unmistakably clear that the disciples, not the Pharisees and other religious leaders, are favored by God. The "great chasm" that separates the symbolic rich man from Jesus' disciples therefore represents God's unchangeable, righteous judgment.

The rich man next requests "father Abraham": "Send [Lazarus] to the house of my father, for I have five brothers." The rich man thus confesses he has a closer relationship to another father, who is actually Satan the Devil. The rich man requests that Lazarus water down God's judgment messages so as not to put his "five brothers," his religious allies, in "this place of torment."

"But Abraham said, 'They have Moses and the Prophets; let them listen to these.'" Yes, if the "five brothers" would escape torment, all they have to do is heed the writings of Moses and the Prophets that identify Jesus as the Messiah and then become his disciples. But the rich man objects: "No, indeed, father Abraham, but if someone from the dead goes to them they will repent."

However, he is told: "If they do not listen to Moses and the Prophets, neither will they be persuaded if someone rises from the dead." God will not provide special signs or miracles to convince people. They must read and apply the Scriptures if they would obtain his favor. **Luke 16:14-31; John 9:28, 29; Matthew 19:3-9; Galatians 3:24; Colossians 2:14; John 8:44.**

■ Why must the deaths of the rich man and Lazarus be symbolic, and what is pictured by their deaths?

■ With the beginning of John's ministry, what change does Jesus indicate takes place?

■ What is to be removed after Jesus' death, and how will this affect the matter of divorce?

■ In Jesus' illustration, who are represented by the rich man and by Lazarus?

■ What are the torments suffered by the rich man, and by what means does he request that they be relieved?

■ What does the "great chasm" represent?

■ Who is the rich man's real father, and who are his five brothers?

89

A Mission of
Mercy Into Judea

SOME weeks earlier, during the Festival of Dedication in Jerusalem, the Jews tried to kill Jesus. So he traveled north, evidently to an area that was not far from the Sea of Galilee.

Recently, he has been heading south again toward Jerusalem, preaching along the way in the villages of Perea, a district east of the Jordan River. After telling the illustration about the rich man and Lazarus, he continues teaching his disciples things that he had taught earlier while in Galilee.

He says, for example, that it would be more advantageous for a person "if a millstone were suspended from his neck and he were thrown into the sea" than for him to cause one of God's "little ones" to stumble. He also emphasizes the need of forgiveness, explaining: "Even if [a brother] sins seven times a day against you and he comes back to you seven times, saying, 'I repent,' you must forgive him."

When the disciples request, "Give us more faith," Jesus answers: "If you had faith the size of a mustard grain, you would say to this black mulberry tree, 'Be uprooted and planted in the sea!' and it would obey you." So even a little faith can accomplish great things.

Next, Jesus relates a true-to-life situation that illustrates the proper attitude of a servant of the almighty God. "Who of you is there that has a slave plowing or minding the flock," Jesus observes, "who will say to him when he gets in from the field, 'Come here at once and recline at the table'? Rather, will he not say to him, 'Get something ready for me to have my evening meal, and put on an apron and minister to me until I am through eating and drinking, and afterward you can eat and drink'? He will not feel gratitude to the slave because he did the things assigned, will he? So you, also, when you have done all the things assigned to you, say, 'We are good-for-nothing slaves. What we have done is what we ought to have done.'" Thus, God's servants should never feel that they are doing God a favor by serving him. Rather, they should always remember the privilege that they have of worshiping him as trusted members of his household.

Apparently it is shortly after Jesus gives this illustration that a messenger arrives. He was sent by Mary and Martha, the sisters of Lazarus, who live in Bethany of Judea. "Lord, see! the one for whom you have affection is sick," the messenger relates.

Jesus replies: "This sickness is not with death as its object, but is for the glory of God, in order that the Son of God may be glorified through it." After remaining two days where he is, Jesus says to his disciples: "Let us go into Judea again." However, they remind him: "Rabbi, just lately the Judeans were seeking to stone you, and are you going there again?"

"There are twelve hours of daylight, are there not?" Jesus asks in response. "If anyone walks in daylight he does not bump against anything, because he sees the light of this world. But if anyone walks in the night, he bumps against something, because the light is not in him."

What Jesus apparently means is that the "hours of daylight," or the time God has allotted for Jesus' earthly ministry, have not yet elapsed and until they do, nobody can harm him. He needs to use to the full the short time of "daylight" left for him, since afterward will come the "night" when his enemies will have killed him.

Jesus adds: "Lazarus our friend has gone to rest, but I am journeying there to awaken him from sleep."

Evidently thinking that Lazarus is resting in sleep and that this is a positive sign that he will recover, the disciples respond: "Lord, if he has gone to rest, he will get well."

Then Jesus tells them outspokenly: "Lazarus has died, and I rejoice on your account that I was not there, in order for you to believe. But let us go to him."

Realizing that Jesus could be killed in Judea, yet desiring to support him, Thomas encourages his fellow disciples: "Let us also go, that we may die with him." So at the risk of their lives, the disciples accompany Jesus on this mission of mercy into Judea.   Luke 13:22; 17:1-10; John 10:22, 31, 40-42; 11:1-16.

- Where has Jesus been preaching recently?
- What teachings does Jesus repeat, and what true-to-life situation does he describe to illustrate what point?
- What news does Jesus receive, and what does he mean by the "daylight" and the "night"?
- What does Thomas mean when he says, 'Let us go that we may die with him'?

90

The Resurrection Hope

JESUS finally arrives at the outskirts of Bethany, a village about two miles from Jerusalem. It has only been a few days since Lazarus' death and burial. His sisters Mary and Martha are still mourning, and many have come to their home to console them.

While they are mourning, someone informs Martha that Jesus is on his way. So she leaves and hurries to meet him, apparently without telling her sister. Coming to Jesus, Martha repeats what she and her sister must have said many times during the past four days: "If you had been here my brother would not have died."

Martha, however, expresses hope, hinting that Jesus might yet do something for her brother. "I know that as many things as you ask God for, God will give you," she says.

"Your brother will rise," Jesus promises.

Martha understands Jesus to be speaking of a future earthly resurrection, to which Abraham and other servants of God also looked forward. So she replies: "I know he will rise in the resurrection on the last day."

However, Jesus gives hope for immediate relief, replying: "I am the resurrection and the life." He reminds Martha that God has given him power over death, saying: "He that exercises faith in me, even though he dies, will come to life; and everyone that is living and exercises faith in me will never die at all."

Jesus is not suggesting to Martha that faithful ones then alive will never die. No, but the point he is making is that exercising faith in him can lead to everlasting life. Such life will be enjoyed by most people as a result of their being resurrected on the last day. But others who are faithful will survive the end of this system of things on earth, and for these Jesus' words will be true in a very literal sense. They will never die at all! After this remarkable statement, Jesus asks Martha, "Do you believe this?"

"Yes, Lord," she answers. "I have believed that you are the Christ the Son of God, the One coming into the world."

Martha then hurries back to summon her sister, telling her privately: "The Teacher is present and is calling you." Immediately Mary leaves the house. When others see her go, they follow, assuming that she is going to the memorial tomb.

Coming to Jesus, Mary falls at his feet weeping. "Lord, if you had been here, my brother would not have died," she says. Jesus is deeply moved when he sees that Mary and the crowds of people following her are weeping. "Where have you laid him?" he asks.

"Lord, come and see," they answer.

Jesus too gives way to tears, causing the Jews to say: "See, what affection he used to have for him!"

Some recall that Jesus, at the time of the Festival of Tabernacles a few months before, had healed a young man born blind, and they ask: "Was not this man that opened the eyes of the blind man able to prevent this one from dying?" John 5:21; 6:40; 9:1-7; 11:17-37.

- When does Jesus finally arrive near Bethany, and what is the situation there?
- What basis does Martha have for belief in a resurrection?
- How is Jesus affected by Lazarus' death?

91

When Lazarus Is Resurrected

JESUS, along with those accompanying him, now arrives at the memorial tomb of Lazarus. Actually, it is a cave with a stone placed at the entrance. "Take the stone away," Jesus says.

Martha objects, not yet understanding what Jesus intends to do. "Lord," she says, "by now he must smell, for it is four days."

But Jesus asks: "Did I not tell you that if you would believe you would see the glory of God?"

So the stone is removed. Then Jesus raises his eyes and prays: "Father, I thank you that you have heard me. True, I knew that you always hear me; but on account of the crowd standing around I spoke, in order that they might believe that you sent me forth." Jesus prays publicly so that the people will know that what he is about to do will be accomplished through power received from God. Then he cries out with a loud voice: "Lazarus, come on out!"

At that, Lazarus comes out. His hands and feet are still bound with burial wrappings, and his face is covered with a cloth. "Loose him and let him go," Jesus says.

On seeing the miracle, many of the Jews that had come to comfort Mary and Martha put faith in Jesus. Others, however, go off to tell the Pharisees what has occurred. They and the chief priests immediately arrange for a meeting of the Jewish high court, the Sanhedrin.

The Sanhedrin includes the present high priest, Caiaphas, as well as Pharisees and Sadducees, chief priests, and former high priests. These lament: "What are we to do, because this man performs many signs? If we let him alone this way, they will all put faith in him, and the Romans will come and take away both our place and our nation."

Although the religious leaders admit that Jesus "performs many signs," the only thing they are concerned about is their own position and authority. The raising of Lazarus is an especially powerful blow to the Sadducees, since they do not believe in the resurrection.

Caiaphas, who is perhaps a Sadducee, now speaks up, saying: "You do not know anything at all, and you do not reason out that it is to your benefit for one man to die in behalf of the people and not for the whole nation to be destroyed."

God influenced Caiaphas to say this, for the apostle John later wrote: "This, though, [Caiaphas] did not say of his own originality." What Caiaphas actually meant was that Jesus should be killed to prevent Him from further undermining their positions of authority and influence. Yet, according to John, 'Caiaphas prophesied that Jesus was destined to die not for the nation only, but in order that God's children might be gathered together.' And, indeed, it is God's purpose that his Son die as a ransom for all.

Caiaphas now succeeds in influencing the Sanhedrin to make plans to kill Jesus. But Jesus, possibly learning of these plans from Nicodemus, a member of the Sanhedrin who is friendly to him, departs from there. **John 11:38-54.**

- Why does Jesus pray publicly before resurrecting Lazarus?
- How do those who saw this resurrection respond to it?
- What reveals the wickedness of members of the Sanhedrin?
- What was the intention of Caiaphas, but what did God use him to prophesy?

92

Ten Lepers Healed During Jesus' Final Trip to Jerusalem

JESUS frustrates the efforts of the Sanhedrin to kill him by leaving Jerusalem and traveling to the city of Ephraim, perhaps only 15 miles or so northeast of Jerusalem. There he remains with his disciples, away from his enemies.

However, the time for the Passover of 33 C.E. is drawing near, and soon Jesus is on the move again. He travels through Samaria and up into Galilee. This is his last visit to this area prior to his death. While in Galilee, likely he and his disciples join others who are on their way to Jerusalem for the Passover celebration. They take the route through the district of Perea, east of the Jordan River.

Early in the trip, while Jesus is entering a village either in Samaria or in Galilee, he is met by ten men who have leprosy. This terrible disease gradually eats away a person's body parts —his fingers, his toes, his ears, his nose, and his lips. To safeguard others from being infected, God's Law says regarding a leper: "He should cover over the mustache and call out, 'Unclean, unclean!' All the days that the plague is in him he will be unclean. . . . He should dwell isolated."

The ten lepers observe the Law's restrictions for lepers and remain a long way off from Jesus. Yet, they cry out with loud voices: "Jesus, Instructor, have mercy on us!"

Seeing them in the distance, Jesus commands: "Go and show yourselves to the priests." Jesus says this because God's Law authorizes the priests to pronounce as cured lepers who have recovered from their illness. In this way such ones receive approval to live again with healthy people.

The ten lepers have confidence in Jesus' miraculous powers. So they hurry off to see the priests, even though they have not yet been healed. While on the way, their faith in Jesus is rewarded. They begin to see and to feel their restored health!

Nine of the cleansed lepers continue on their way, but the other leper, a Samaritan, returns to look for Jesus. Why? Because he is so grateful for what has happened to him. He praises God with a loud voice, and when he finds Jesus, he falls at his feet, thanking him.

In reply Jesus says: "The ten were cleansed, were they not? Where, then, are the other nine? Were none found that turned back to give glory to God but this man of another nation?"

Then he tells the Samaritan man: "Rise and be on your way; your faith has made you well."

When we read about Jesus' healing of the ten lepers, we should take to heart the lesson implied by his question: "Where, then, are the other nine?" The ingratitude that was manifested by the nine is a serious shortcoming. Will we, like the Samaritan, show ourselves grateful for the things we receive from God, including the certain promise of everlasting life in God's righteous new world? John 11:54, 55; Luke 17:11-19; Leviticus 13:16, 17, 45, 46; Revelation 21:3, 4.

■ How does Jesus frustrate efforts to kill him?

■ Where does Jesus next travel, and what is his destination?

■ Why do the lepers stand at a distance, and why does Jesus tell them to go to the priests?

■ What lesson should we learn from this experience?

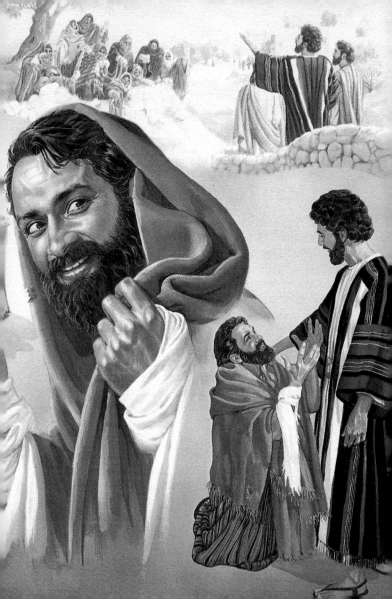

93 When the Son of Man Is Revealed

WHILE Jesus is still in the north (either in Samaria or in Galilee), Pharisees ask him about the arrival of the Kingdom. They believe that it will come with great pomp and ceremony, but Jesus says: "The kingdom of God is not coming with striking observableness, neither will people be saying, 'See here!' or, 'There!' For, look! the kingdom of God is in your midst."

Jesus' words "in your midst" have at times been translated "within you." So some have thought that Jesus meant that the Kingdom of God reigns in the hearts of God's servants. But, obviously, the Kingdom of God is not within the hearts of these unbelieving Pharisees to whom Jesus is speaking. Yet, it is *in their midst,* since the designated King of God's Kingdom, Jesus Christ, is right among them.

It is probably after the Pharisees leave that Jesus talks further with his disciples about the coming of the Kingdom. He has particularly in mind his future presence in Kingdom power when he warns: "People will say to you, 'See there!' or, 'See here!' Do not go out or chase after [these false Messiahs]. For even as the lightning, by its flashing, shines from one part under heaven to another part under heaven, so the Son of man will be." Hence, Jesus is indicating that just as lightning is seen over a wide area, the evidence of his presence in Kingdom power will be clearly visible to all wishing to observe it.

Jesus then draws comparisons with ancient events to show what the attitudes of people will be during his future presence. He explains: "Moreover, just as it occurred in the days of Noah, so it will be also in the days of the Son of man . . . Likewise, just as it occurred in the days of Lot: they were eating, they were drinking, they were buying, they were selling, they were planting, they were building. But on the day that Lot came out of Sodom it rained fire and sulphur from heaven and destroyed them all. The same way it will be on that day when the Son of man is to be revealed."

Jesus is not saying that people in Noah's day and in Lot's day were destroyed simply because they pursued the normal activities of eating, drinking, buying, selling, planting, and building. Even Noah and Lot and their families did these things. But the others went about such daily activities without paying any attention to God's will, and it was for this reason that they were destroyed. For the same reason, people will be destroyed when Christ is revealed during the great tribulation on this system of things.

Emphasizing the importance of responding quickly to the evidence of his future presence in Kingdom power, Jesus adds: "On that day let the person that is on the housetop but whose movable things are in the house not come down to pick these up, and the person out in the field, let him likewise not return to the things behind. Remember the wife of Lot."

When the evidence of Christ's presence appears, people cannot let attachment to their material possessions hinder them from taking prompt action. On her way out of Sodom, Lot's wife apparently looked back longingly for the things left behind, and she became a pillar of salt.

Continuing his description of the situation that would exist during his future presence, Jesus tells his disciples: "In that night two men will be in one bed; the one will be taken along, but the other will be abandoned. There will be two women grinding at the same mill; the one will be taken along, but the other will be abandoned."

Being taken along corresponds to Noah's entering with his family into the ark and the angels' taking Lot and his family out of Sodom. It means salvation. On the other hand, being abandoned means suffering destruction.

At this point, the disciples ask: "Where, Lord?"

"Where the body is, there also the eagles will be gathered together," Jesus answers. Those "taken along" for salvation are like farsighted eagles in that they gather together to "the body." The body has reference to the true Christ at his invisible presence in Kingdom power and to the spiritual feast that Jehovah provides. **Luke 17:20-37; Genesis 19:26.**

- How was the Kingdom in the midst of the Pharisees?
- In what way is Christ's presence like lightning?
- Why will people be destroyed for their actions during Christ's presence?
- What does it mean to be taken along, and to be abandoned?

94

The Need for Prayer and for Humility

EARLIER, when he was in Judea, Jesus told an illustration regarding the importance of being persistent in prayer. Now, on his final trip to Jerusalem, he again emphasizes the need not to give up in praying. Jesus is probably still in Samaria or Galilee when he tells his disciples this further illustration:

"In a certain city there was a certain judge that had no fear of God and had no respect for man. But there was a widow in that city and she kept going to him, saying, 'See that I get justice from my adversary at law.' Well, for a while he was unwilling, but afterward he said to himself, 'Although I do not fear God or respect a man, at any rate, because of this widow's continually making me trouble, I will see that she gets justice, so that she will not keep coming and pummeling me to a finish.'"

Jesus then makes the application of his story, saying: "Hear what the judge, although unrighteous, said! Certainly, then, shall not God cause justice to be done for his chosen ones who cry out to him day and night, even though he is long-suffering toward them?"

Jesus does not mean to imply that Jehovah God is in any way like that unrighteous judge. Rather, if even an unrighteous judge will

respond to persistent entreaties, there should be no question that God, who is altogether righteous and good, will answer if his people do not give up in praying. So Jesus continues: "I tell you, [God] will cause justice to be done to them speedily."

Justice is frequently denied the lowly and the poor, whereas the powerful and the rich are often favored. God, however, not only will see to it that the wicked are justly punished but will also ensure that his servants are treated justly by giving them everlasting life. But how many people firmly believe that God will cause justice to be done speedily?

Referring especially to faith related to the power of prayer, Jesus asks: "When the Son of man arrives, will he really find the faith on the earth?" Although the question is left unanswered, the implication may be that such faith would not be common when Christ arrives in Kingdom power.

Among those listening to Jesus are some who feel quite self-assured in their faith. They trust in themselves that they are righteous, and they look down on others. Certain ones of Jesus' disciples may even be included in the group. So he directs the following illustration to such ones:

"Two men went up into the temple to pray, the one a Pharisee and the other a tax collector. The Pharisee stood and began to pray these things to himself, 'O God, I thank you I am not as the rest of men, extortioners, unrighteous, adulterers, or even as this tax collector. I fast twice a week, I give the tenth of all things I acquire.'"

The Pharisees are noted for their public displays of righteousness to impress others. The usual days for their self-imposed fasts are Mondays and Thursdays, and they scrupulously pay the tenth of even the small herbs of the field. A few months earlier, their contempt for the common people had been manifest during the Festival of Tabernacles when they said: "This crowd that does not know the Law [that is, the Pharisaical interpretation given to it] are accursed people."

Continuing his illustration, Jesus tells of such an "accursed" person: "But the tax collector standing at a distance was not willing even to raise his eyes heavenward, but kept beating his breast, saying, 'O God, be gracious to me a sinner.'" Because the tax collector has humbly acknowledged his shortcomings, Jesus says: "I tell you, This man went down to his home proved more righteous than that man; because everyone that exalts himself will be humiliated, but he that humbles himself will be exalted."

Thus Jesus again emphasizes the need to be humble. Being reared in a society in which the self-righteous Pharisees are so influential and position and rank are always stressed, it is not surprising that even Jesus' disciples are affected. Yet, what fine lessons in humility Jesus teaches! **Luke 18:1-14; John 7:49.**

■ Why does the unrighteous judge grant the widow's request, and what lesson is taught by Jesus' illustration?

■ What faith will Jesus look for when he arrives?

■ To whom does Jesus direct his illustration about the Pharisee and the tax collector?

■ What attitude of the Pharisees is to be avoided?

95

Lessons on Divorce and on Love for Children

JESUS and his disciples are on their way to Jerusalem to attend the Passover of 33 C.E. They cross the Jordan River and take the route through the district of Perea. Jesus was in Perea a few weeks earlier, but then he was summoned to Judea because his friend Lazarus was sick. While then in Perea, Jesus spoke to the Pharisees about divorce, and now they bring the matter up again.

Among the Pharisees there are different schools of thought about divorce. Moses said that a woman could be divorced because of "something indecent on her part." Some believe that this refers only to unchastity. But others consider "something indecent" to include very minor offenses. So, to test Jesus, the Pharisees ask: "Is it lawful for a man to divorce his wife on every sort of ground?" They are confident that whatever Jesus says will involve him in difficulty with the Pharisees who hold a different view.

Jesus handles the question masterfully, not appealing to any human opinion, but referring back to the original design of marriage. "Did you not read," he asks, "that he who created them from the beginning made them male and female and said, 'For this reason a man will leave his father and his mother and will stick to his wife, and the two will be one flesh'? So that they are no longer two, but one flesh. Therefore, what God has yoked together let no man put apart."

God's original purpose, Jesus shows, is that marriage mates stick together, that they not get a divorce. If that is so, the Pharisees respond, "why, then, did Moses prescribe giving a certificate of dismissal and divorcing her?"

"Moses, out of regard for your hardheartedness, made the concession to you of divorcing your wives," Jesus answers, "but such has not been the case from the beginning." Yes, when God established the true standard for marriage in the garden of Eden, he made no provision for divorce.

Jesus goes on to tell the Pharisees: "I say to you that whoever divorces his wife, except on the ground of fornication [from Greek, *por·nei'a*], and marries another commits adultery." He thereby shows that *por·nei'a,* which is gross sexual immorality, is the only ground approved by God for a divorce.

Realizing that marriage should be a lasting union with only this ground for divorce, the disciples are moved to say: "If

such is the situation of a man with his wife, it is not advisable to marry." There is no question that one who is contemplating marriage should seriously consider the permanence of the marital bond!

Jesus goes on to talk about singleness. He explains that some boys are born eunuchs, being incapable of marriage because of not developing sexually. Others have been made eunuchs by men, being cruelly disabled sexually. Finally, some suppress the desire to marry and to enjoy sex relations so that they can devote themselves more fully to matters relating to the Kingdom of the heavens. "Let him that can make room for [singleness] make room for it," Jesus concludes.

People now begin to bring their young children to Jesus. The disciples, however, scold the children and try to send them away, no doubt wanting to protect Jesus from unnecessary stress. But Jesus says: "Let the young children come to me; do not try to stop them, for the kingdom of God belongs to suchlike ones. Truly I say to you, Whoever does not receive the kingdom of God like a young child will by no means enter into it."

What fine lessons Jesus here provides! To receive God's Kingdom, we must imitate the humility and teachableness of young children. But Jesus' example also illustrates how important it is, especially for parents, to spend time with their children. Jesus now shows his love for little ones by taking them into his arms and blessing them. Matthew 19:1-15; Deuteronomy 24:1; Luke 16:18; Mark 10:1-16; Luke 18:15-17.

- What different views do the Pharisees have on divorce, and so how do they test Jesus?

- How does Jesus deal with the Pharisees' effort to test him, and what does he give as the only ground for divorce?

- Why do Jesus' disciples say it is not advisable to marry, and what recommendation does Jesus provide?

- What does Jesus teach us by his dealings with young children?

96

Jesus and a Rich Young Ruler

AS JESUS goes on through the district of Perea toward Jerusalem, a young man runs up and falls on his knees before him. The man is called a ruler, probably meaning that he holds a prominent position in a local synagogue or even that he is a member of the Sanhedrin. Also, he is very rich. "Good Teacher," he asks, "what must I do to inherit everlasting life?"

"Why do you call me good?" Jesus replies. "Nobody is good, except one, God." Likely the young man uses "good" as a title, so Jesus lets him know that such a title belongs only to God.

"If, though," Jesus continues, "you want to enter into life, observe the commandments continually."

"Which ones?" the man asks.

Citing five of the Ten Commandments, Jesus answers: "Why, You must not murder, You must not commit adultery, You must not steal, You must not bear false witness, Honor your father and your mother." And adding an even more important commandment, Jesus says: "You must love your neighbor as yourself."

"All these things I have kept from my youth on," the man answers with all sincerity. "What yet am I lacking?"

Listening to the man's intense, earnest request, Jesus feels love for him. But Jesus perceives the man's attachment to material possessions and so points out his need: "One thing is missing about you: Go, sell what things you have and give to the poor, and you will have treasure in heaven, and come be my follower."

Jesus watches, no doubt with pity, as the man rises and turns away deeply saddened. His wealth blinds him to the value of true treasure. "How difficult," Jesus laments, "it will be for those with money to enter into the kingdom of God!"

Jesus' words astound the disciples. But they are surprised even more when he goes on to state a general rule: "It is easier, in fact, for a camel to get through the eye of a sewing needle than for a rich man to get into the kingdom of God."

"Who, in fact, can be saved?" the disciples want to know.

Looking straight at them, Jesus replies: "With men it is impossible, but not so with God, for all things are possible with God."

Noting that they have made a choice very different from that of the rich young ruler, Peter says: "Look! We have left all things and followed you." So he asks: "What actually will there be for us?"

"In the re-creation," Jesus promises, "when the Son of man sits down upon his glorious throne, you who have followed me will also yourselves sit upon twelve thrones, judging the twelve tribes of Israel." Yes, Jesus is showing that there will be a re-creation of conditions on earth so that things will be as they were in the garden of Eden. And Peter and the other disciples will receive the reward of ruling with Christ over this earth-wide Paradise. Surely, such a grand reward is worth any sacrifice!

However, even now there are rewards, as Jesus firmly states: "No one has left house or brothers or sisters or mother or father or children or fields for my sake and for the sake of the good news who will not get a hundredfold now in this period of time, houses and brothers and sisters and mothers and children and fields, with persecutions, and in the coming system of things everlasting life."

As Jesus promises, wherever in the world his disciples go, they enjoy a relationship with fellow Christians that is closer and more precious than that enjoyed with natural family members. The rich young ruler apparently loses out on both this reward and that of everlasting life in God's heavenly Kingdom.

Afterward Jesus adds: "However, many that are first will be last, and the last first." What does he mean?

He means that many people who are "first" in enjoying religious privileges, such as the rich young ruler, will not enter the Kingdom. They will be "last." But many, including Jesus' humble disciples, who are looked down upon by the self-righteous Pharisees as being "last"—as being people of the earth, or 'am ha·'a'rets—will become "first." Their becoming "first" means they will receive the privilege of becoming corulers with Christ in the Kingdom. **Mark 10:17-31; Matthew 19: 16-30; Luke 18:18-30.**

- Evidently, what kind of ruler is the rich young man?
- Why does Jesus object to being called good?
- How does the young ruler's experience illustrate the danger of being rich?
- What rewards does Jesus promise his followers?
- How do the first become last, and the last first?

97

Workers in the Vineyard

"**M**ANY that are first," Jesus just said, "will be last and the last first." Now he illustrates this by telling a story. "The kingdom of the heavens," he begins, "is like a man, a householder, who went out early in the morning to hire workers for his vineyard."

Jesus continues: "When [the householder] had agreed with the workers for a denarius a day, he sent them forth into his vineyard. Going out also about the third hour, he saw others standing unemployed in the marketplace; and to those he said, 'You also, go into the vineyard, and whatever is just I will give you.' So off they went. Again he went out about the sixth and the ninth hour and did likewise. Finally, about the eleventh hour he went out and found others standing, and he said to them, 'Why have you been standing here all day unemployed?' They said to him, 'Because nobody has hired us.' He said to them, 'You too go into the vineyard.'"

The householder, or owner of the vineyard, is Jehovah God, and the vineyard is the nation of Israel. The workers in the vineyard are persons brought into the Law covenant; they are specifically those Jews living in the days of the apostles. It is only with the full-day workers that a wage agreement is made. The wage is a denarius for the day's work. Since "the third hour" is 9:00 a.m., those called at the 3rd, 6th, 9th, and 11th hours work, respectively, only 9, 6, 3, and 1 hours.

The 12-hour, or full-day, workers represent the Jewish leaders who have been occupied continually in religious service. They are unlike Jesus' disciples, who have, for most of their lives, been employed in fishing or other secular

occupations. Not until the
fall of 29 C.E. did the "householder"
send Jesus Christ to gather these to be his disciples. They thus became "the last," or the 11th-hour
vineyard workers.

Finally, the symbolic workday ends with the death of Jesus,
and the time comes to pay the workers. The unusual rule of
paying the last first is followed, as is explained: "When it
became evening, the master of the vineyard said to his man
in charge, 'Call the workers and pay them their wages,
proceeding from the last to the first.' When the eleventh-hour
men came, they each received a denarius. So, when the first
came, they concluded they would receive more; but they also
received pay at the rate of a denarius. On receiving it they
began to murmur against the householder and said, 'These
last put in one hour's work; still you made them equal to us
who bore the burden of the day and the burning heat!' But in
reply to one of them he said, 'Fellow, I do you no wrong. You

agreed with me for a denarius, did you not? Take what is yours and go. I want to give to this last one the same as to you. Is it not lawful for me to do what I want with my own things? Or is your eye wicked because I am good?'" In conclusion, Jesus repeated a point made earlier, saying: "In this way the last ones will be first, and the first ones last."

The receiving of the denarius occurs, not at Jesus' death, but at Pentecost 33 C.E., when Christ, the "man in charge," pours out holy spirit on his disciples. These disciples of Jesus are like "the last," or the 11th-hour, workers. The denarius does not represent the gift of the holy spirit itself. The denarius is something for the disciples to use here on earth. It is something that means their livelihood, their everlasting life. It is the privilege of being a spiritual Israelite, anointed to preach about God's Kingdom.

Soon those hired first observe that Jesus' disciples have been paid, and they see them using the symbolic denarius. But they want more than the holy spirit and its associated Kingdom privileges. Their murmuring and objections take the form of persecuting Christ's disciples, "the last" workers in the vineyard.

Is that first-century fulfillment the only fulfillment of Jesus' illustration? No, the clergy of Christendom in this 20th century have, by reason of their positions and responsibilities, been "first" to be hired for work in God's symbolic vineyard. They considered dedicated preachers associated with the Watch Tower Bible and Tract Society to be "the last" ones to have any valid assignment in God's service. But it is, in fact, these very ones, whom the clergy despised, who received the denarius—the honor of serving as anointed ambassadors of God's heavenly Kingdom.   Matthew 19:30–20:16.

- What is represented by the vineyard? Who are represented by the vineyard's owner and by the 12-hour and 1-hour workers?
- When did the symbolic workday end, and when was payment made?
- What is represented by the payment of the denarius?

98

The Disciples Argue as Jesus' Death Nears

JESUS and his disciples are near the Jordan River, where they cross from the district of Perea into Judea. Many others are traveling with them to the Passover of 33 C.E., which is only a week or so away.

Jesus is walking on ahead of the disciples, and they are amazed at his bold determination. Recall that a few weeks earlier when Lazarus died and Jesus was about to go from Perea into Judea, Thomas encouraged the others: "Let us also go, that we may die with him." Recall also that after Jesus resurrected Lazarus, the Sanhedrin laid plans to have Jesus killed. No wonder that fear grips the disciples as they now enter Judea again.

To prepare them for what lies ahead, Jesus takes the 12 aside privately and tells them: "Here we are, advancing up to Jerusalem, and the Son of man will be delivered to the chief priests and the scribes, and they will condemn him to death and will deliver him to men of the nations, and they will make fun of him and will spit upon him and scourge him and kill him, but three days later he will rise."

This is the third time in recent months that Jesus has told his disciples about his death and resurrection. And although they listen to him, they fail to comprehend. Perhaps it is because they believe in the restoration on earth of the kingdom of Israel, and they are looking forward to enjoying glory and honor in an earthly kingdom with Christ.

Among the Passover-bound travelers is Salome, the mother of the apostles James and John. Jesus has called these men "Sons of Thunder," no doubt because of their fiery dispositions. For some time these two have harbored the ambition to be prominent in Christ's Kingdom, and they have made their desires known to their mother. She now approaches Jesus in their behalf, bows before him, and requests a favor.

"What do you want?" Jesus asks.

She replies: "Give the word that these my two sons may sit down, one at your right hand and one at your left, in your kingdom."

Realizing the source of the request, Jesus says to James and John: "You men do not know what you are asking for. Can you drink the cup that I am about to drink?"

"We can," they answer. Even though Jesus has just told them that he faces terrible persecution and finally execution, they apparently do not comprehend that this is what he means by "the cup" he is about to drink.

Nevertheless, Jesus tells them: "You will indeed drink my cup, but this sitting down at my right hand and at my left is not mine to give, but it belongs to those for whom it has been prepared by my Father."

In time the other ten apostles learn what James and John have requested, and they are angry. Perhaps James and John were prominent in the earlier argument among the apostles about who is the greatest. Their present request reveals that they have not applied the counsel Jesus has given on this matter. Sadly, their desire for prominence is still strong.

So to deal with this latest controversy and the ill will it has created, Jesus calls the 12 together. Counseling them lovingly, he says: "You know that the rulers of the nations lord it over them and the great men wield authority over them. This is not the way among you; but whoever wants to become great among you must be your minister, and whoever wants to be first among you must be your slave."

Jesus has set the example they should imitate, as he explains: "Just as the Son of man came, not to be ministered to, but to minister and to give his soul a ransom in exchange for many." Jesus not only has ministered in behalf of others but will do so to the extent of dying for mankind! The disciples need that same Christlike disposition of desiring to serve rather than to be served and to be a lesser one rather than to be in a position of prominence. Matthew 20:17-28; Mark 3:17; 9:33-37; 10:32-45; Luke 18:31-34; John 11:16.

- Why does fear now grip the disciples?
- How does Jesus prepare his disciples for what lies ahead?
- What request is made of Jesus, and how are the other apostles affected?
- How does Jesus deal with the problem among his apostles?

SOON Jesus and the crowds traveling with him arrive at Jericho, which is a city about a day's journey from Jerusalem. Apparently Jericho is a double city, the old Jewish city being about a mile from the newer Roman city. As the crowds make their way out of the old city and approach the new one, two blind beggars hear the commotion. One of them is named Bartimaeus.

On learning that it is Jesus who is passing by, Bartimaeus and his companion begin shouting: "Lord, have mercy on us, Son of David!" When the crowd sternly tells them to be quiet, they cry out even more and with louder voices: "Lord, have mercy on us, Son of David!"

Hearing the disturbance, Jesus stops. He asks those with him to call the ones doing all the shouting. These go to the blind beggars and say to one of them: "Take courage, get up, he is calling you." With unbounded excitement, the blind man throws off his outer garment, leaps to his feet, and goes to Jesus.

"What do you want me to do for you?" Jesus asks.

"Lord, let our eyes be opened," the two blind men plead.

Moved with pity, Jesus touches their eyes. According to Mark's account, Jesus says to one of them: "Go, your faith has made you well." Immediately the blind beggars receive sight, and doubtless both of them begin glorifying God. When all the people see what has happened, they also give praise to God. Without delay, Bartimaeus and his companion begin to follow Jesus.

As Jesus passes through Jericho, the crowds are tremendous. Everyone wants to see the one who has healed the blind men. The people press in upon Jesus from every direction, and as a result, some cannot even get a glimpse of him. Among these is Zacchaeus, chief over the tax collectors in and around Jericho. He is too short to see what is going on.

So Zacchaeus runs ahead and climbs a fig-mulberry tree along the route that Jesus is taking. From this vantage point, he can get a good view of everything. As the crowds approach, Jesus calls up into the tree: "Zacchaeus, hurry and get down, for today I must stay in your house." Zacchaeus climbs down with rejoicing and hurries home to get things prepared for his distinguished visitor.

However, when people see what is happening, they all begin

grumbling. They consider it improper for Jesus to be the guest of such a man. You see, Zacchaeus became rich by dishonestly extorting money in his tax-collecting business.

Many people follow, and when Jesus enters into the home of Zacchaeus, they complain: "With a man that is a sinner he went in to lodge." Yet Jesus sees in Zacchaeus the potential for repentance. And Jesus is not disappointed, for Zacchaeus stands up and announces: "Look! The half of my belongings, Lord, I am giving to the poor, and whatever I extorted from anyone by false accusation I am restoring fourfold."

Zacchaeus proves that his repentance is genuine by giving half of his belongings to the poor and by using the other half to pay back those he cheated. Apparently he can calculate from his tax records just how much he owes these persons. So he vows to make a fourfold restoration, in keeping with God's law that says: 'In case a man should steal a sheep, he is to compensate with four of the flock for the sheep.'

Jesus is pleased with the way that Zacchaeus promises to dispense his belongings, for He says: "This day salvation has come to this house, because he also is a son of Abraham. For the Son of man came to seek and to save what was lost."

Recently, Jesus had illustrated the situation of 'the lost' with his story about the prodigal son. Now we have a real-life example of a lost one who has been found. Even though the religious leaders and those who follow them mutter and complain about Jesus' attention to persons like Zacchaeus, Jesus continues to look for and restore these lost sons of Abraham. *Matthew 20:29-34; Mark 10:46-52; Luke 18:35–19:10; Exodus 22:1.*

- Where, apparently, does Jesus meet the blind beggars, and what does he do for them?
- Who is Zacchaeus, and why does he climb a tree?
- How does Zacchaeus prove his repentance?
- What lesson can we learn from Jesus' treatment of Zacchaeus?

100

The Illustration
of the Minas

JESUS is perhaps still at the home of Zacchaeus, where he has stopped en route to Jerusalem. His disciples believe that when they get to Jerusalem, he will declare that he is the Messiah and set up his Kingdom. To correct this idea and to show that the Kingdom is yet a long way off, Jesus gives an illustration.

"A certain man of noble birth," he relates, "traveled to a distant land to secure kingly power for himself and to return." Jesus is the "man of noble birth," and heaven is the "distant land." When Jesus arrives there, his Father will grant him kingly power.

Before leaving, however, the man of noble birth calls ten slaves and gives each of them a silver mina, saying: "Do business till I come." The ten slaves in the initial fulfillment represent Jesus' early disciples. In an enlarged application, they picture all who are prospective heirs with him in the heavenly Kingdom.

The silver minas are valuable pieces of money, each amounting to about three months' wages for an agricultural worker. But what do the minas represent? And what kind of business are the slaves to do with them?

The minas represent assets that spirit-begotten disciples could make use of in producing more heirs of the heavenly Kingdom until Jesus' coming as King in the promised Kingdom. After his resurrection and appearance to his disciples, he gave them the symbolic minas for making more disciples and thus adding to the Kingdom-of-heaven class.

"But," Jesus continues, "his citizens hated [the man of noble birth] and sent out a body of ambassadors after him, to say, 'We do not want this man to become king over us.'" The citizens are Israelites, or Jews, not including his disciples. After Jesus' departure to heaven, these Jews by persecuting his disciples made known that they did not want him to be their king. In this way they were acting like the citizens who sent out the body of ambassadors.

How do the ten slaves use their minas? Jesus explains: "Eventually when he got back after having secured the kingly power, he commanded to be called to him these slaves to whom he had given the silver money, in order to ascertain what they had gained by business activity. Then the first one presented himself, saying, 'Lord, your mina gained ten minas.' So he said to him, 'Well done, good slave! Because in a very small matter you have proved yourself faithful, hold authority over ten cities.' Now the second came, saying, 'Your mina, Lord, made five minas.' He said to this one also, 'You, too, be in charge of five cities.'"

The slave with ten minas pictures a class, or group, of disciples from Pentecost 33 C.E. until now that includes the apostles. The slave that gained five minas also represents a group during the same time period that, according to their opportunities and abilities, increase their king's assets on earth. Both groups zealously preach the good news, and as a result, many righthearted ones become Christians. Nine of the slaves did successful business and increased their holdings.

"But," Jesus goes on, "a different one came, saying, 'Lord, here is your mina, that I kept laid away in a cloth. You see, I was in fear of you, because you are a harsh man; you take up what you did not deposit and you reap what you did not sow.' He said to him, 'Out of your own mouth I judge you, wicked slave. You knew, did you, that I am a harsh man, taking up what I did not deposit and reaping what I did not sow? Hence why is it you did not put my silver money in a bank? Then on my arrival I would have collected it with interest.' With that he said to those standing by, 'Take the mina from him and give it to him that has the ten minas.'"

For the wicked slave, loss of the symbolic mina means loss of a place in the heavenly Kingdom. Yes, he loses the privilege of ruling, as it were, over ten cities or five cities. Note, too, that the slave is not pronounced wicked for any badness he does but, rather, for failing to work for the increase of the wealth of his master's kingdom.

When the wicked slave's mina is given to the first slave, the objection is made: "Lord, he has ten minas!" Yet, Jesus answers: "To everyone that has, more will be given; but from the one that does not have, even what he has will be taken away. Moreover, these enemies of mine that did not want me to become king over them bring here and slaughter them before me."   **Luke 19:11-27; Matthew 28:19, 20.**

- What prompts Jesus' illustration of the minas?
- Who is the man of noble birth, and what is the land to which he goes?
- Who are the slaves, and what is represented by the minas?
- Who are the citizens, and how do they show their hatred?
- Why is one slave called wicked, and what does loss of his mina mean?

101

At Bethany, in
the House of Simon

WHEN Jesus leaves Jericho, he heads for Bethany. The trip takes most of the day, since it is a climb of some 12 miles over difficult terrain. Jericho is about 820 feet below sea level, and Bethany is some 2,500 feet above sea level. Bethany, you may recall, is the home of Lazarus and his sisters. The little village is about two miles from Jerusalem, being located on the eastern slope of the Mount of Olives.

Many have already arrived in Jerusalem for the Passover. They have come early to cleanse themselves ceremonially. Perhaps they have touched a dead body or done something else that makes them unclean. So they follow the procedures to cleanse themselves in order to celebrate the Passover acceptably. As these early arrivers gather at the temple, many speculate about whether Jesus will come to the Passover.

Jerusalem is a hotbed of controversy regarding Jesus. It is common knowledge that the religious leaders want to seize him to put him to death. In fact, they have given orders that if anyone learns his

whereabouts, they are to report it to them. Three times in recent months—at the Festival of Tabernacles, at the Festival of Dedication, and after he resurrected Lazarus—these leaders have tried to kill him. So, the people wonder, will Jesus appear in public yet another time? "What is your opinion?" they ask one another.

In the meantime, Jesus arrives at Bethany six days before the Passover, which falls on Nisan 14 according to the Jewish calendar. Jesus reaches Bethany sometime Friday evening, which is at the beginning of Nisan 8. He could not have made the trip to Bethany on Saturday because travel on the Sabbath —from sundown Friday to sundown Saturday—is restricted by Jewish law. Jesus probably goes to the home of Lazarus, as he has done before, and spends Friday night there.

However, another resident of Bethany invites Jesus and his companions for a meal Saturday evening. The man is Simon, a former leper, who earlier had perhaps been healed by Jesus. In keeping with her industrious character, Martha is ministering to the guests. But, typically, Mary is attentive to Jesus, this time in a way that stirs controversy.

Mary opens an alabaster case, or small flask,

that holds about a pound of perfumed oil, "genuine nard." This is very precious. Indeed, its value is equivalent to about a year's wages! When Mary pours the oil on Jesus' head and on his feet and wipes his feet with her hair, the aromatic scent fills the whole house.

The disciples are angry and ask: "Why this waste?" Then Judas Iscariot says: "Why was it this perfumed oil was not sold for three hundred denarii and given to the poor people?" But Judas is not really concerned about the poor, for he has been stealing from the money box kept by the disciples.

Jesus comes to Mary's defense. "Let her alone," he commands. "Why do you try to make trouble for her? She did a fine deed toward me. For you always have the poor with you, and whenever you want to you can always do them good, but me you do not have always. She did what she could; she undertook beforehand to put perfumed oil on my body in view of the burial. Truly I say to you, Wherever the good news is preached in all the world, what this woman did shall also be told as a remembrance of her."

Jesus has been in Bethany now more than 24 hours, and word of his presence has spread about. Therefore, many come to Simon's house to see Jesus, but they also come to see Lazarus, who is present too. So the chief priests take counsel to kill not only Jesus but Lazarus as well. This is because many people are putting faith in Jesus because of seeing alive the one whom he raised from the dead! Truly, how wicked these religious leaders are! **John 11:55–12:11; Matthew 26:6-13; Mark 14:3-9; Acts 1:12.**

- **What discussion is going on at the temple in Jerusalem, and why?**
- **Why must Jesus have arrived in Bethany on Friday rather than on Saturday?**
- **When Jesus arrives in Bethany, where does he likely spend the Sabbath?**
- **What act of Mary stirs controversy, and how does Jesus defend her?**
- **What illustrates the great wickedness of the chief priests?**

102

Christ's Triumphal Entry Into Jerusalem

THE following morning, Sunday, Nisan 9, Jesus leaves Bethany with his disciples and heads over the Mount of Olives toward Jerusalem. In a short time, they draw close to Bethphage, located on the Mount of Olives. Jesus instructs two of his disciples:

"Be on your way into the village that is within sight of you, and you will at once find an ass tied, and a colt with her; untie them and bring them to me. And if someone says anything to you, you must say, 'The Lord needs them.' At that he will immediately send them forth."

Although at first the disciples fail to discern that these instructions have anything to do with the fulfillment of Bible prophecy, later they realize that they do. The prophet Zechariah foretold that God's promised King would ride into Jerusalem on an ass, yes, "even upon a full-grown animal the son of a she-ass." King Solomon had similarly ridden to his anointing on the offspring of an ass.

When the disciples enter Bethphage and take the colt and its mother, some of those standing by say: "What are you doing?" But when told that the animals are for the Lord, the men let the disciples take them to Jesus. The disciples place their outer garments on the mother ass and on her offspring, but Jesus mounts the colt.

As Jesus rides toward Jerusalem, the crowd increases. Most of the people spread their outer garments on the road, while others cut branches from the trees and spread them out. "Blessed is the One coming as the King in Jehovah's name!" they cry. "Peace in heaven, and glory in the highest places!"

Some Pharisees in the crowd are upset by these proclamations and complain to Jesus: "Teacher, rebuke your disciples." But Jesus replies: "I tell you, If these remained silent, the stones would cry out."

As Jesus draws close to Jerusalem, he views the city and begins to weep over it, saying: "If you, even you, had discerned in this day the things having to do with peace—but now they have been hid from your eyes." For her willful disobedience, Jerusalem must pay the price, as Jesus foretells:

"Your enemies [the Romans under General Titus] will build around you a fortification with pointed stakes and will encircle you and distress you from every side, and they will dash you and your children within you to the ground, and they will not leave a stone upon a stone in you." This destruction of Jerusalem foretold by Jesus actually occurs 37 years later, in the year 70 C.E.

Just a few weeks earlier, many in the crowd had seen Jesus resurrect Lazarus. Now these keep telling others about that miracle. So when Jesus enters Jerusalem, the whole city is set in commotion. "Who is this?" people want to know. And the crowds keep telling: "This is the prophet Jesus, from Nazareth of Galilee!" Seeing what is happening, the Pharisees lament that they are getting absolutely nowhere, for, as they say: "The world has gone after him."

As is his custom on visits to Jerusalem, Jesus goes to the temple to teach. There the blind and the lame come to him, and he cures them! When the chief priests and the scribes see the marvelous things Jesus is doing and when they hear the boys in the temple crying out, "Save, we pray, the Son of David!" they become angry. "Do you hear what these are saying?" they protest.

"Yes," Jesus replies. "Did you never read this, 'Out of the mouth of babes and sucklings you have furnished praise'?"

Jesus continues teaching, and he looks around upon all things in the temple. Soon it is late. So he leaves, along with the 12, and travels back the two miles or so to Bethany. There he spends Sunday night, probably in the home of his friend Lazarus.   **Matthew 21:1-11, 14-17; Mark 11:1-11; Luke 19:29-44; John 12:12-19; Zechariah 9:9.**

- When and in what manner does Jesus enter Jerusalem as King?
- How vital is it that the crowds praise Jesus?
- How does Jesus feel when he views Jerusalem, and what prophecy does he utter?
- What happens when Jesus goes to the temple?

103

Visiting the Temple Again

JESUS and his disciples have just spent their third night in Bethany since arriving from Jericho. Now the early morning light of Monday, Nisan 10, finds them already on the road to Jerusalem. Jesus is hungry. So when he catches sight of a fig tree with leaves, he goes over to it to see whether it might have some figs.

The tree's leaves are unseasonally early, since the season for figs is not until June, and it is now only late March. However, Jesus evidently feels that since the leaves are early, the figs might also be early. But he is disappointed. The leaves have given the tree a deceptive appearance. Jesus then curses the tree, saying: "Let no one eat fruit from you anymore forever." The consequences of Jesus' action and its significance are learned the following morning.

Continuing on, Jesus and his disciples soon reach Jerusalem. He goes to the temple, which he had inspected the previous afternoon. Today, however, he takes action, just as he did three years earlier when he came to the Passover in 30 C.E. Jesus throws out those selling and buying in the temple and overturns the tables of the money changers and the benches of those selling doves. He does not even allow anyone to carry a utensil through the temple.

Condemning those who are changing money and selling animals in the temple, he says: "Is it not written, 'My house will be called a house of prayer for all the nations'? But you have made it a cave of robbers." They are robbers because they demand exorbitant prices from those who have little alternative but to buy from them the animals needed for sacrifice. So Jesus views these business dealings as a form of extortion or robbery.

When the chief priests, scribes, and principal ones of the people hear what Jesus has done, they again seek a way to have him killed. They thereby prove that they are irreformable. Yet, they do not know how to destroy Jesus, since all the people keep hanging on to him to hear him.

Besides natural Jews, Gentiles have also come to the Passover. These are proselytes, meaning that they have converted to the religion of the Jews. Certain Greeks, evidently proselytes, now approach Philip and ask to see Jesus. Philip goes to Andrew, perhaps to ask whether such a meeting would be

appropriate. Jesus is apparently still at the temple, where the Greeks are able to see him.

Jesus knows he has only a few days of life left, so he nicely illustrates his situation: "The hour has come for the Son of man to be glorified. Most truly I say to you, Unless a grain of wheat falls into the ground and dies, it remains just one grain; but if it dies, it then bears much fruit."

One grain of wheat has little value. Yet, what if it is put into the soil and "dies," ending its life as a seed? It then germinates and in time grows into a stalk that produces many, many grains of wheat. Similarly, Jesus is just one perfect man. But if he dies faithful to God, he becomes the means of imparting everlasting life to faithful ones who have the same spirit of self-sacrifice that he has. Thus, Jesus says: "He that is fond of his soul destroys it, but he that hates his soul in this world will safeguard it for everlasting life."

Jesus obviously is not thinking only of himself, for he next explains: "If anyone would minister to me, let him follow me, and where I am there my minister will be also. If anyone would minister to me, the Father will honor him." What a marvelous reward for following Jesus and ministering to him! It is the reward of being honored by the Father to associate with Christ in the Kingdom.

Thinking about the great suffering and agonizing death that awaits him, Jesus continues: "Now my soul is troubled, and what shall I say? Father, save me out of this hour." If what awaits him could only be avoided! But, no, as he says: "This is why I have come to this hour." Jesus is in agreement with the entire arrangement of God, including his own sacrificial death. **Matthew 21:12, 13, 18, 19; Mark 11:12-18; Luke 19: 45-48; John 12:20-27.**

- Why does Jesus expect to find figs even though it is not the season for them?
- Why does Jesus call those selling in the temple "robbers"?
- In what way is Jesus like a grain of wheat that dies?
- How does Jesus feel about the suffering and death that await him?

104

God's Voice Heard a Third Time

WHILE at the temple, Jesus has been agonizing over the death that he soon must face. His main concern is how his Father's reputation will be affected, so he prays: "Father, glorify your name."

At that, a mighty voice comes from the heavens, proclaiming: "I both glorified it and will glorify it again."

The crowd standing around are bewildered. "An angel has spoken to him," some begin to say. Others claim that it thundered. But, indeed, it is Jehovah God who spoke! This, however, is not the first time God's voice was heard in connection with Jesus.

At Jesus' baptism, three and a half years earlier, John the Baptizer heard God say of Jesus: "This is my

Son, the beloved, whom I have approved." Then, sometime after the previous Passover, when Jesus was transfigured before them, James, John, and Peter heard God declare: "This is my Son, the beloved, whom I have approved; listen to him." And now, for the third time, on Nisan 10, four days before Jesus' death, God's voice is again heard by men. But this time Jehovah speaks so that multitudes can hear!

Jesus explains: "This voice has occurred, not for my sake, but for your sakes." It provides proof that Jesus is indeed God's Son, the promised Messiah. "Now there is a judging of this world," Jesus continues, "now the ruler of this world will be cast out." Jesus' faithful life course, in effect, confirms that Satan the Devil, the ruler of the world, deserves to be "cast out," executed.

Pointing to the consequences of his approaching death, Jesus says: "And yet I, if I am lifted up from the earth, will draw men of all sorts to me." His death is in no way a defeat, for by means of it, he will draw others to himself so that they may enjoy everlasting life.

But the crowd protests: "We heard from the Law that the Christ remains forever; and how is it you say that the Son of man must be lifted up? Who is this Son of man?"

Despite all the evidence, including hearing God's own voice, most do not believe that Jesus is the *true* Son of man, the promised Messiah. Yet, as he did six months earlier at the Festival of Tabernacles, Jesus again speaks of himself as "the light" and encourages his listeners: "While you have the light, exercise faith in the light, in order to become sons of light." After saying these things, Jesus goes off and hides, evidently because his life is in danger.

The Jews' lack of faith in Jesus fulfills the words of Isaiah about the 'eyes of people being blinded and their hearts being hardened so that they do not turn around to be healed.' Isaiah saw in vision the heavenly courts of Jehovah, including Jesus in his prehuman glory along with Jehovah. Yet, the Jews, in fulfillment of what Isaiah wrote, stubbornly reject the evidence that this One is their promised Deliverer.

On the other hand, many even of the rulers (evidently members of the Jewish high court, the Sanhedrin) actually put faith in Jesus. Nicodemus and Joseph of Arimathea are two of these rulers. But the rulers, at least for the present, fail to declare their faith, for fear of being expelled from their positions in the synagogue. How much such ones miss out on!

Jesus goes on to note: "He that puts faith in me puts faith, not in me only, but in him also that sent me; and he that beholds me beholds also him that sent me. . . . But if anyone hears my sayings and does not keep them, I do not judge him; for I came, not to judge the world, but to save the world. . . . The word that I have spoken is what will judge him in the last day."

Jehovah's love for the world of mankind moved him to send Jesus so that those who put faith in him might be saved. Whether people are saved will be determined by whether they obey the things God instructed Jesus to speak. The judgment will take place "in the last day," during Christ's Thousand Year Reign.

Jesus concludes by saying: "I have not spoken out of my own impulse, but the Father himself who sent me has given me a commandment as to what to tell and what to speak. Also, I know that his commandment means everlasting life. Therefore the things I speak, just as the Father has told me them, so I speak them." **John 12:28-50; 19:38, 39; Matthew 3:17; 17:5; Isaiah 6:1, 8-10.**

- On what three occasions was God's voice heard with regard to Jesus?
- How did the prophet Isaiah see Jesus' glory?
- Who are the rulers that put faith in Jesus, but why do they not confess him openly?
- What is "the last day," and on what basis will people be judged then?

105

Beginning of a Crucial Day

WHEN Jesus leaves Jerusalem on Monday evening, he returns to Bethany on the eastern slope of the Mount of Olives. Two days of his final ministry in Jerusalem have been completed. Jesus no doubt again spends the night with his friend Lazarus. Since arriving from Jericho on Friday, this is the fourth night he has spent in Bethany.

Now, early Tuesday morning, Nisan 11, he and his disciples are on the road again. This proves to be a crucial day of Jesus' ministry, the busiest thus far. It is the last day he appears in the temple. And it is the last day of his public ministry before his trial and execution.

Jesus and his disciples take the same route over the Mount of Olives toward Jerusalem. Along that road from Bethany, Peter notices the tree that Jesus cursed the previous morning. "Rabbi, see!" he exclaims, "the fig tree that you cursed has withered up."

But why did Jesus kill the tree? He indicates why when he goes on to say: "Truly I say to you, If only you have faith and do not doubt, not only will you do what I did to the fig tree, but also if you say to this mountain [the Mount of Olives on which they are standing], 'Be lifted up and cast into the sea,' it will happen. And all the things you ask in prayer, having faith, you will receive."

So by causing the tree to wither, Jesus is providing for his disciples an object lesson on their need to have faith in God. As he states: "All the things you pray and ask for have faith that you have practically received, and you will have them." What an important lesson for them to learn, especially in view of the awesome

tests that are soon to come! Yet, there is another connection between the withering of the fig tree and the quality of faith.

The nation of Israel, like this fig tree, has a deceptive appearance. Although the nation is in a covenant relationship with God and may outwardly appear to observe his regulations, it has proved to be without faith, barren of good fruitage. Because of lack of faith, it is even in the process of rejecting God's own Son! Hence, by causing the unproductive fig tree to wither, Jesus is graphically demonstrating what the end result will be for this fruitless, faithless nation.

Shortly, Jesus and his disciples enter Jerusalem, and as is their custom, they go to the temple, where Jesus begins teaching. The chief priests and older men of the people, no doubt having in mind Jesus' action the previous day against the money changers, challenge him: "By what authority do you do these things? And who gave you this authority?"

In reply Jesus says: "I, also, will ask you one thing. If you tell it to me, I also will tell you by what authority I do these things: The baptism by John, from what source was it? From heaven or from men?"

The priests and older men begin consulting among themselves as to how they will answer. "If we say, 'From heaven,' he will say to us, 'Why, then, did you not believe him?' If, though, we say, 'From men,' we have the crowd to fear, for they all hold John as a prophet."

The leaders do not know what to answer. So they reply to Jesus: "We do not know."

Jesus, in turn, says: "Neither am I telling you by what authority I do these things." **Matthew 21:19-27; Mark 11:19-33; Luke 20:1-8.**

- What is significant about Tuesday, Nisan 11?
- What lessons does Jesus provide when he causes the fig tree to wither?
- How does Jesus answer those who ask by what authority he does things?

106

Exposed by Vineyard Illustrations

JESUS is at the temple. He has just confounded the religious leaders who demanded to know by whose authority he was doing things. Before they recover from their confusion, Jesus asks: "What do you think?" And then by means of an illustration, he shows them what kind of persons they really are.

"A man had two children," Jesus relates. "Going up to the first, he said, 'Child, go work today in the vineyard.' In answer this one said, 'I will, sir,' but did not go out. Approaching the second, he said the same. In reply this one said, 'I will not.' Afterwards he felt regret and went out. Which of the two did the will of his father?" Jesus asks.

"The latter," his opponents answer.

So Jesus explains: "Truly I say to you that the tax collectors and the harlots are going ahead of you into the kingdom of God." The tax collectors and the harlots, in effect, initially refused to serve God. But then, like the second child, they repented and did serve him. On the other hand, the religious leaders, like the first child, professed to serve God, yet, as Jesus notes: "John [the Baptizer] came to you in a way of righteousness, but you did not believe him. However, the tax collectors and the harlots believed him, and you, although you saw this, did not feel regret afterwards so as to believe him."

Jesus next shows that the failure of those religious leaders is not simply in neglecting to serve God. No, but they are actually evil, wicked men. "There was a man, a householder," Jesus relates, "who planted a vineyard and put a fence around it and dug a winepress in it and erected a tower, and let it out to cultivators, and traveled abroad. When the season of the fruits came around, he dispatched his slaves to the cultivators to get his fruits. However, the cultivators took his slaves, and one they beat up, another they killed, another they stoned. Again he dispatched other slaves, more than the first, but they did the same to these."

The "slaves" are the prophets that the "householder," Jehovah God, sent to "the cultivators" of his "vineyard." These cultivators are leading representatives of the nation of Israel, which nation the Bible identifies as God's "vineyard."

Since "the cultivators" mistreat and kill the "slaves," Jesus explains: "Lastly [the owner of the vineyard] dispatched his son to them, saying, 'They will respect my son.' On seeing the son the cultivators said among themselves, 'This is the heir; come, let us kill him and get his inheritance!' So they took him and threw him out of the vineyard and killed him."

Now, addressing the religious leaders, Jesus asks: "When the owner of the vineyard comes, what will he do to those cultivators?"

"Because they are evil," the religious leaders answer, "he will bring an evil destruction upon them and will let out the vineyard to other cultivators, who will render him the fruits when they become due."

They thus unwittingly proclaim judgment upon themselves, since they are included among the Israelite "cultivators" of Jehovah's national "vineyard" of Israel. The fruitage that Jehovah expects from such cultivators is faith in his Son, the true Messiah. For their failing to provide such fruitage, Jesus warns: "Did you never read in the Scriptures [at Psalm 118:22, 23], 'The stone that the builders rejected is the one that has become the chief cornerstone. From Jehovah this has come to be, and it is marvelous in our eyes'? This is why I say to you, The kingdom of God will be taken from you and be given to a nation producing its fruits. Also, the person falling upon this stone will be shattered. As for anyone upon whom it falls, it will pulverize him."

The scribes and chief priests now recognize that Jesus is speaking about them, and they want to kill him, the rightful "heir." So the privilege of being rulers in God's Kingdom will be taken from them as a nation, and a new nation of 'vineyard cultivators' will be created, one that will produce suitable fruits.

Because the religious leaders fear the crowds, who consider Jesus a prophet, they do not try to kill him on this occasion. **Matthew 21:28-46; Mark 12:1-12; Luke 20:9-19; Isaiah 5:1-7.**

■ Whom do the two children in Jesus' first illustration represent?

■ In the second illustration, who are represented by the "householder," the "vineyard," "the cultivators," the "slaves," and "the heir"?

■ What will become of the 'vineyard cultivators,' and who will replace them?

107

Illustration of the Marriage Feast

BY MEANS of two illustrations, Jesus has exposed the scribes and the chief priests, and they want to kill him. But Jesus is far from through with them. He goes on to tell them yet another illustration, saying:

"The kingdom of the heavens has become like a man, a king, that made a marriage feast for his son. And he sent forth his slaves to call those invited to the marriage feast, but they were unwilling to come."

Jehovah God is the King who prepares a marriage feast for his Son, Jesus Christ. Eventually, the bride of 144,000 anointed followers will be united with Jesus in heaven. The King's subjects are the people of Israel, who, on being brought into the Law covenant in 1513 B.C.E., received the opportunity of becoming "a kingdom of priests." Thus, on that occasion, they were originally extended the invitation to the marriage feast.

However, the first call to those invited did not go out until the fall of 29 C.E., when Jesus and his disciples (the king's slaves) began their work of Kingdom preaching. But the natural Israelites who received this call issued by the slaves from 29 C.E. to

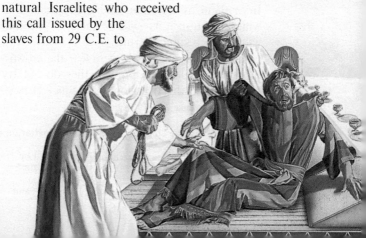

33 C.E. were unwilling to come. So God gave the nation of invited ones another opportunity, as Jesus relates:

"Again he sent forth other slaves, saying, 'Tell those invited: "Look! I have prepared my dinner, my bulls and fattened animals are slaughtered, and all things are ready. Come to the marriage feast."'" This second and final call of those invited began at Pentecost 33 C.E., when holy spirit was poured out on Jesus' followers. This call continued until 36 C.E.

The great majority of the Israelites, however, also spurned this call. "Unconcerned they went off," Jesus says, "one to his own field, another to his commercial business; but the rest, laying hold of his slaves, treated them insolently and killed them." "But," Jesus continues, "the king grew wrathful, and sent his armies and destroyed those murderers and burned their city." This occurred in 70 C.E., when Jerusalem was razed to the ground by the Romans, and those murderers were killed.

Jesus then explains what occurred in the meantime: "Then [the king] said to his slaves, 'The marriage feast indeed is ready, but those invited were not worthy. Therefore go to the roads leading out of the city, and anyone you find invite to the marriage feast.'" The slaves did this, and "the

room for the wedding ceremonies was filled with those reclining at the table."

This work of gathering guests from the roads outside the city of the invited ones began in 36 C.E. The Roman army officer Cornelius and his family were the first of the uncircumcised non-Jews gathered. The ingathering of these non-Jews, all of whom are replacements for those who originally refused the call, has continued on down into the 20th century.

It is during the 20th century that the room for the wedding ceremonies becomes filled. Jesus relates what then occurs, saying: "When the king came in to inspect the guests he caught sight there of a man not clothed with a marriage garment. So he said to him, 'Fellow, how did you get in here not having on a marriage garment?' He was rendered speechless. Then the king said to his servants, 'Bind him hand and foot and throw him out into the darkness outside. There is where his weeping and the gnashing of his teeth will be.'"

The man without a marriage garment pictures imitation Christians of Christendom. God has never recognized these as having the proper identification as spiritual Israelites. God never did anoint them with holy spirit as Kingdom heirs. So they are thrown outside into darkness where they will suffer destruction.

Jesus concludes his illustration by saying: "For there are many invited, but few chosen." Yes, there were many invited from the nation of Israel to become members of Christ's bride, but only a few natural Israelites were chosen. Most of the 144,000 guests who receive the heavenly reward prove to be non-Israelites. **Matthew 22:1-14; Exodus 19:1-6; Revelation 14:1-3.**

- Who are those originally invited to the wedding feast, and when were they extended the invitation?
- When does the call first go out to those invited, and who are the slaves used to issue it?
- When is the second call extended, and who afterward are invited?
- Who are pictured by the man without a wedding garment?
- Who are the many called, and the few chosen?

108

They Fail to Entrap Jesus

BECAUSE Jesus has been teaching in the temple and has just told his religious enemies three illustrations that expose their wickedness, the Pharisees are angered and take counsel to entrap him into saying something for which they can have him arrested. They concoct a plot and send their disciples, along with party followers of Herod, to try to trip him up.

"Teacher," these men say, "we know you are truthful and teach the way of God in truth, and you do not care for

anybody, for you do not look upon men's outward appearance. Tell us, therefore, What do you think? Is it lawful to pay head tax to Caesar or not?"

Jesus is not fooled by the flattery. He realizes that if he says, 'No, it is not lawful or right to pay this tax,' he will be guilty of sedition against Rome. Yet, if he says, 'Yes, you should pay this tax,' the Jews, who despise their subjugation to Rome, will hate him. So he answers: "Why do you put me to the test, hypocrites? Show me the head tax coin."

When they bring him one, he asks: "Whose image and inscription is this?"

"Caesar's," they reply.

"Pay back, therefore, Caesar's things to Caesar, but God's things to God." Well, when these men hear Jesus' masterful answer, they marvel. And they go off and leave him alone.

Seeing the failure of the Pharisees to get something against Jesus, the Sadducees, who say there is no resurrection, approach him and ask: "Teacher, Moses said, 'If any man dies without having children, his brother must take his wife in marriage and raise up offspring for his brother.' Now there were seven brothers with us; and the first married and deceased, and, not having offspring, he left his wife for his brother. It went the same way also with the second and the third, until through all seven. Last of all the woman died. Consequently, in the resurrection, to which of the seven will she be wife? For they all got her."

In reply Jesus says: "Is not this why you are mistaken, your not knowing either the Scriptures or the power of God? For when they rise from the dead, neither do men marry nor are women given in marriage, but are as angels in the heavens. But concerning the dead, that they are raised up, did you not read in the book of Moses, in the account about the thorn-bush, how God said to him, 'I am the God of Abraham and

God of Isaac and God of Jacob'? He is a God, not of the dead, but of the living. You are much mistaken."

Again the crowds are astounded by Jesus' answer. Even some of the scribes acknowledge: "Teacher, you spoke well."

When the Pharisees see that Jesus has silenced the Sadducees, they come to him in one group. To test him further, one scribe among them asks: "Teacher, which is the greatest commandment in the Law?"

Jesus replies: "The first is, 'Hear, O Israel, Jehovah our God is one Jehovah, and you must love Jehovah your God with your whole heart and with your whole soul and with your whole mind and with your whole strength.' The second is this, 'You must love your neighbor as yourself.' There is no other commandment greater than these." In fact, Jesus adds: "On these two commandments the whole Law hangs, and the Prophets."

"Teacher, you well said in line with truth," the scribe agrees. "'He is One, and there is no other than He'; and this loving him with one's whole heart and with one's whole understanding and with one's whole strength and this loving one's neighbor as oneself is worth far more than all the whole burnt offerings and sacrifices."

Discerning that the scribe has answered intelligently, Jesus tells him: "You are not far from the kingdom of God."

For three days now—Sunday, Monday, and Tuesday—Jesus has been teaching in the temple. The people have listened to him with pleasure, yet the religious leaders want to kill him, but so far their attempts have been frustrated.
Matthew 22:15-40; Mark 12:13-34; Luke 20:20-40.

■ What plot do the Pharisees concoct to entrap Jesus, and what would result if he should give a yes or a no answer?

■ How does Jesus foil the attempts of the Sadducees to entrap him?

■ What further attempt do the Pharisees make to test Jesus, and what is the outcome?

■ During his final ministry in Jerusalem, how many days does Jesus teach in the temple, and with what effect?

109

Jesus Denounces His Opposers

JESUS has so thoroughly confounded his religious opposers that they fear to ask him anything further. So he takes
the initiative to expose their ignorance. "What do you
think about the Christ?" he inquires. "Whose son is he?"

"David's," the Pharisees answer.

Although Jesus does not deny that David is the physical
ancestor of the Christ, or Messiah, he asks: "How, then, is it
that David by inspiration [at Psalm 110] calls him 'Lord,'
saying, 'Jehovah said to my Lord: "Sit at my right hand until
I put your enemies beneath your feet"'? If, therefore, David
calls him 'Lord,' how is he his son?"

The Pharisees are silent, for they do not know the true
identity of the Christ, or anointed one. The Messiah is not
simply a human descendant of David, as the Pharisees apparently believe, but he existed in heaven and was David's
superior, or Lord.

Turning now to the crowds and to his disciples, Jesus warns
about the scribes and the Pharisees. Since these teach God's
Law, having "seated themselves in the seat of Moses," Jesus
urges: "All the things they tell you, do and observe." But he
adds: "Do not do according to their deeds, for they say but
do not perform."

They are hypocrites, and Jesus denounces them in much
the same language that he did while dining in the house
of a Pharisee months earlier. "All the works they do," he
says, "they do to be viewed by men." And he provides
examples, noting:

"They broaden the scripture-containing cases that they
wear as safeguards." These relatively small cases, worn on the
forehead or on the arm, contain four portions of the Law:
Exodus 13:1-10, 11-16; and Deuteronomy 6:4-9; 11:13-21. But

the Pharisees increase the size of these cases to give the impression that they are zealous about the Law.

Jesus continues that they "enlarge the fringes of their garments." At Numbers 15:38-40 the Israelites are commanded to make fringes on their garments, but the Pharisees make theirs larger than anyone else does. Everything is done for show! "They like the most prominent place," Jesus declares.

Sadly, his own disciples have been affected by this desire for prominence. So he counsels: "But you, do not you be called Rabbi, for one is your teacher, whereas all you are brothers.

Moreover, do not call anyone your father on earth, for one is your Father, the heavenly One. Neither be called 'leaders,' for your Leader is one, the Christ." The disciples must rid themselves of the desire to be number one! "The greatest one among you must be your minister," Jesus admonishes.

He next pronounces a series of woes on the scribes and the Pharisees, repeatedly calling them hypocrites. They "shut up the kingdom of the heavens before men," he says, and "they are the ones devouring the houses of the widows and for a pretext making long prayers."

"Woe to you, blind guides," Jesus says. He condemns the Pharisees' lack of spiritual values, evidenced by the arbitrary distinctions they make. For example, they say, 'It is nothing if anyone swears by the temple, but one is under obligation if he swears by the gold of the temple.' By their putting more emphasis on the gold of the temple than on the spiritual value of that place of worship, they reveal their moral blindness.

Then, as he did earlier, Jesus condemns the Pharisees for neglecting "the weightier matters of the Law, namely, justice and mercy and faithfulness" while giving great attention to paying a tithe, or tenth part, of insignificant herbs.

Jesus calls the Pharisees "blind guides, who strain out the gnat but gulp down the camel!" They strain a gnat from their wine not simply because it is an insect but because it is ceremonially unclean. Yet, their disregarding the weightier matters of the Law is comparable to swallowing a camel, also a ceremonially unclean animal.   **Matthew 22:41–23:24; Mark 12: 35-40; Luke 20:41-47; Leviticus 11:4, 21-24.**

■ Why are the Pharisees silent when Jesus questions them about what David said in Psalm 110?

■ Why do the Pharisees enlarge their Scripture-containing cases and the fringes on their garments?

■ What counsel does Jesus give his disciples?

■ What arbitrary distinctions do the Pharisees make, and how does Jesus condemn them for neglecting weightier matters?

110

Ministry at the Temple Completed

JESUS is making his last appearance at the temple. In fact, he is concluding his public ministry on earth except for the events of his trial and execution, which are three days in the future. Now he continues his castigation of the scribes and the Pharisees.

Three more times he exclaims: "Woe to you, scribes and Pharisees, hypocrites!" First, he proclaims woe on them because they cleanse "the outside of the cup and of the dish, but inside they are full of plunder and immoderateness." So he admonishes: "Cleanse first the inside of the cup and of the dish, that the outside of it also may become clean."

Next he pronounces woe on the scribes and the Pharisees for the inner rottenness and putrefaction that they attempt to hide by outward piety. "You resemble whitewashed graves," he says, "which outwardly indeed appear beautiful but inside are full of dead men's bones and of every sort of uncleanness."

Finally, their hypocrisy is manifest in their willingness to build tombs for the prophets and decorate them to draw attention to their own deeds of charity. Yet, as Jesus reveals, they "are sons of those who murdered the prophets." Indeed, anyone who dares expose their hypocrisy is in danger!

Going on, Jesus utters his strongest words of denunciation. "Serpents, offspring of vipers," he says, "how are you to flee from the judgment of Gehenna?" Gehenna is the valley used as the garbage dump of Jerusalem. So Jesus is saying that for pursuing their wicked course, the scribes and the Pharisees will suffer everlasting destruction.

Regarding those whom he sends forth as his representatives, Jesus says: "Some of them you will kill and impale, and some of them you will scourge in your synagogues and persecute from city to city; that there may come upon you all the righteous blood spilled on earth, from the blood of righteous Abel to the blood of Zechariah son of Barachiah [called Jehoiada in Second Chronicles], whom you murdered between the sanctuary and the altar. Truly I say to you, All these things will come upon this generation."

Because Zechariah chastised Israel's leaders, "they conspired against him and pelted him with stones at the king's commandment in the courtyard of Jehovah's house." But, as Jesus foretells, Israel will pay for all such righteous blood spilled. They pay 37 years later, in 70 C.E., when the Roman armies destroy Jerusalem and over a million Jews perish.

As Jesus considers this frightful situation, he is distressed. "Jerusalem, Jerusalem," he proclaims once again, "how often I wanted to gather your children together, the way a hen gathers her chicks together under her wings! But you people did not want it. Look! Your house is abandoned to you."

Jesus then adds: "You will by no means see me from henceforth until you say, 'Blessed is he that comes in Jehovah's name!'" That day will be at Christ's presence when he comes into his heavenly Kingdom and people see him with eyes of faith.

Jesus now moves to a place where he can watch the treasury chests in the temple and the crowds dropping money into them. The rich drop in many coins. But then a poor widow comes along and drops in two small coins of very little value.

Calling his disciples over, Jesus says: "Truly I say to you that this poor widow dropped in more than all those dropping money into the treasury chests." They must wonder how this can be. So Jesus explains: "They all dropped in out of their surplus, but she, out of her want, dropped in all of what she had, her whole living." After saying these things, Jesus departs from the temple for the last time.

Marveling at the size and the beauty of the temple, his disciples exclaim: "Teacher, see! what sort of stones and what sort of buildings!" Indeed, the stones are reportedly over 35 feet long, more than 15 feet wide, and over 10 feet high!

"Do you behold these great buildings?" Jesus replies. "By no means will a stone be left here upon a stone and not be thrown down."

After saying these things, Jesus and his apostles cross the Kidron Valley and climb the Mount of Olives. From here they can look down on the magnificent temple. **Matthew 23:25–24:3; Mark 12:41–13:3; Luke 21: 1-6; 2 Chronicles 24:20-22.**

- What does Jesus do during his final visit to the temple?
- How is the hypocrisy of the scribes and the Pharisees manifested?
- What is meant by "the judgment of Gehenna"?
- Why does Jesus say that the widow contributed more than the rich?

111 Sign of the Last Days

BY NOW it is Tuesday afternoon. As Jesus is seated on the Mount of Olives, looking at the temple below, Peter, Andrew, James, and John come to him privately. They are concerned about the temple, since Jesus has just foretold that not a stone will be left upon a stone in it.

But apparently they have even more on their minds as they approach Jesus. A few weeks earlier, he had spoken about his "presence," during which time "the Son of man is to be revealed." And on an earlier occasion, he had told them about "the conclusion of the system of things." So the apostles are very curious.

"Tell us," they say, "when will these things be [resulting in destruction for Jerusalem and her temple], and what will be the sign of your presence and of the conclusion of the system of things?" In effect, theirs is a three-part question. First, they want to know about the end of Jerusalem and its temple, then regarding Jesus' presence in Kingdom power, and finally about the end of the entire system of things.

In his lengthy response, Jesus answers all three parts of the question. He provides a sign that identifies when the Jewish system of things will end; but he provides more. He also gives a sign that will alert his future disciples so they can know that they are living during his presence and near the end of the entire system of things.

As the years go by, the apostles observe the fulfillment of Jesus' prophecy. Yes, the very things he foretold start to occur in their day. Thus, Christians who are alive 37 years later, in 70 C.E., are not caught unawares by the destruction of the Jewish system with its temple.

However, Christ's presence and the conclusion of the system of things do not take place in 70 C.E. His presence in Kingdom power occurs much later. But when? A consideration of Jesus' prophecy reveals this.

Jesus foretells that there will be "wars and reports of wars." "Nation will rise against nation," he says, and there will be food shortages, earthquakes, and pestilences. His disciples will be hated and killed. False prophets will arise and mislead many. Lawlessness will increase, and the love of the greater number will cool off. At the same time, the good news of God's Kingdom will be preached as a witness to all the nations.

Although Jesus' prophecy has a limited fulfillment prior to the destruction of Jerusalem in 70 C.E., the major fulfillment of it takes place during his presence and the conclusion of the system of things. A careful review of world events since 1914 reveals that Jesus' momentous prophecy has been undergoing its major fulfillment since that year.

Another part of the sign that Jesus gives is the appearance of "the disgusting thing that causes desolation." In 66 C.E. this disgusting thing appears in the form of the "encamped armies" of Rome that surround Jerusalem and undermine the temple wall. "The disgusting thing" is standing where it ought not.

In the major fulfillment of the sign, the disgusting thing is the League of Nations and its successor, the United Nations. This organization for world peace is viewed by Christendom as a substitute for God's Kingdom. How disgusting! In time, therefore, the political powers associated with the UN will turn on Christendom (antitypical Jerusalem) and will desolate her.

Jesus thus foretells: "There will be great tribulation such as has not occurred since the world's beginning until now, no, nor will occur again." While Jerusalem's destruction in 70 C.E. is indeed a great tribulation, with over a million reportedly being killed, it is not a greater tribulation than the global Flood in Noah's day. So the major fulfillment of this portion of Jesus' prophecy is yet to be realized.

Confidence During the Last Days

As Tuesday, Nisan 11, draws to a close, Jesus continues the discussion with his apostles regarding the sign of his presence in Kingdom power and of the end of the system of things. He warns them about chasing after false Christs. Attempts will be made, he says, "to mislead, if possible, even the chosen ones." But, like farsighted eagles, these chosen ones will gather to where the true spiritual food is to be found, namely, with the true Christ at his invisible presence. They will not be misled and be gathered together to a false Christ.

False Christs can make only a visible appearance. In contrast, Jesus' presence will be invisible. It will occur during a frightful time in human history, as Jesus says: "The sun will be darkened, and the moon will not give its light." Yes, this will be the blackest period of mankind's existence. It will be as if the sun were darkened during the daytime, and as if the moon did not give its light by night.

"The powers of the heavens will be shaken," Jesus continues. He thus indicates that the physical heavens will take on a foreboding appearance. The heavens will not simply be the domain of birds, but they will be filled with warplanes, rockets, and space probes. The fear and violence will exceed anything experienced in previous human history.

As a result, Jesus says, there will be "anguish of nations, not knowing the way out because of the roaring of the sea and its agitation, while men become faint out of fear and expectation of the things coming upon the inhabited earth." Indeed, this blackest period of human existence will lead up to the time when, as Jesus says, "the sign of the Son of man will appear in heaven, and then all the tribes of the earth will beat themselves in lamentation."

But not all will be lamenting when 'the Son of man comes with power' to destroy this wicked system of things. The "chosen ones," the 144,000 who will share with Christ in his heavenly Kingdom, will not lament, nor will their companions, the ones whom Jesus earlier called his "other sheep." Despite living during the blackest period in human history, these respond to Jesus' encouragement: "As these things start to occur, raise yourselves erect and lift your heads up, because your deliverance is getting near."

So that his disciples who would be living during the last days could determine the nearness of the end, Jesus gives this illustration: "Note the fig tree and all the other trees: When they are already in the bud, by observing it you know for yourselves that now the summer is near. In this way you also, when you see these things occurring, know that the kingdom of God is near. Truly I say to you, This generation will by no means pass away until all things occur."

Thus, when his disciples see the many different features of the sign being fulfilled, they should realize that the end of the system of things is near and that God's Kingdom will soon wipe out all wickedness. In fact, the end will occur within the lifetime of the people who see the fulfillment of all the things Jesus foretells! Admonishing those disciples who would be alive during the momentous last days, Jesus says:

"Pay attention to yourselves that your hearts never become weighed down with overeating and heavy drinking and anxieties of life, and suddenly that day be instantly upon you as a snare. For it will come in upon all those dwelling upon the face of all the earth. Keep awake, then, all the time making supplication that you may succeed in escaping all these things that are destined to occur, and in standing before the Son of man."

The Wise and the Foolish Virgins

Jesus has been answering his apostles' request for a sign of his presence in Kingdom power. Now he provides further features of the sign in three parables, or illustrations.

The fulfillment of each illustration would be observable by those living during his presence. He introduces the first one with the words: "Then the kingdom of the heavens will become like ten virgins that took their lamps and went out to meet the bridegroom. Five of them were foolish, and five were discreet."

By the expression "the kingdom of the heavens will become like ten virgins," Jesus does not mean that half of those who inherit the heavenly Kingdom are foolish persons and half are discreet ones! No, but he means that in connection with the Kingdom of the heavens, there is a feature like this or like that, or that matters in connection with the Kingdom will be like such and such a thing.

The ten virgins symbolize all Christians who are in line for or who profess to be in line for the heavenly Kingdom. It was at Pentecost 33 C.E. that the Christian congregation was promised in marriage to the resurrected, glorified Bridegroom, Jesus Christ. But the marriage was to take place in heaven at some unspecified time in the future.

In the illustration, the ten virgins go out with the purpose of welcoming the bridegroom and of joining the wedding procession. When he arrives, they will light the processional route with their lamps, thus honoring him as he brings his bride to the house prepared for her. However, Jesus explains: "The foolish took their lamps but took no oil with them, whereas the discreet took oil in their receptacles with their lamps. While the bridegroom was delaying, they all nodded and went to sleep."

The extended delay of the bridegroom indicates that Christ's presence as ruling King is to be in the distant future. He finally comes to his throne in the year 1914. During the long night prior thereto, all the virgins fall asleep. But they are not condemned for this. The condemnation of the foolish virgins is for their not having oil for their receptacles. Jesus explains how the virgins awaken before the bridegroom arrives: "Right in the middle of the night there arose a cry, 'Here is the bridegroom! Be on your way out to meet him.' Then all those virgins rose and put their lamps in order. The foolish said to the discreet, 'Give us some of your oil, because our lamps are about to go out.' The discreet answered with the words, 'Perhaps there may not be quite enough for us and you. Be on your way, instead, to those who sell it and buy for yourselves.'"

The oil symbolizes that which keeps true Christians shining as illuminators. This is the inspired Word of God, on which Christians keep a tight grip, together with the holy spirit, which helps them to understand that Word. The spiritual oil enables the discreet virgins to shed forth light in welcoming the bridegroom during the procession to the marriage feast. But the foolish virgin class

do not have in themselves, in their receptacles, the needed spiritual oil. So Jesus describes what happens:

"While [the foolish virgins] were going off to buy [oil], the bridegroom arrived, and the virgins that were ready went in with him to the marriage feast; and the door was shut. Afterwards the rest of the virgins also came, saying, 'Sir, sir, open to us!' In answer he said, 'I tell you the truth, I do not know you.'"

After Christ arrives in his heavenly Kingdom, the discreet virgin class of true anointed Christians awake to their privilege of shedding light in this bedarkened world in praise of the returned Bridegroom. But those pictured by the foolish virgins are unprepared to provide this welcoming praise. So when the time comes, Christ does not open the door to the marriage feast in heaven to them. He leaves them outside in the blackness of the world's deepest night, to perish with all other workers of lawlessness. "Keep on the watch, therefore," Jesus concludes, "because you know neither the day nor the hour."

The Illustration of the Talents

Jesus continues the discussion with his apostles on the Mount of Olives by telling them another illustration, the second in a series of three. A few days earlier, while he was at Jericho, he gave the illustration of the minas to show that the Kingdom was yet a long time in the future. The illustration he relates now, while having a number of similar features, describes in its fulfillment activities during Christ's presence in Kingdom power. It illustrates that his disciples must work while still on earth to increase "his belongings."

Jesus begins: "For it [that is, circumstances connected with the Kingdom] is just as when a man, about to travel abroad, summoned slaves of his and committed to them his belongings." Jesus is the man who, before traveling abroad to heaven, commits to his slaves—disciples in line for the heavenly Kingdom—his belongings. These belongings are not physical possessions, but they represent a cultivated field into which he has built a potential for bringing forth more disciples.

Jesus entrusts his belongings to his slaves shortly before ascending to heaven. How does he do that? By instructing them to keep on working in the cultivated field by preaching the Kingdom message to the most distant parts of the earth. As Jesus says: "To one he gave five talents, to another two, to still another one, to each one according to his own ability, and he went abroad."

The eight talents—Christ's belongings—are thus distributed according to the abilities, or spiritual possibilities, of the slaves. The slaves stand for classes of disciples. In the first century, the class that received the five talents evidently included the apostles. Jesus goes on to relate that the slaves who received the five and the two talents both doubled them by their Kingdom preaching and making of disciples. However, the slave who received the one talent hid it in the ground.

"After a long time," Jesus continues, "the master of those slaves came and settled accounts with them." It was not until the 20th century, some 1,900 years later, that Christ returned to settle accounts, so it was, indeed, "after a long time." Then Jesus explains:

"The one that had received five talents came forward and brought five additional talents, saying, 'Master, you committed five talents to me; see, I gained five talents more.' His master said to him, 'Well done, good and faithful slave! You were faithful over a few things. I will appoint you over many things. Enter into the joy of your master.'" The slave that received two talents likewise doubled his talents, and he received the same commendation and reward.

How, though, do these faithful slaves enter into the joy of their Master? Well, the joy of their Master, Jesus Christ, is that of receiving possession of the Kingdom when he went abroad to his Father in heaven. As for the faithful slaves in modern times, they have great joy in being entrusted with further Kingdom responsibilities, and as they finish their earthly course, they will have the culminating joy of being resurrected to the heavenly Kingdom. But what about the third slave?

"Master, I knew you to be an exacting man," this slave complains. "So I grew afraid and went off and hid your talent in the ground. Here you have what is yours." The slave deliberately refused to work in the cultivated field by preaching

and making disciples. So the master calls him "wicked and sluggish" and pronounces the judgment: "Take away the talent from him . . . And throw the good-for-nothing slave out into the darkness outside. There is where his weeping

and the gnashing of his teeth will be." Those of this evil slave class, being cast outside, are deprived of any spiritual joy.

This sets forth a solemn lesson for *all* who profess to be followers of Christ. If they are to enjoy his commendation and reward, and avoid being thrown into the darkness outside and ultimate destruction, they must work for the increase of the belongings of their heavenly Master by having a full share in the preaching work. Are you diligent in this regard?

When Christ Arrives in Kingdom Power

Jesus is still with his apostles on the Mount of Olives. In answer to their request for a sign of his presence and the conclusion of the system of things, he now tells them the last in a series of three illustrations. "When the Son of man arrives in his glory, and all the angels with him," Jesus begins, "then he will sit down on his glorious throne."

Humans cannot see angels in their heavenly glory. So the arrival of the Son of man, Jesus Christ, with the angels must be invisible to human eyes. The arrival occurs in the year 1914. But for what purpose? Jesus explains: "All the nations will be gathered before him, and he will separate people one from another, just as a shepherd separates the sheep from the goats. And he will put the sheep on his right hand, but the goats on his left."

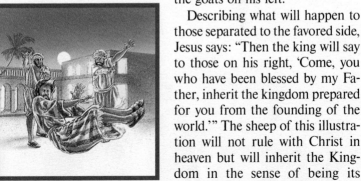

Describing what will happen to those separated to the favored side, Jesus says: "Then the king will say to those on his right, 'Come, you who have been blessed by my Father, inherit the kingdom prepared for you from the founding of the world.'" The sheep of this illustration will not rule with Christ in heaven but will inherit the Kingdom in the sense of being its earthly subjects. "The founding of the world" took place when Adam and Eve first produced children who could benefit from God's provision to redeem mankind.

But why are the sheep separated to the King's favored right hand? "For I became hungry," the king replies, "and you gave me something to eat; I got thirsty and you gave me something to drink. I was a stranger and you received me hospitably; naked, and you clothed me. I fell sick and you looked after me. I was in prison and you came to me."

Since the sheep are on earth, they want to know how they could have done such fine deeds for their heavenly King. "Lord, when did we see you hungry and feed you," they ask, "or thirsty, and give you something to drink? When did we see you a stranger and receive you hospitably, or naked, and clothe you? When did we see you sick or in prison and go to you?"

"Truly I say to you," the King replies, "to the extent that you did it to one of the least of these my brothers, you did it

to me." Christ's brothers are the remaining ones on earth of the 144,000 who will rule with him in heaven. And doing good to them, Jesus says, is the same as doing good to him.

Next, the King addresses the goats. "Be on your way from me, you who have been cursed, into the everlasting fire prepared for the Devil and his angels. For I became hungry, but you gave me nothing to eat, and I got thirsty, but you gave me nothing to drink. I was a stranger, but you did not receive me hospitably; naked, but you did not clothe me; sick and in prison, but you did not look after me."

The goats, however, complain: "Lord, when did we see you hungry or thirsty or a stranger or naked or sick or in prison and did not minister to you?" The goats are judged adversely on the same basis that the sheep are judged favorably. "To the extent that you did not do it to one of these least ones [of my brothers]," Jesus answers, "you did not do it to me."

So Christ's presence in Kingdom power, just prior to the end of this wicked system of things in the great tribulation,

will be a time of judgment. The goats "will depart into everlasting cutting-off, but the righteous ones [the sheep] into everlasting life." **Matthew 24:2–25:46; 13:40, 49; Mark 13:3-37; Luke 21:7-36; 19:43, 44; 17:20-30; 2 Timothy 3:1-5; John 10:16; Revelation 14:1-3.**

■ What prompts the apostles' question, but apparently what else do they have on their minds?

■ What part of Jesus' prophecy is fulfilled in 70 C.E., but what does not occur then?

■ When does Jesus' prophecy have a first fulfillment, but when does it have a major fulfillment?

■ What is the disgusting thing in its first and final fulfillments?

■ Why does the great tribulation not have its final fulfillment with the destruction of Jerusalem?

■ What world conditions mark Christ's presence?

■ When will 'all the tribes of the earth beat themselves in lamentation,' but what will Christ's followers be doing?

■ What illustration does Jesus provide to help his future disciples discern when the end is near?

■ What admonition does Jesus provide for those of his disciples who would be living during the last days?

■ Who are symbolized by the ten virgins?

■ When was the Christian congregation promised in marriage to the bridegroom, but when does the bridegroom arrive to take his bride to the marriage feast?

■ What does the oil represent, and what does possession of it enable the discreet virgins to do?

■ Where does the marriage feast take place?

■ What grand reward do the foolish virgins lose out on, and what is their fate?

■ What lesson does the illustration of the talents teach?

■ Who are the slaves, and what are the belongings with which they are entrusted?

■ When does the master come to settle accounts, and what does he find?

■ What is the joy the faithful slaves enter into, and what happens to the third slave, the wicked one?

■ Why must Christ's presence be invisible, and what work does he do at that time?

■ In what sense do the sheep inherit the Kingdom?

■ When did "the founding of the world" take place?

■ On what basis are people judged either as sheep or as goats?

112

Jesus' Final Passover Is At Hand

A S TUESDAY, Nisan 11, draws to a close, Jesus finishes teaching the apostles on the Mount of Olives. What a busy, strenuous day it has been! Now, perhaps while returning to Bethany for the night, he tells his apostles: "You know that two days from now the passover occurs, and the Son of man is to be delivered up to be impaled."

Jesus apparently spends the following day, Wednesday, Nisan 12, in quiet retirement with his apostles. On the day before, he had rebuked the religious leaders publicly, and he realizes that they are seeking to kill him. So on Wednesday he does not openly show himself, since he does not want anything to interfere with his celebrating the Passover with his apostles the following evening.

In the meantime, the chief priests and the older men of the people have gathered in the courtyard of the high priest, Caiaphas. Smarting from Jesus' attack the previous day, they are making plans to seize him by crafty device and have him put to death. Yet they keep saying: "Not at the festival, in order that no uproar may arise among the people." They are in fear of the people, whose favor Jesus enjoys.

While the religious leaders are wickedly conspiring to kill Jesus, they receive a visitor. To their surprise, it is one of Jesus' own apostles, Judas Iscariot, the one into whom Satan has implanted the base idea of betraying his Master! How pleased they are when Judas inquires: "What will you give me to betray him to you?" They gladly agree to pay him 30 silver pieces, the price of a slave according to the Mosaic Law covenant. From then on, Judas seeks a good opportunity to betray Jesus to them without a crowd around.

Nisan 13 begins at sundown Wednesday. Jesus arrived from Jericho on Friday, so this is the sixth and final night that he spends in Bethany. The next day, Thursday, final preparations will need to be made for the Passover, which commences at sundown. That is when the Passover lamb must be slaughtered and then roasted whole. Where will they celebrate the feast, and who will make the preparations?

Jesus has not provided such details, perhaps to prevent Judas from informing the chief priests so that they might apprehend Jesus during the Passover celebration. But now, probably early Thursday afternoon, Jesus dispatches Peter and John from Bethany, saying: "Go and get the passover ready for us to eat."

"Where do you want us to get it ready?" they ask.

"When you enter into the city," Jesus explains, "a man carrying an earthenware vessel of water will meet you. Follow him into the house into which he enters. And you must say to the landlord of the house, 'The Teacher says to you: "Where is the guest room in which I may eat the passover with my disciples?"' And that man will show you a large upper room furnished. Get it ready there."

No doubt the landlord is a disciple of Jesus who perhaps anticipates Jesus' request to use his house for this special occasion. At any rate, when Peter and John arrive in Jerusalem, they find everything just as Jesus foretold. So the two of them see to it that the lamb is ready and that all the other arrangements are made to care for the needs of the 13 Passover celebrants, Jesus and his 12 apostles. **Matthew 26:1-5, 14-19; Mark 14:1, 2, 10-16; Luke 22:1-13; Exodus 21:32.**

- What does Jesus apparently do Wednesday, and why?
- What meeting is held at the home of the high priest, and for what purpose does Judas visit the religious leaders?
- Whom does Jesus send into Jerusalem on Thursday, and for what purpose?
- What do these sent ones find that once again reveals Jesus' miraculous powers?

113

Humility
at the Last Passover

PETER and John, under instructions from Jesus, have already arrived in Jerusalem to make preparations for the Passover. Jesus, apparently along with the ten other apostles, arrives later in the afternoon. The sun is sinking on the horizon as Jesus and his party descend the Mount of Olives. This is Jesus' last daytime view of the city from this mountain until after his resurrection.

Soon Jesus and his party arrive in the city and make their way to the home where they will celebrate the Passover. They climb the stairs to the large upper room, where they find all preparations made for their private celebration of the Passover. Jesus has looked forward to this occasion, as he says: "I have greatly desired to eat this passover with you before I suffer."

Traditionally, four cups of wine are drunk by Passover participants. After accepting what is evidently the third cup, Jesus gives thanks and says: "Take this and pass it from one to the other among yourselves; for I tell you, From now on I will not drink again from the product of the vine until the kingdom of God arrives."

Sometime during the course of the meal, Jesus gets up, lays aside his outer garments, takes a towel, and fills a basin with water. Ordinarily, a host would see to it that a guest's feet were washed. But since on this occasion no host is present, Jesus cares for this personal service. Any one of the apostles could have seized the opportunity to do it; yet, apparently because some rivalry still exists among them, no one does. Now they are embarrassed as Jesus begins to wash their feet.

When Jesus comes to him, Peter protests: "You will certainly never wash my feet."

"Unless I wash you, you have no part with me," says Jesus.

"Lord," Peter responds, "not my feet only, but also my hands and my head."

"He that has bathed," Jesus answers, "does not need to have more than his feet washed, but is wholly clean. And you men are clean, but not all." He says this because he knows that Judas Iscariot is planning to betray him.

When Jesus has washed the feet of all 12, including the feet of his betrayer, Judas, he puts his outer garments on and reclines at the table again. Then he asks: "Do you know what I have done to you? You address me, 'Teacher,' and, 'Lord,' and you speak rightly, for I am such. Therefore, if I, although Lord and Teacher, washed your feet, you also ought to wash the feet of one another. For I set the pattern for you, that, just as I did to you, you should do also. Most truly I say to you, A slave is not greater than his master, nor is one that is sent forth greater than the one that sent him. If you know these things, happy you are if you do them."

What a beautiful lesson in humble service! The apostles should not be seeking the first place, thinking that they are so important that others should always serve them. They need to follow the pattern set by Jesus. This is not one of ritual foot washing. No, but it is one of willingness to serve without partiality, no matter how menial or unpleasant the task may be. Matthew 26:20, 21; Mark 14:17, 18; Luke 22:14-18; 7:44; John 13:1-17.

- What is unique about Jesus' view of Jerusalem as he enters the city to celebrate the Passover?
- During the Passover, evidently what cup does Jesus pass to the 12 apostles after saying a blessing?
- What personal service was customarily provided guests when Jesus was on earth, and why was it not provided during the Passover celebrated by Jesus and the apostles?
- What was Jesus' purpose in performing the menial service of washing his apostles' feet?

114

The Memorial Supper

AFTER Jesus washes his apostles' feet, he quotes the scripture at Psalm 41:9, saying: "He that used to feed on my bread has lifted up his heel against me." Then, becoming troubled in spirit, he explains: "One of you will betray me."

The apostles begin to grieve and say to Jesus one by one: "It is not I, is it?" Even Judas Iscariot joins in asking. John, who is lying next to Jesus at the table, leans back on Jesus' breast and asks: "Lord, who is it?"

"It is one of the twelve, who is dipping with me into the common bowl," Jesus answers. "True, the Son of man is going away, just as it is written concerning him, but woe to that man through whom the Son of man is betrayed! It would have been finer for that man if he had not been born." After that, Satan again enters Judas, taking advantage of the opening in his heart, which has become wicked. Later that night, Jesus fittingly calls Judas "the son of destruction."

Jesus now tells Judas: "What you are doing get done more quickly." None of the other apostles understand what Jesus means. Some imagine that since Judas is holding the money box, Jesus is telling him: "Buy what things we need for the festival," or that he should go and give something to the poor.

After Judas leaves, Jesus introduces an entirely new celebration, or commemoration, with his faithful apostles. He takes a loaf, says a prayer of thanks, breaks it, and gives it to them, saying: "Take, eat." He explains: "This means my body which is to be given in your behalf. Keep doing this in remembrance of me."

When each has eaten of the bread, Jesus takes a cup of wine, evidently the fourth cup used in the Passover service. He also says a prayer of thanks over it, passes it to them, asks them to drink from it, and states: "This cup means the new covenant by virtue of my blood, which is to be poured out in your behalf."

So this is, in fact, a memorial of Jesus' death. Each year on Nisan 14 it is to be repeated, as Jesus says, in remembrance of him. It will call to the memory of the celebrants what Jesus and his heavenly Father have done to provide escape for humankind from the condemnation of death. For the Jews who become Christ's followers, the celebration will replace the Passover.

The new covenant, which is made operative by Jesus' shed blood, replaces the old Law covenant. It is mediated by Jesus Christ between two parties—on the one hand, Jehovah God, and

on the other, 144,000 spirit-begotten Christians. Besides providing for the forgiveness of sins, the covenant allows for the formation of a heavenly nation of king-priests.   **Matthew 26:21-29; Mark 14:18-25; Luke 22:19-23; John 13:18-30; 17:12; 1 Corinthians 5:7.**

■ What Bible prophecy does Jesus quote regarding a companion, and what application does he make of it?

■ Why do the apostles become deeply grieved, and what does each of them ask?

■ What does Jesus tell Judas to do, but how do the other apostles interpret these instructions?

■ What celebration does Jesus introduce after Judas leaves, and what purpose does it serve?

■ Who are the parties to the new covenant, and what does the covenant accomplish?

115

An Argument Erupts

EARLIER in the evening, Jesus taught a beautiful lesson in humble service by washing his apostles' feet. Afterward, he introduced the Memorial of his approaching death. Now, especially in view of what has just taken place, a surprising incident occurs. His apostles become involved in a heated argument over which one of them seems to be the greatest! Apparently, this is part of an ongoing dispute.

Recall that after Jesus was transfigured on the mountain, the apostles argued over who among them was the greatest. Moreover, James and John requested prominent positions in the Kingdom, resulting in further contention among the apostles. Now, on his last night with them, how saddened Jesus must be to see them bickering again! What does he do?

Rather than scold the apostles for their behavior, once again Jesus patiently reasons with them: "The kings of the nations lord it over them, and those having authority over them are called Benefactors. You, though, are not to be that way. . . . For which one is greater, the one reclining at the table or the one ministering? Is it not the one reclining at the table?" Then, reminding them of his example, he says: "But I am in your midst as the one ministering."

Despite their imperfections, the apostles have stuck with Jesus during his trials. So he says: "I make a covenant with you, just as my Father has made a covenant with me, for a kingdom." This personal covenant between Jesus and his loyal followers joins them to him to share his royal dominion. Only a limited number of 144,000 are finally taken into this covenant for a Kingdom.

Although the apostles are presented with this marvelous prospect of sharing with Christ in Kingdom rule, they are at present spiritually weak. "All of you will be stumbled in connection with me on this night," says Jesus. However, telling Peter that He has prayed in his behalf, Jesus urges: "When once you have returned, strengthen your brothers."

"Little children," Jesus explains, "I am with you a little longer. You will look for me; and just as I said to the Jews, 'Where I go you cannot come,' I say also to you at present. I am giving you a new commandment, that you love one another; just as I have loved you, that you also love one another. By this all will know that you are my disciples, if you have love among yourselves."

"Lord, where are you going?" Peter asks.

"Where I am going you cannot follow me now," Jesus responds, "but you will follow afterwards."

"Lord, why is it I cannot follow you at present?" Peter wants to know. "I will surrender my soul in your behalf."

"Will you surrender your soul in my behalf?" Jesus asks. "Truly I say to you, You today, yes, this night, before a cock crows twice, even you will disown me three times."

"Even if I should have to die with you," Peter protests, "I will by no means disown you." And while the other apostles join in saying the same thing, Peter boasts: "Although all the others are stumbled in connection with you, never will I be stumbled!"

Referring to the time when he sent the apostles out on a preaching tour of Galilee without purse and food pouch, Jesus asks: "You did not want for anything, did you?"

"No!" they reply.

"But now let the one that has a purse take it up, likewise also a food pouch," he says, "and let the one having no sword sell his outer garment and buy one. For I tell you that this which is written must be accomplished in me, namely, 'And he was reckoned with lawless ones.' For that which concerns me is having an accomplishment."

Jesus is pointing to the time when he will be impaled with evildoers, or lawless ones. He is also indicating that his followers will thereafter face severe persecution. "Lord, look! here are two swords," they say.

"It is enough," he answers. As we will see, having the swords with them will soon permit Jesus to teach another vital lesson. **Matthew 26:31-35; Mark 14:27-31; Luke 22:24-38; John 13: 31-38; Revelation 14:1-3.**

- Why is the apostles' argument so surprising?
- How does Jesus handle the argument?
- What is accomplished by the covenant Jesus makes with his disciples?
- What new commandment does Jesus give, and how important is it?
- What overconfidence does Peter display, and what does Jesus say?
- Why are Jesus' instructions about carrying a purse and a food pouch different from those he gave earlier?

116

Preparing the Apostles for His Departure

THE memorial meal is over, but Jesus and his apostles are still in the upstairs room. Although Jesus will soon be gone, he has many things yet to say. "Do not let your hearts be troubled," he comforts them. "Exercise faith in God." But he adds: "Exercise faith also in me."

"In the house of my Father there are many abodes," Jesus continues. "I am going my way to prepare a place for you . . . that where I am you also may be. And where I am going you know the way." The apostles do not comprehend that Jesus is talking about going away to heaven, so Thomas asks: "Lord, we do not know where you are going. How do we know the way?"

"I am the way and the truth and the life," Jesus answers. Yes, only by accepting him and imitating his life course can anyone enter the heavenly house of the Father because, as Jesus says: "No one comes to the Father except through me."

"Lord, show us the Father," Philip requests, "and it is enough for us." Philip apparently wants Jesus to provide a

visible manifestation of God, such as was granted in ancient times in visions to Moses, Elijah, and Isaiah. But, really, the apostles have something much better than visions of that type, as Jesus observes: "Have I been with you men so long a time, and yet, Philip, you have not come to know me? He that has seen me has seen the Father also."

Jesus so perfectly reflects the personality of his Father that living with and observing him is, in effect, like actually seeing the Father. Yet, the Father is superior to the Son, as Jesus acknowledges: "The things I say to you men I do not speak of my own originality." Jesus properly gives all credit for his teachings to his heavenly Father.

How encouraging it must be for the apostles to hear Jesus now tell them: "He that exercises faith in me, that one also will do the works that I do; and he will do works greater than these"! Jesus does not mean that his followers will exercise greater miraculous powers than he did. No, but he means that they will carry on the ministry for a much longer time, over a much greater area, and to far more people.

Jesus will not abandon his disciples after his departure. "Whatever it is that you ask in my name," he promises, "I will do this." Further, he says: "I will request the Father and he will give you another helper to be with you forever, the spirit of the truth." Later, after he ascends to heaven, Jesus pours out on his disciples the holy spirit, this other helper.

Jesus' departure is near, as he says: "A little longer and the world will behold me no more." Jesus will be a spirit creature that no human can see. But again Jesus promises his faithful apostles: "You will behold me, because I live and you will live." Yes, not only will Jesus appear to them in human form after his resurrection but in due time he will resurrect them to life with him in heaven as spirit creatures.

Jesus now states the simple rule: "He that has my commandments and observes them, that one is he who loves me.

In turn he that loves me will be loved by my Father, and I will love him and will plainly show myself to him."

At this the apostle Judas, the one who is also called Thaddaeus, interrupts: "Lord, what has happened that you intend to show yourself plainly to us and not to the world?"

"If anyone loves me," Jesus replies, "he will observe my word, and my Father will love him . . . He that does not love me does not observe my words." Unlike his obedient followers, the world ignores Christ's teachings. So he does not reveal himself to them.

During his earthly ministry, Jesus has taught his apostles many things. How will they remember them all, especially since, even up to this moment, they fail to grasp so much? Happily, Jesus promises: "The helper, the holy spirit, which the Father will send in my name, that one will teach you all things and bring back to your minds all the things I told you."

Again comforting them, Jesus says: "I leave you peace, I give you my peace. . . . Do not let your hearts be troubled." True, Jesus is departing, but he explains: "If you loved me, you would rejoice that I am going my way to the Father, because the Father is greater than I am."

Jesus' remaining time with them is short. "I shall not speak much with you anymore," he says, "for the ruler of the world is coming. And he has no hold on me." Satan the Devil, the one who was able to enter Judas and get a hold on him, is the ruler of the world. But there is no sinful weakness in Jesus that Satan can play on to turn him away from serving God.

Enjoying an Intimate Relationship

Following the memorial meal, Jesus has been encouraging his apostles with an informal heart-to-heart talk. It may be past midnight. So Jesus urges: "Get up, let us go from here." However, before they leave, Jesus, moved by his love for them, continues speaking, providing a motivating illustration.

"I am the true vine, and my Father is the cultivator," he begins. The Great Cultivator, Jehovah God, planted this symbolic vine when he anointed Jesus with holy spirit at his baptism in the fall of 29 C.E. But Jesus goes on to show that the vine symbolizes more than just him, observing: "Every branch in me not bearing fruit he takes away, and every one bearing fruit he cleans, that it may bear more fruit. . . . Just as the branch cannot bear fruit of itself unless it remains in the vine, in the same way neither can you, unless you remain in union with me. I am the vine, you are the branches."

At Pentecost, 51 days later, the apostles and others become branches of the vine when holy spirit is poured out on them. Eventually, 144,000 persons become branches of the figurative grapevine. Along with the vine stem, Jesus Christ, these make up a symbolic vine that produces the fruits of God's Kingdom.

Jesus explains the key to producing fruit: "He that remains in union with me, and I in union with him, this one bears much fruit; because apart from me you can do nothing at all." If, however, a person fails to produce fruit, Jesus says, "he is cast out as a branch and is dried up; and men gather those branches up and pitch them into the fire and they are burned." On the other hand, Jesus promises: "If you remain in union with me and my sayings remain in you, ask whatever you wish and it will take place for you."

Further, Jesus says to his apostles: "My Father is glorified in this, that you keep bearing much fruit and prove yourselves my disciples." The fruit God desires from the branches is their manifestation of Christlike qualities, particularly love. Moreover, since Christ was a proclaimer of God's Kingdom, the desired fruit also includes their activity of making disciples as he did.

"Remain in my love," Jesus now urges. Yet, how can his apostles do so? "If you observe my commandments," he says, "you will remain in my love." Continuing, Jesus explains: "This is my commandment, that you love one another just as I have loved you. No one has love greater than this, that someone should surrender his soul in behalf of his friends."

In a few hours, Jesus will demonstrate this surpassing love by giving his life in behalf of his apostles, as well as all others who will exercise faith in him. His example should move his followers to have the same self-sacrificing love for one another. This love will identify them, as Jesus stated earlier: "By this all will know that you are my disciples, if you have love among yourselves."

Identifying his friends, Jesus says: "You are my friends if you do what I am commanding you. I no longer call you slaves, because a slave does not know what his master does. But I have called you friends, because all the things I have heard from my Father I have made known to you."

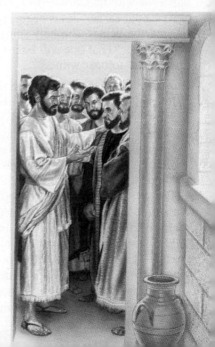

What a precious relationship to have—to be intimate friends of Jesus! But to continue to enjoy this relationship, his followers must "keep bearing fruit." If they do, Jesus says, "no matter what you ask the Father in my name he [will] give it to you." Surely, that is a grand reward for bearing Kingdom fruit! After again urging the apostles to "love one another,"

Jesus explains that the world will hate them. Yet, he comforts them: "If the world hates you, you know that it has hated me before it hated you." Jesus next reveals why the world hates his followers, saying: "Because you are no part of the world, but I have chosen you out of the world, on this account the world hates you."

Explaining further the reason for the world's hatred, Jesus continues: "They will do all these things against you on account of my name, because they do not know him [Jehovah God] that sent me." Jesus' miraculous works, in effect, convict those who hate him, as he notes: "If I had not done among them the works that no one else did, they would have no sin; but now they have both seen and hated me as well as my Father." Thus, as Jesus says, the scripture is fulfilled: "They hated me without cause."

As he did earlier, Jesus again comforts them by promising to send the helper, the holy spirit, which is God's powerful active force. "That one will bear witness about me; and you, in turn, are to bear witness."

Further Departing Admonition

Jesus and the apostles are poised to leave the upper room. "I have spoken these things to you that you may not be stumbled," he continues. Then he gives the solemn warning: "Men will expel you from the synagogue. In fact, the hour is coming when everyone that kills you will imagine he has rendered a sacred service to God."

The apostles are evidently deeply disturbed by this warning. Although Jesus had earlier said that the world would hate them, he had not revealed so directly that they would be killed. "I did not tell you [this] at first," Jesus explains, "because I was with you." Yet, how fine it is to forearm them with this information before he departs!

"But now," Jesus continues, "I am going to him that sent me, and yet not one of you asks me, 'Where are you going?'"

Earlier in the evening, they had inquired about where he was going, but now they are so shaken by what he has told them that they fail to ask further about this. As Jesus says: "Because I have spoken these things to you grief has filled your hearts." The apostles are grieved not only because they have learned that they will suffer terrible persecution and be killed but because their Master is leaving them.

So Jesus explains: "It is for your benefit I am going away. For if I do not go away, the helper will by no means come to you; but if I do go my way, I will send him to you." As a human, Jesus can only be in one place at a time, but when he is in heaven, he can send the helper, God's holy spirit, to his followers wherever they may be on earth. So Jesus' leaving will be beneficial.

The holy spirit, Jesus says, "will give the world convincing evidence concerning sin and concerning righteousness and concerning judgment." The world's sin, its failure to exercise faith in God's Son, will be exposed. In addition, convincing evidence of the righteousness of Jesus will be demonstrated by his ascension to the Father. And the failure of Satan and his wicked world to break Jesus' integrity is convincing evidence that the ruler of the world has been adversely judged.

"I have many things yet to say to you," Jesus continues, "but you are not able to bear them at present." Therefore Jesus promises that when he pours out the holy spirit, which is God's active force, it will guide them into an understanding of these things in accordance with their ability to grasp them.

The apostles fail particularly to understand that Jesus will die and then appear to them after he is resurrected. So they ask one another: "What does this mean that he says to us, 'In a little while you will not behold me, and, again, in a little while you will see me,' and, 'because I am going to the Father'?"

Jesus realizes that they want to question him, so he explains: "Most truly I say to you, You will weep and wail, but the world will rejoice; you will be grieved, but your grief will be turned into joy." Later that day, in the afternoon, when Jesus is killed, the worldly religious leaders rejoice, but the disciples grieve. Their grief is changed to joy, however, when Jesus is resurrected! And their joy continues when he empowers them at Pentecost to be his witnesses by pouring out upon them God's holy spirit!

Comparing the apostles' situation to that of a woman during her birth pangs, Jesus says: "A woman, when she is giving birth, has grief, because her hour has arrived." But Jesus observes that she no longer remembers her tribulation once her child is born, and he encourages his apostles, saying: "You also, therefore, are now, indeed, having grief; but I shall see you again [when I am resurrected] and your hearts will rejoice, and your joy no one will take from you."

Up to this time, the apostles have never made requests in Jesus' name. But he now says: "If you ask the Father for anything he will give it to you in my name. . . . For the Father himself has affection for you, because you have had affection for me and have believed that I came out as the Father's representative. I came out from the Father and have come into the world. Further, I am leaving the world and am going my way to the Father."

Jesus' words are a great encouragement to the apostles. "By this we believe that you came out from God," they say. "Do you believe at present?" Jesus asks. "Look! The hour is coming, indeed, it has come, when you will be scattered each one to his own house and you will leave me alone." Unbelievable as it may seem, this occurs before the night is finished!

"I have said these things to you that by means of me you may have peace." Jesus concludes: "In the world you are having tribulation, but take courage! I have conquered the world." Jesus conquered the world by faithfully accomplishing God's will despite everything that Satan and his world tried to do to break Jesus' integrity.

Concluding Prayer in the Upper Room

Moved by deep love for his apostles, Jesus has been preparing them for his imminent departure. Now, after admonishing and comforting them at length, he raises his eyes to heaven and petitions his Father: "Glorify your son, that your son may glorify you, according as you have given him authority over all flesh, that, as regards the whole number whom you have given him, he may give them everlasting life."

What a stirring theme Jesus introduces—everlasting life! Having been given "authority over all flesh," Jesus can impart the benefits of his ransom sacrifice to all dying humankind. Yet, he grants "everlasting life" only to those whom the Father approves. Building on this theme of everlasting life, Jesus continues his prayer:

"This means everlasting life, their taking in knowledge of you, the only true God, and of the one whom you sent forth, Jesus Christ." Yes, salvation is dependent upon our taking in knowledge of both God and his Son. But more is needed than just head knowledge.

A person must come to know them intimately, developing an understanding friendship with them. One must feel as they do about matters and see things through their eyes. And above all, a person must strive to imitate their matchless qualities in dealing with others.

Jesus next prays: "I have glorified you on the earth, having finished the work you have given me to do." Having thus fulfilled his assignment up to this point and being confident of his future success, he petitions: "Father, glorify me alongside yourself with the glory that I had alongside you before the world was." Yes, he now asks to be restored to his previous heavenly glory by means of a resurrection.

Summarizing his principal work on earth, Jesus says: "I have made your name manifest to the men you gave me out of the world. They were yours, and you gave them to me, and they have observed your word." Jesus used God's name, Jehovah, in his ministry and demonstrated a correct pronunciation of it, but he did more than that to make God's name manifest to his apostles. He also expanded their knowledge and appreciation of Jehovah, of his personality, and of his purposes.

Crediting Jehovah as his Superior, the One under whom he serves, Jesus humbly acknowledges: "The sayings that you gave me I have given to them, and they have received them and have certainly come to know that I came out as your representative, and they have believed that you sent me."

Making a distinction between his followers and the rest of mankind, Jesus next prays: "I make request, not concerning the world, but concerning those you have given me . . . When

I was with them I used to watch over them . . . , and I have kept them, and not one of them is destroyed except the son of destruction," namely, Judas Iscariot. At this very moment, Judas is on his despicable mission to betray Jesus. Thus, Judas is unknowingly fulfilling the Scriptures.

"The world has hated them," Jesus continues to pray. "I request you, not to take them out of the world, but to watch over them because of the wicked one. They are no part of the world, just as I am no part of the world." Jesus' followers are in the world, this organized human society ruled by Satan, but they are and must always remain separate from it and its wickedness.

"Sanctify them by means of the truth," Jesus continues, "your word is truth." Here Jesus calls the inspired Hebrew Scriptures, from which he continually quoted, "the truth." But what he taught his disciples and what they later wrote under inspiration as the Christian Greek Scriptures is likewise "the truth." This truth can sanctify a person, change his life completely, and make him a person separate from the world.

Jesus now prays "not concerning these only, but also concerning those putting faith in [him] through their word." So Jesus prays for those who will be his anointed followers and other future disciples who yet will be gathered into "one flock." What does he request for all of these?

"That they may all be one, just as you, Father, are in union with me and I am in union with you, . . . that they may be one just as we are one." Jesus and his Father are not literally one person, but they are in agreement on all things. Jesus prays that his followers enjoy this same oneness so that "the world may have the knowledge that you sent me forth and that you loved them just as you loved me."

In behalf of those who would be his anointed followers, Jesus now makes a request of his heavenly Father. For what? "That, where I am, they also may be with me, in order to behold my glory that you have given me, because you loved me before the founding of the world," that is, before Adam and Eve conceived offspring. Long before that, God loved his only-begotten Son, who became Jesus Christ.

Concluding his prayer, Jesus again emphasizes: "I have made your name known to them and will make it known, in order that the love with which you loved me may be in them and I in union with them." For the apostles, learning the name of God has involved personally coming to know the love of God. John 14: 1–17:26; 13:27, 35, 36; 10:16; Luke 22:3, 4; Exodus 24:10; 1 Kings 19:9-13; Isaiah 6:1-5; Galatians 6:16; Psalm 35:19; 69:4; Proverbs 8:22, 30.

- Where is Jesus going, and what answer does Thomas receive regarding the way there?
- By his request, what does Philip apparently want Jesus to provide?
- Why has one who has seen Jesus also seen the Father?
- How will Jesus' followers do greater works than he did?
- In what sense does Satan have no hold on Jesus?
- When did Jehovah plant the symbolic vine, and when and how do others become part of the vine?
- Eventually, how many branches does the symbolic vine have?
- What fruit does God desire from the branches?
- How can we be friends of Jesus?
- Why does the world hate Jesus' followers?
- What warning by Jesus disturbs his apostles?
- Why do the apostles fail to question Jesus about where he is going?
- What do the apostles particularly fail to understand?
- How does Jesus illustrate that the situation of the apostles will change from grief to joy?
- What does Jesus say the apostles will soon do?
- How does Jesus conquer the world?
- In what sense is Jesus given "authority over all flesh"?
- What does it mean to take in knowledge of God and his Son?
- In what ways does Jesus make God's name manifest?
- What is "the truth," and how does it "sanctify" a Christian?
- How are God, his Son, and all true worshipers one?
- When was "the founding of the world"?

117

Agony in the Garden

WHEN Jesus finishes praying, he and his 11 faithful apostles sing songs of praise to Jehovah. Then they descend from the upper room, emerge into the cool darkness of the night, and head back across the Kidron Valley toward Bethany. But along the way, they stop at a favorite spot, the garden of Gethsemane. This is located on or in the vicinity of the Mount of Olives. Jesus has often met with his apostles here amid the olive trees.

Leaving eight of the apostles—perhaps near the garden's entrance—he instructs them: "Sit down here while I go over there and pray." He then takes the other three—Peter, James, and John—and proceeds farther into the garden. Jesus becomes grieved and sorely troubled. "My soul is deeply grieved, even to death," he tells them. "Stay here and keep on the watch with me."

Going a little way forward, Jesus drops to the ground and with his face to the ground begins earnestly praying: "My Father, if it is possible, let this cup pass away from me. Yet, not as I will, but as you will." What does he mean? Why is he "deeply grieved, even to death"? Is he backing down from his decision to die and provide the ransom?

Not at all! Jesus is not appealing to be spared from death. Even the thought of avoiding a sacrificial death, once suggested by Peter, is repugnant to him. Rather, he is in agony because he fears that the way he will soon die—as a despicable criminal—will bring reproach upon his Father's name. He now senses that in a few hours he is going to be impaled upon a stake as the worst kind of person—a blasphemer against God! This is what sorely troubles him.

After praying at length, Jesus returns and finds the three apostles sleeping. Addressing Peter, he says: "Could you men not so much as watch one hour with me? Keep on the watch and pray continually, that you may not enter into temptation." Acknowledging, however, the stress they have been under and the lateness of the hour, he says: "The spirit, of course, is eager, but the flesh is weak."

Jesus then goes off a second time and requests that God remove from him "this cup," that is, Jehovah's assigned portion, or will, for him. When he returns, he again finds the three sleeping when they should have been praying that they not enter into temptation. When Jesus speaks to them, they do not know what to say in reply.

Finally, a third time, Jesus goes away, about the distance of a stone's throw, and on bended knees, with strong outcries and tears, he prays: "Father, if you wish, remove this cup from me." Jesus keenly feels severe pains because of the reproach that his death as a criminal will bring on his Father's name. Why, to be charged as a blasphemer—one who curses God—is almost too much to bear!

Nevertheless, Jesus continues to pray: "Not what I want, but what you want." Jesus obediently submits his will to God's. At this, an angel from heaven appears and strengthens him with some encouraging words. Likely, the angel tells Jesus that he has his Father's smile of approval.

Yet, what a weight is on Jesus' shoulders! His own eternal life and that of the whole human race hangs in the balance. The emotional stress is enormous. So Jesus continues praying more earnestly, and his sweat becomes as drops of blood as it falls to the ground. "Although this is a very rare phenomenon," observes *The Journal of the American Medical Association,* "bloody sweat . . . may occur in highly emotional states."

Afterward, Jesus returns for a third time to his apostles, and once more finds them sleeping. They are exhausted from sheer grief. "At such a time as this you are sleeping and taking your rest!" he exclaims. "It is enough! The hour has come!

Look! The Son of man is betrayed into the hands of sinners. Get up, let us go. Look! My betrayer has drawn near."

While he is yet speaking, Judas Iscariot approaches, accompanied by a large crowd carrying torches and lamps and weapons. **Matthew 26:30, 36-47; 16:21-23; Mark 14:26, 32-43; Luke 22: 39-47; John 18:1-3; Hebrews 5:7.**

- After leaving the upper room, where does Jesus lead the apostles, and what does he do there?
- While Jesus is praying, what are the apostles doing?
- Why is Jesus in agony, and what request does he make of God?
- What is indicated by Jesus' sweat becoming as drops of blood?

118

Betrayal and Arrest

IT IS well past midnight as Judas leads a large crowd of soldiers, chief priests, Pharisees, and others into the garden of Gethsemane. The priests have agreed to pay Judas 30 pieces of silver to betray Jesus.

Earlier, when Judas was dismissed from the Passover meal, he had evidently gone directly to the chief priests. These immediately assembled their own officers, as well as a band of soldiers. Judas had perhaps first led them to where Jesus and his apostles had celebrated the Passover. Discovering that they had left, the large crowd bearing weapons and carrying lamps and torches followed Judas out of Jerusalem and across the Kidron Valley.

As Judas leads the procession up the Mount of Olives, he feels sure he knows where to find Jesus. During the past week, as Jesus and the apostles traveled back and forth between Bethany and Jerusalem, they often stopped in the garden of Gethsemane to rest and to converse. But, now, with Jesus possibly concealed in the darkness beneath the olive trees, how will the soldiers identify him? They may never have seen him before. Therefore Judas provides a sign, saying: "Whoever it is I kiss, this is he; take him into custody and lead him away safely."

Judas leads the great crowd into the garden, sees Jesus with his apostles, and goes straight up to him. "Good day, Rabbi!" he says and kisses him very tenderly.

"Fellow, for what purpose are you present?" Jesus retorts. Then, answering his own question, he says: "Judas, do you betray the Son of man with a kiss?" But enough of his betrayer! Jesus steps forward into the light of the burning torches and lamps and asks: "Whom are you looking for?"

"Jesus the Nazarene," comes the answer.

"I am he," Jesus replies, as he stands courageously before

them all. Astonished by his boldness and not knowing what to expect, the men draw back and fall to the ground.

"I told you I am he," Jesus calmly continues. "If, therefore, it is I you are looking for, let these go." Shortly before in the upper room, Jesus had told his Father in prayer that he had kept his faithful apostles and not one of them had been lost "except the son of destruction." So, in order that his word might be fulfilled, he asks that his followers be let go.

As the soldiers regain their composure, stand up, and start to bind Jesus, the apostles recognize what is about to happen. "Lord, shall we strike with the sword?" they ask. Before Jesus replies, Peter, wielding one of the two swords the apostles have brought, attacks Malchus, a slave of the high priest. Peter's blow misses the slave's head but cuts off his right ear.

"Let it go as far as this," Jesus says as he intervenes. Touching the ear of Malchus, he heals the wound. Then he teaches an important lesson, commanding Peter: "Return your sword to its place, for all those who take the sword will perish by the sword. Or do you think that I cannot appeal to my Father to supply me at this moment more than twelve legions of angels?"

Jesus is willing to be arrested, for he explains: "How would the Scriptures be fulfilled that it must take place this way?" And he adds: "The cup that the Father has given me, should I not by all means drink it?" He is in complete agreement with God's will for him!

Then Jesus addresses the crowd. "Have you come out with swords and clubs as against a robber to arrest me?" he asks. "Day after day I used to sit in the temple teaching, and yet you did not take me into custody. But all this has taken place for the scriptures of the prophets to be fulfilled."

At that the soldier band and the military commander and the officers of the Jews seize Jesus and bind him. On seeing this, the apostles abandon Jesus and flee. However, a young man—perhaps it is the disciple Mark—remains among the crowd. He may have been at the home where Jesus celebrated the Passover and afterward followed the crowd from there. Now, however, he is recognized, and an attempt is made to seize him. But he leaves behind his linen garment and gets away.   Matthew 26:47-56; Mark 14:43-52; Luke 22:47-53; John 17:12; 18:3-12.

- Why does Judas feel sure he will find Jesus in the garden of Gethsemane?
- How does Jesus manifest concern for his apostles?
- What action does Peter take in Jesus' defense, but what does Jesus say to Peter about it?
- How does Jesus reveal that he is in complete agreement with God's will for him?
- When the apostles abandon Jesus, who remains, and what happens to him?

119

Taken to Annas,
Then to Caiaphas

JESUS, bound as a common criminal, is led to Annas, the influential former high priest. Annas was high priest when Jesus as a 12-year-old lad amazed the rabbinic teachers at the temple. Several of Annas' sons later served as high priest, and presently his son-in-law Caiaphas holds that position.

Jesus is probably first led to the home of Annas because of that chief priest's longtime prominence in Jewish religious life. This stopover to see Annas allows time for High Priest Caiaphas to assemble the Sanhedrin, the 71-member Jewish high court, as well as to gather false witnesses.

Chief priest Annas now questions Jesus about his disciples and about his teaching. However, Jesus says in reply: "I have spoken to the world publicly. I always taught in a synagogue and in the temple, where all the Jews come together; and I spoke nothing in secret. Why do you question me? Question those who have heard what I spoke to them. See! These know what I said."

At this, one of the officers standing near Jesus slaps him in the face, saying: "Is that the way you answer the chief priest?"

"If I spoke wrongly," Jesus replies, "bear witness concerning the wrong; but if rightly, why do you hit me?" After this exchange, Annas sends Jesus away bound to Caiaphas.

By now all the chief priests and the older men and the scribes, yes, the whole Sanhedrin, are beginning to assemble. Their place of meeting is evidently the home of Caiaphas. To hold such a trial on the night of a Passover is clearly against Jewish law. But this does not deter the religious leaders from their wicked purpose.

Weeks before, when Jesus resurrected Lazarus, the Sanhedrin had already determined among themselves that he must die. And just two days earlier, on Wednesday, the religious authorities took counsel together to seize Jesus by crafty device to kill him. Imagine, he had actually been condemned before his trial!

Efforts are now under way to find witnesses who will provide false evidence so that a case may be built against Jesus. However, no witnesses can be found who are in agreement in their testimony. Eventually, two come forward and assert: "We heard him say, 'I will throw down this temple that was made with hands and in three days I will build another not made with hands.'"

"Do you say nothing in reply?" Caiaphas asks. "What is it these are testifying against you?" But Jesus remains silent. Even in this false charge, to the humiliation of the Sanhedrin, the witnesses cannot make their stories agree. So the high priest tries a different tactic.

Caiaphas knows how sensitive Jews are about anyone claiming to be the very Son of God. On two earlier occasions, they had rashly labeled Jesus a blasphemer worthy of death, once having mistakenly imagined that he was claiming to be equal to God. Caiaphas now craftily demands: "By the living God I put you under oath to tell us whether you are the Christ the Son of God!"

Regardless of what the Jews think, Jesus really is the Son of God. And to remain silent could be construed as a denial of his being the Christ. So Jesus courageously replies: "I am; and you persons will see the Son of man sitting at the right hand of power and coming with the clouds of heaven."

At this, Caiaphas, in a dramatic display, rips his garments and exclaims: "He has blasphemed! What further need do we have of witnesses? See! Now you have heard the blasphemy. What is your opinion?"

"He is liable to death," the Sanhedrin proclaims. Then they begin to make fun of him, and they say many things in blasphemy against him. They slap his face and spit into it. Others cover his whole face and hit him with their fists and say sarcastically: "Prophesy to us, you Christ. Who is it that struck you?" This abusive, illegal behavior occurs during the nighttime trial. **Matthew 26:57-68; 26:3, 4; Mark 14:53-65; Luke 22: 54, 63-65; John 18:13-24; 11:45-53; 10:31-39; 5:16-18.**

- Where is Jesus led first, and what happens to him there?
- Where is Jesus next taken, and for what purpose?
- How is Caiaphas able to get the Sanhedrin to proclaim that Jesus is deserving of death?
- What abusive, illegal behavior occurs during the trial?

AFTER abandoning Jesus in the garden of Gethsemane and fleeing in fear with the rest of the apostles, Peter and John stop in their flight. Perhaps they catch up with Jesus when he is being taken to the home of Annas. When Annas sends him over to High Priest Caiaphas, Peter and John follow at a good distance, apparently torn between fear for their own lives and their deep concern as to what will happen to their Master.

Arriving at Caiaphas' spacious residence, John is able to gain entrance into the courtyard, since he is known to the high priest. Peter, however, is left standing outside at the door. But soon John returns and speaks to the doorkeeper, a servant girl, and Peter is permitted to enter.

By now it is cold, and the house attendants and the officers of the high priest have built a charcoal fire. Peter joins them to keep warm while awaiting the outcome of Jesus' trial. There, in the light of the bright fire, the doorkeeper who had let Peter in gets a better look at him. "You, too, were with Jesus the Galilean!" she exclaims.

Upset at being identified, Peter denies before all of them ever knowing Jesus. "Neither do I know him nor do I understand what you are saying," he says.

At that, Peter goes out near the gateway. There, another girl notices him and also says to those standing by: "This man was with Jesus the Nazarene." Once more Peter denies it, swearing: "I do not know the man!"

Peter remains in the courtyard, trying to be as inconspicuous as possible. Perhaps at this point he is startled by the crowing of a cock in the early morning darkness. In the meantime, Jesus' trial is in progress, evidently being conducted in a part of the house above the courtyard. No doubt Peter

and the others waiting below see the comings and goings of various witnesses that are brought in to testify.

About an hour has passed since Peter was last identified as an associate of Jesus. Now a number of those standing around come up to him and say: "Certainly you also are one of them, for, in fact, your dialect gives you away." One of the group is a relative of Malchus, whose ear Peter cut off. "I saw you in the garden with him, did I not?" he says.

"I do not know the man!" Peter vehemently asserts. In fact, he tries to convince them that they are all mistaken by cursing and swearing to the matter, in effect, calling down evil upon himself if he is not telling the truth.

Just as Peter makes this third denial, a cock crows. And at that moment, Jesus, who has apparently come out onto a balcony above the courtyard, turns and looks at him. Immediately, Peter recalls what Jesus said only a few hours earlier in the upper room: "Before a cock crows twice, even you will disown me three times." Crushed by the weight of his sin, Peter goes outside and weeps bitterly.

How could this happen? How, after being so certain of his spiritual strength, could Peter deny his Master three times in quick succession? The circumstances no doubt catch Peter unawares. Truth is being distorted, and Jesus is being depicted as a vile criminal. What is right is being made to appear wrong, the innocent one as guilty. So because of the pressures of the occasion, Peter is thrown off balance. Suddenly his proper sense of loyalty is upset; to his sorrow he is paralyzed by fear of man. May that never happen to us! **Matthew 26:57, 58, 69-75; Mark 14:30, 53, 54, 66-72; Luke 22:54-62; John 18:15-18, 25-27.**

- How do Peter and John gain entrance to the courtyard of the high priest?
- While Peter and John are in the courtyard, what is going on in the house?
- How many times does a cock crow, and how many times does Peter deny knowing Christ?
- What does it mean that Peter curses and swears?
- What causes Peter to deny that he knows Jesus?

121

Before the Sanhedrin, Then to Pilate

THE night is drawing to a close. Peter has denied Jesus for the third time, and the members of the Sanhedrin have finished with their mock trial and have dispersed. However, as soon as it becomes dawn Friday morning, they meet again, this time at their Sanhedrin hall. Their purpose likely is to give some appearance of legality to the night trial. When Jesus is brought before them, they say, as they did during the night: "If you are the Christ, tell us."

"Even if I told you, you would not believe it," Jesus answers. "Moreover, if I questioned you, you would not answer." However, Jesus courageously points to his identity, saying: "From now on the Son of man will be sitting at the powerful right hand of God."

"Are you, therefore, the Son of God?" all of them want to know.

"You yourselves are saying that I am," Jesus replies.

For these men intent on murder, this answer is sufficient. They consider it blasphemy. "Why do we need further witness?" they ask. "For we ourselves have heard it out of his own mouth." So they bind Jesus, lead him away, and hand him over to the Roman governor Pontius Pilate.

Judas, Jesus' betrayer, has been observing the proceedings. When he sees that Jesus has been condemned, he feels remorse. So he goes to the chief priests and older men to return the 30 pieces of silver, explaining: "I sinned when I betrayed righteous blood."

"What is that to us? You must see to that!" they heartlessly re-ply. So Judas throws the silver pieces into the temple and goes off and tries to hang himself. However, the branch to which Judas ties the rope apparently breaks, and his body plunges to the rocks below, where it bursts apart.

The chief priests are not sure what to do with the silver pieces. "It is not lawful to drop them into the sacred treasury," they conclude, "because they are the price of blood." So, after consulting together, they purchase with the money the potter's field to bury strangers. The field thus comes to be called "Field of Blood."

It is still early in the morning when Jesus is taken to the governor's palace. But the Jews who have accompanied him refuse to enter because they believe that such intimacy with Gentiles will defile them. So to accommodate them, Pilate comes out. "What accusation do you bring against this man?" he asks.

"If this man were not a wrongdoer, we would not have delivered him up to you," they answer.

Desiring to avoid involvement, Pilate responds: "Take him yourselves and judge him according to your law."

Revealing their murderous intent, the Jews claim: "It is not lawful for us to kill anyone." Indeed, if they killed Jesus during the Passover Festival, it would likely cause a public uproar, since many hold Jesus in high regard. But if they can get the Romans to execute him on a political charge, this will tend to absolve them of responsibility before the people.

So the religious leaders, not mentioning their earlier trial during which they condemned Jesus for blasphemy, now trump up different charges. They make the three-part accusation: "This man we found [1] subverting our nation and [2] forbidding the paying of taxes to Caesar and [3] saying he himself is Christ a king."

It is the charge that Jesus claims to be a king that concerns Pilate. He, therefore, enters the palace again, calls Jesus to him, and asks: "Are you the king of the Jews?" In other words, have you broken the law by declaring yourself to be a king in opposition to Caesar?

Jesus wants to know how much Pilate already has heard about him, so he asks: "Is it of your own originality that you say this, or did others tell you about me?"

Pilate professes ignorance about him and a desire to learn the facts. "I am not a Jew, am I?" he responds. "Your own nation and the chief priests delivered you up to me. What did you do?"

Jesus in no way attempts to dodge the issue, which is that of kingship. The answer that Jesus now gives no doubt surprises Pilate. **Luke 22:66–23:3; Matthew 27:1-11; Mark 15:1; John 18:28-35; Acts 1:16-20.**

- For what purpose does the Sanhedrin meet again in the morning?
- How does Judas die, and what is done with the 30 pieces of silver?
- Rather than kill him themselves, why do the Jews want the Romans to kill Jesus?
- What charges do the Jews make against Jesus?

122

From Pilate to Herod and Back Again

ALTHOUGH Jesus makes no attempt to conceal from Pilate that he is a king, he explains that his Kingdom is no threat to Rome. "My kingdom is no part of this world," Jesus says. "If my kingdom were part of this world, my attendants would have fought that I should not be delivered up to the Jews. But, as it is, my kingdom is not from this source." Jesus thus acknowledges three times that he has a Kingdom, although it is not of an earthly source.

Yet, Pilate presses him further: "Well, then, are you a king?" That is, are you a king even though your Kingdom is no part of this world?

Jesus lets Pilate know that he has drawn the right conclusion, answering: "You yourself are saying that I am a king. For this I have been born, and for this I have come into the world, that I should bear witness to the truth. Everyone that is on the side of the truth listens to my voice."

Yes, the very purpose of Jesus' existence on earth is to bear witness to "the truth," specifically the truth about his Kingdom. Jesus is prepared to be faithful to that truth even if it costs him his life. Although Pilate asks: "What is truth?" he does not wait for further explanation. He has heard enough to render judgment.

Pilate returns to the crowd waiting outside the palace. Evidently with Jesus at his side, he tells the chief priests and those with them: "I find no crime in this man."

Angered by the decision, the crowds begin to insist: "He stirs up the people by teaching throughout all Judea, even starting out from Galilee to here."

The unreasoning fanaticism of the Jews must amaze Pilate. So, as the chief priests and older men continue shouting,

Pilate turns to Jesus and asks: "Do you not hear how many things they are testifying against you?" Yet, Jesus makes no attempt to answer. His calm in the face of the wild accusations causes Pilate to marvel.

Learning that Jesus is a Galilean, Pilate sees a way out of responsibility for him. The ruler of Galilee, Herod Antipas (son of Herod the Great), is in Jerusalem for the Passover, so Pilate sends Jesus to him. Earlier, Herod Antipas had John the Baptizer beheaded, and then Herod became frightened when he heard about the miraculous works Jesus was performing, fearing that Jesus was actually John who had been raised from the dead.

Now, Herod is overjoyed at the prospect of seeing Jesus. This is not because he is concerned about Jesus' welfare or that he wants to make any real attempt to learn whether the charges against him are true or not. Rather, he is simply curious and hopes to see Jesus perform some miracle.

Jesus, however, refuses to satisfy Herod's curiosity. In fact, as Herod questions him, he does not say a word. Disappointed, Herod and his soldier guards make fun of Jesus. They clothe him with a bright garment and mock him. Then they send him back to Pilate. As a result, Herod and Pilate, who had formerly been enemies, become good friends.

When Jesus returns, Pilate calls the chief priests, the Jewish rulers, and the people together and says: "You brought this man to me as one inciting the people to revolt, and, look! I examined him in front of you but found in this man no ground for the charges you are bringing against him. In fact, neither did Herod, for he sent him back to us; and, look! nothing deserving of death has been committed by him. I will therefore chastise him and release him."

Thus Pilate has twice declared Jesus innocent. He is eager to free him, for he realizes that it is only because of envy that the priests have handed him over. As Pilate continues to try to release Jesus, he receives even stronger motivation to do so. While he is on his judgment seat, his wife sends a message, urging him: "Have nothing to do with that righteous man, for I suffered a lot today in a dream [evidently of divine origin] because of him."

Yet, how can Pilate release this innocent man, as he knows he should? John 18:36-38; Luke 23:4-16; Matthew 27:12-14, 18, 19; 14: 1, 2; Mark 15:2-5.

■ How does Jesus answer the question regarding his kingship?

■ What is "the truth" about which Jesus spent his earthly life bearing witness?

■ What is Pilate's judgment, how do the people respond, and what does Pilate do with Jesus?

■ Who is Herod Antipas, why is he overjoyed to see Jesus, and what does he do with him?

■ Why is Pilate eager to free Jesus?

123

"Look! The Man!"

IMPRESSED by Jesus' demeanor and recognizing his innocence, Pilate pursues another way to release him. "You have a custom," he tells the crowds, "that I should release a man to you at the passover."

Barabbas, a notorious murderer, is also being held as prisoner, so Pilate asks: "Which one do you want me to release to you, Barabbas or Jesus the so-called Christ?"

Persuaded by the chief priests who have stirred them up, the people ask for Barabbas to be released but for Jesus to be killed. Not giving up, Pilate responds, asking again: "Which of the two do you want me to release to you?"

"Barabbas," they shout.

"What, then, shall I do with Jesus the so-called Christ?" Pilate asks in dismay.

With one deafening roar, they answer: "Let him be impaled!" "Impale! Impale him!"

Knowing that they are demanding the death of an innocent man, Pilate pleads: "Why, what bad thing did this man do? I found nothing deserving of death in him; I will therefore chastise and release him."

Despite his attempts, the enraged crowd, egged on by their religious leaders, keep yelling: "Let him be impaled!" Worked into a frenzy by the priests, the crowd wants blood. And to think, only five days before, some of them were probably among those who welcomed Jesus into Jerusalem as King! All the while, Jesus' disciples, if they are present, remain silent and inconspicuous.

Pilate, seeing his appeals are doing no good but, rather, that an uproar is arising, takes water and washes his hands before the crowd, and says: "I am innocent of the blood of this man. You yourselves must see to it." At that, the people answer: "His blood come upon us and upon our children."

So, in accord with their demands—and wishing to satisfy the crowd more than to do what he knows is right—Pilate releases Barabbas to them. He takes Jesus and has him stripped and then scourged. This was no ordinary whipping. *The Journal of the American Medical Association* describes the Roman practice of scourging:

"The usual instrument was a short whip (flagrum or flagellum) with several single or braided leather thongs of variable lengths, in which small iron balls or sharp pieces of sheep bones were tied at intervals. . . . As the Roman soldiers repeatedly struck the victim's back with full force, the iron balls would cause deep contusions, and the leather thongs and sheep bones would cut into the skin and subcutaneous tissues. Then, as the flogging continued, the lacerations would tear into the underlying skeletal muscles and produce quivering ribbons of bleeding flesh."

After this torturous beating, Jesus is taken into the governor's palace, and the whole body of troops is called together. There the soldiers heap further abuse on him by braiding a crown of thorns and pushing it down on his head. They put a reed in his right hand, and they clothe him with a purple garment, the type that is worn by royalty. Then they say to him mockingly: "Good day, you King of the Jews!" Also, they spit on him and slap him in the face. Taking the sturdy reed from his hand, they use it to hit him on the head, driving even further into his scalp the sharp thorns of his humiliating "crown."

Jesus' remarkable dignity and strength in the face of this mistreatment so impresses Pilate that he is moved to make another attempt to redeem him. "See! I bring him outside to you in order for you to know I find no fault in him," he tells the crowds. Possibly he imagines that the sight of Jesus' tortured condition will soften their hearts. As Jesus stands before the heartless mob, wearing the thorny crown and the

purple outer garment and with his bleeding face etched with pain, Pilate proclaims: "Look! The man!"

Though bruised and battered, here stands the most outstanding figure of all history, truly the greatest man who ever lived! Yes, Jesus shows a quiet dignity and calm that bespeak a greatness that even Pilate must acknowledge, for his words are apparently a mingling of both respect and pity. **John 18: 39–19:5; Matthew 27:15-17, 20-30; Mark 15:6-19; Luke 23:18-25.**

- In what way does Pilate attempt to have Jesus released?
- How does Pilate try to absolve himself of responsibility?
- What is involved in being scourged?
- How is Jesus ridiculed after being scourged?
- What further attempt does Pilate make to release Jesus?

124

Handed Over and Led Away

WHEN Pilate, moved by the quiet dignity of the tortured Jesus, again tries to release him, the chief priests become even angrier. They are determined to let nothing interfere with their wicked purpose. So they renew their shouting: "Impale him! Impale him!"

"Take him yourselves and impale him," Pilate responds. (Contrary to their earlier claims, the Jews may have authority to execute criminals for religious offenses that are of sufficient gravity.) Then, for at least the fifth time, Pilate declares Jesus innocent, saying: "I do not find any fault in him."

The Jews, seeing that their political charges have failed to produce results, fall back on the religious charge of blasphemy used hours earlier at Jesus' trial before the Sanhedrin. "We have a law," they say, "and according to the law he ought to die, because he made himself God's son."

This charge is new to Pilate, and it causes him to become more fearful. By now he realizes that Jesus is no ordinary man, even as his wife's dream and Jesus' remarkable strength of personality indicate. But "God's son"? Pilate knows that Jesus is from Galilee. Yet, could he possibly have lived before? Taking him back into the palace again, Pilate asks: "Where are you from?"

Jesus remains silent. Earlier he had told Pilate that he is a king but that his Kingdom is no part of this world. No further explanation now would serve a useful purpose. However, Pilate's pride is hurt by the refusal to answer, and he flares up at Jesus with the words: "Are you not speaking to me? Do you not know I have authority to release you and I have authority to impale you?"

"You would have no authority at all against me unless it had been granted to you from above," Jesus responds respectfully. He is referring to the grant by God of authority to human rulers to administer earthly affairs. Jesus adds: "This is why the man that handed me over to you has greater sin." Indeed, the high priest Caiaphas and his accomplices and Judas Iscariot all bear heavier responsibility than Pilate for the unjust treatment of Jesus.

Impressed even more by Jesus and fearful that Jesus may have a divine origin, Pilate renews his efforts to release him. The Jews, however, rebuff Pilate. They repeat their political charge, craftily threatening: "If you release this man, you are not a friend of Caesar. Every man making himself a king speaks against Caesar."

Despite the dire implications, Pilate brings Jesus outside once more. "See! Your king!" he appeals yet again.

"Take him away! Take him away! Impale him!"

"Shall I impale your king?" Pilate asks in desperation.

The Jews have chafed under the rule of the Romans. Indeed, they despise Rome's domination! Yet, hypocritically, the chief priests say: "We have no king but Caesar."

Fearing for his political position and reputation, Pilate finally caves in under the Jews' relentless demands. He hands Jesus over. The soldiers strip Jesus of the purple cloak and clothe him with his outer garments. As Jesus is led off to be impaled, he is made to bear his own torture stake.

By now it is midmorning on Friday, Nisan 14; perhaps it is approaching noon. Jesus has been up since early Thursday morning, and he has suffered one agonizing experience after another. Understandably, his strength soon gives out under the weight of the stake. So a passerby, a certain Simon of Cyrene in Africa, is impressed into service to carry it for him. As they proceed along, many people, including women, follow, beating themselves in grief and bewailing Jesus.

Turning to the women, Jesus says: "Daughters of Jerusalem, stop weeping for me. On the contrary, weep for yourselves and for your children; because, look! days are coming in which people will say, 'Happy are the barren women, and the wombs that did not give birth and the breasts that did not nurse!' . . . Because if they do these things when the tree is moist, what will occur when it is withered?"

Jesus is referring to the tree of the Jewish nation, which still has some moisture of life in it because of Jesus' presence and the existence of a remnant that believe in him. But when these are taken out from the nation, only a spiritually dead tree will remain, yes, a withered national organization. Oh, what cause for weeping there will be when the Roman armies, serving as God's executioners, devastate the Jewish nation! John 19:6-17; 18:31; Luke 23:24-31; Matthew 27:31, 32; Mark 15:20, 21.

■ What charge against Jesus do the religious leaders make when their political charges fail to produce results?

■ Why does Pilate become more fearful?

■ Who bear the greater sin for what happens to Jesus?

■ Finally, how do the priests get Pilate to hand Jesus over for execution?

■ What does Jesus tell the women who weep for him, and what does he mean by referring to the tree as being "moist" and then "withered"?

125

Agony on the Stake

ALONG with Jesus two robbers are being led out to be executed. Not far from the city, the procession comes to a halt at the place called Golgotha, or Skull Place.

The prisoners are stripped of their garments. Then wine drugged with myrrh is provided. Apparently it is prepared by the women of Jerusalem, and the Romans do not deny this pain-dulling potion to those being impaled. However, when Jesus tastes it, he refuses to drink. Why? Evidently he wants to have full possession of all his faculties during this supreme test of his faith.

Jesus is now stretched out on the stake with his hands placed above his head. The soldiers then pound large nails into his hands and into his feet. He wrenches with pain as the nails pierce flesh and ligaments. When the stake is swung upright, the pain is excruciating, for the weight of the body tears at the nail wounds. Yet, rather than threaten, Jesus prays for the Roman soldiers: "Father, forgive them, for they do not know what they are doing."

Pilate has posted on the stake a sign that reads: "Jesus the Nazarene the King of the Jews." Apparently, he writes this not only because he respects Jesus but because he loathes the Jewish priests for their having wrung Jesus' death sentence from him. So that all may read the sign, Pilate has it written in three languages—in Hebrew, in the official Latin, and in the common Greek.

The chief priests, including Caiaphas and Annas, are dismayed. This positive proclamation spoils their hour of triumph. Therefore they protest: "Do not write 'The King of the Jews,' but that he said, 'I am King of the Jews.'" Chafing from having served as the pawn of the priests, Pilate answers with resolute contempt: "What I have written I have written."

The priests, along with a large crowd, now gather at the site of the execution, and the priests refute the testimony of the sign. They repeat the false testimony that was given earlier at the Sanhedrin trials. Not surprisingly, therefore, passersby begin speaking abusively, wagging their heads in mockery and saying: "O you would-be thrower-down of the temple and builder of it in three days, save yourself! If you are a son of God, come down off the torture stake!"

"Others he saved; himself he cannot save!" the chief priests and their religious cronies chime in. "He is King of Israel; let him now come down off the torture stake and we will believe on him. He has put his trust in God; let Him now rescue him if He wants him, for he said, 'I am God's Son.'"

Caught up in the spirit, the soldiers too make fun of Jesus. They mockingly offer him sour wine, apparently holding it just beyond his parched lips. "If you are the king of the Jews," they taunt, "save yourself." Even the robbers—one impaled to Jesus' right, and the other to his left—ridicule him. Think of it! The greatest man who ever lived, yes, the one who shared with Jehovah God in creating all things, resolutely suffers all this abuse!

The soldiers take Jesus' outer garments and divide them into four parts. They cast lots to see whose these will become. The inner garment, however, is without a seam, being of superior quality. So the soldiers say to one another: "Let us not tear it, but let us determine by lots over it whose it will be." Thus, unwittingly, they fulfill the scripture that says: "They apportioned my outer garments among themselves, and upon my apparel they cast lots."

In time, one of the robbers comes to appreciate that Jesus truly must be a king. Therefore, rebuking his companion, he says: "Do you not fear God at all, now that you are in the same judgment? And we, indeed, justly so, for we are receiving in full what we deserve for things we did; but this man did nothing out of the way." Then he addresses Jesus, with the petition: "Remember me when you get into your kingdom."

"Truly I tell you today," Jesus replies, "You will be with me in Paradise." This promise will be fulfilled when Jesus rules as King in heaven and resurrects this repentant evildoer to life on earth in the Paradise that Armageddon survivors and their companions will have the privilege of cultivating. Matthew 27: 33-44; Mark 15:22-32; Luke 23:27, 32-43; John 19:17-24.

- Why does Jesus refuse to drink the wine drugged with myrrh?
- Why, apparently, is a sign posted on Jesus' stake, and what exchange does it initiate between Pilate and the chief priests?
- What further abuse does Jesus receive on the stake, and what evidently prompts it?
- How is prophecy fulfilled in what is done with Jesus' garments?
- What change does one of the robbers make, and how will Jesus fulfill his request?

126

"Certainly This Was God's Son"

JESUS has not been on the stake long when, at midday, a mysterious, three-hour-long darkness occurs. A solar eclipse is not responsible, since these take place only at the time of the new moon and the moon is full at Passover time. Moreover, solar eclipses last only a few minutes. So the darkness is of divine origin! It probably gives pause to those mocking Jesus, even causing their taunts to cease.

If the eerie phenomenon occurs before the one evildoer chastises his companion and asks Jesus to remember him, it may be a factor in his repentance. Perhaps it is during the darkness that four women, namely, Jesus' mother and her sister Salome, Mary Magdalene, and Mary the mother of the apostle James the Less, make their way close to the torture stake. John, Jesus' beloved apostle, is with them there.

How the heart of Jesus' mother is 'pierced through' as she watches the son she nursed and nurtured hanging there in agony! Yet Jesus thinks, not of his own pain, but of her welfare. With great effort, he nods toward John and says to his mother: "Woman, see! Your son!" Then, nodding toward Mary, he says to John: "See! Your mother!"

Jesus thereby entrusts the care of his mother, who is evidently now a widow, to his specially loved apostle. He does this because Mary's other sons have not as yet manifested faith in him. Thus he sets a fine example in making provision not only for his mother's physical needs but also for her spiritual ones.

At about three in the afternoon, Jesus says: "I am thirsty." Jesus senses that his Father has, as it were, withdrawn protection from him in order that his integrity might be tested to the limit. So he calls out with a loud voice: "My God, my God, why have you forsaken me?" At hearing this, some who are standing nearby exclaim: "See! He is calling Elijah." Immediately one of them runs and, placing a sponge soaked with sour wine on the end of a hyssop stalk, gives him a drink. But others say: "Let him be! Let us see whether Elijah comes to take him down."

When Jesus receives the sour wine, he cries out: "It has been accomplished!" Yes, he has finished everything that his Father has sent him to earth to do. Finally, he says: "Father, into your hands I entrust my spirit." Jesus thereby commits to God his life-force in confidence that God will restore it to him again. Then he bows his head and dies.

The moment Jesus breathes his last, a violent earthquake occurs, splitting open the rock-masses. The quake is so powerful that the memorial tombs outside Jerusalem are broken open and corpses are thrown out of them. Passersby who see the dead bodies that have been exposed enter the city and report it.

Furthermore, at the moment Jesus dies, the huge curtain that divides the Holy from the Most Holy in God's temple is rent in two, from top to bottom. Apparently this beautifully ornamented curtain is some 60 feet high and very heavy! The astonishing miracle not only manifests God's wrath against the killers of His Son but signifies that the way into the Most Holy, heaven itself, is now made possible by Jesus' death.

Well, when people feel the earthquake and see the things happening, they grow very much afraid. The army officer in charge at the execution gives glory to God. "Certainly this was God's Son," he proclaims. Likely he had been present when the claim of divine sonship was discussed at Jesus' trial before

Pilate. And now he is convinced that Jesus is the Son of God, yes, that he is indeed the greatest man who ever lived.

Others too are overcome by these miraculous events, and they begin returning home beating their breasts as a gesture of their intense grief and shame. Observing the spectacle at a distance are many female disciples of Jesus who are deeply moved by these momentous events. The apostle John is also present.   **Matthew 27:45-56; Mark 15:33-41; Luke 23:44-49; 2:34, 35; John 19:25-30.**

- Why can a solar eclipse not be responsible for the three hours of darkness?

- Shortly before his death, what fine example does Jesus provide for those with aged parents?

- What are Jesus' last four statements before he dies?

- What does the earthquake accomplish, and what is the significance of the temple curtain's being rent in two?

- How is the army officer in charge at the execution affected by the miracles?

127 Buried Friday—An Empty Tomb Sunday

B Y NOW it is late Friday afternoon, and the Sabbath of Nisan 15 will begin at sundown. Jesus' dead body hangs limp on the stake, but the two robbers alongside him are still alive. Friday afternoon is called Preparation because this is when people prepare meals and complete any other pressing work that cannot wait until after the Sabbath.

The Sabbath soon to begin is not only a regular Sabbath (the seventh day of the week) but also a double, or "great," Sabbath. It is called this because Nisan 15, which is the first day of the seven-day Festival of Unfermented Cakes (and is always a Sabbath, no matter on what day of the week it comes), falls on the same day as the regular Sabbath.

According to God's Law, bodies are not to be left hanging on a stake overnight. So the Jews ask Pilate that the death of those being executed be hastened by breaking their legs. The soldiers, therefore, break the legs of the two robbers. But since Jesus appears to be dead, his legs are not broken. This fulfills the scripture: "Not a bone of his will be crushed."

However, to remove any doubt that Jesus is really dead, one of the soldiers jabs a spear into his side. The spear pierces the region of his heart, and immediately blood and water come out. The apostle John, who is an eyewitness, reports that this fulfills another scripture: "They will look to the One whom they pierced."

Also present at the execution is Joseph from the city of Arimathea, a reputable member of the Sanhedrin. He refused to vote in favor of the high court's unjust action against Jesus. Joseph is actually a disciple of Jesus, although he has been afraid to identify himself as one. Now, however, he exercises courage and goes to Pilate to ask for Jesus' body. Pilate summons the army officer in charge, and after the officer confirms that Jesus is dead, Pilate has the corpse handed over.

Joseph takes the body and wraps it in clean fine linen in preparation for burial. He is assisted by Nicodemus, another member of the Sanhedrin. Nicodemus also has failed to confess his faith in Jesus because of fear of losing his position. But now he brings a roll containing about a hundred Roman pounds of myrrh and expensive aloes. Jesus' body is wrapped in bandages containing these spices, just the way the Jews have the custom of preparing bodies for burial.

The body is then laid in Joseph's new memorial tomb that is carved in the rock in the garden nearby. Finally, a large stone is rolled in front of the tomb. To accomplish the burial before the Sabbath, preparation of the body is hasty. Therefore, Mary Magdalene and Mary the mother of James the Less, who have perhaps been helping with the preparation, hurry home to prepare more spices and perfumed oils. After the Sabbath, they plan to treat Jesus' body further in order to preserve it for a longer period of time.

The next day, which is Saturday (the Sabbath), the chief priests and the Pharisees go to Pilate and say: "Sir, we have called to mind that that impostor said while yet alive, 'After three days I am to be raised up.' Therefore command the grave to be made secure until the third day, that his disciples may never come and steal him and say to the people, 'He was raised up from the dead!' and this last imposture will be worse than the first."

"You have a guard," Pilate answers. "Go make it as secure as you know how." So they go and make the grave secure by sealing the stone and posting Roman soldiers as guards.

Early Sunday morning Mary Magdalene and Mary the mother of James, along with Salome, Joanna, and other women, bring spices to the tomb to treat Jesus' body. En route they say to one another: "Who will roll the stone away from the door of the memorial tomb for us?" But on arriving, they find that an earthquake has occurred and Jehovah's angel has rolled the stone away. The guards are gone, and the tomb is empty! **Matthew 27:57–28:2; Mark 15:42–16:4; Luke 23:50–24:3, 10; John 19:14, 31–20:1; 12:42; Leviticus 23:5-7; Deuteronomy 21:22, 23; Psalm 34:20; Zechariah 12:10.**

- Why is Friday called Preparation, and what is a "great" Sabbath?
- What scriptures are fulfilled in connection with Jesus' body?
- What do Joseph and Nicodemus have to do with Jesus' burial, and what is their relationship to Jesus?
- What request do the priests make of Pilate, and how does he respond?
- What occurs early Sunday morning?

128

Jesus Is Alive!

WHEN the women find Jesus' tomb empty, Mary Magdalene runs off to tell Peter and John. However, the other women evidently remain at the tomb. Soon, an angel appears and invites them inside.

Here the women see yet another angel, and one of the angels says to them: "Do not you be fearful, for I know you are looking for Jesus who was impaled. He is not here, for he was raised up, as he said. Come, see the place where he was lying. And go quickly and tell his disciples that he was raised up from the dead." So with fear and great joy, these women also run off.

By this time, Mary has found Peter and John, and she reports to them: "They have taken away the Lord out of the memorial tomb, and we do not know where they have laid him." Immediately the two apostles take off running. John is fleeter of foot—evidently being younger—and he reaches the tomb first. By this time the women have left, so no one is around. Stooping down, John peers into the tomb and sees the bandages, but he remains outside.

When Peter arrives, he does not hesitate but goes right on in. He sees the bandages lying there and also the cloth used to wrap Jesus' head. It is rolled up in one place. John now also enters the tomb, and he believes Mary's report. But neither Peter nor John grasps that Jesus has been raised up, even though He had often told them that He would be. Puzzled, the two return home, but Mary, who has come back to the tomb, remains.

In the meantime, the other women are hurrying to tell the disciples that Jesus has been resurrected, as the angels commanded them to do. While they are running along as fast as they can, Jesus meets them and says: "Good day!" Falling at his feet, they do obeisance to him. Then Jesus says: "Have no fear! Go, report to my brothers, that they may go off into Galilee; and there they will see me."

Earlier, when the earthquake occurred and the angels appeared, the soldiers on guard were stunned and became as dead men. Upon recovering, they immediately went into the city and told the chief priests what had happened. After consulting with the "older men" of the Jews, the decision was made to try to hush up the matter by bribing the soldiers. They were instructed: "Say, 'His disciples came in the night and stole him while we were sleeping.'"

Since Roman soldiers may be punished with death for falling asleep at their posts, the priests promised: "If this [report of your falling asleep] gets to the governor's ears, we will persuade him and will set you free from worry." Since the size of the bribe was sufficiently large, the soldiers did as they were instructed. As a result, the false report about the theft of Jesus' body became widely spread among the Jews.

Mary Magdalene, who remains behind at the tomb, is overcome by grief. Where could Jesus be? Stooping forward to look into the tomb, she sees the two angels in white, who have reappeared! One is sitting at the head and the other at the foot of where Jesus' body had been lying. "Woman, why are you weeping?" they ask.

"They have taken my Lord away," Mary answers, "and I do not know where they have laid him." Then she turns around and sees someone who repeats the question: "Woman, why are you weeping?" And this one also asks: "Whom are you looking for?"

Imagining this person to be the caretaker of the garden in which the tomb is situated, she says to him: "Sir, if you have carried him off, tell me where you have laid him, and I will take him away."

"Mary!" the person says. And immediately she knows, by the familiar way he speaks to her, that it is Jesus. *Rab·bo'ni!* (meaning "Teacher!") she exclaims. And with unbounded joy, she grabs hold of him. But Jesus says: "Stop clinging to me. For I have not yet ascended to the Father. But be on your way to my brothers and say to them, 'I am ascending to my Father and your Father and to my God and your God.'"

Mary now runs to where the apostles and fellow disciples have gathered. She adds her account to the report that the other women have already given about seeing the resurrected Jesus. Yet, these men, who did not believe the first women, apparently do not believe Mary either. **Matthew 28:3-15; Mark 16:5-8; Luke 24:4-12; John 20:2-18.**

- After finding the tomb empty, what does Mary Magdalene do, and what experience do the other women have?
- How do Peter and John react at finding the tomb empty?
- What do the other women encounter on their way to report Jesus' resurrection to the disciples?
- What had happened to the soldier guard, and what was the response to their report to the priests?
- What happens when Mary Magdalene is alone at the tomb, and what is the response of the disciples to the reports of the women?

129

Further Appearances

THE disciples are still downhearted. They do not comprehend the significance of the empty tomb, nor do they believe the reports of the women. So later on Sunday, Cleopas and another disciple leave Jerusalem for Emmaus, a distance of about seven miles.

En route, while they are discussing the events of the day, a stranger joins them. "What are these matters that you are debating between yourselves as you walk along?" he asks.

The disciples stop, their faces downcast, and Cleopas replies: "Are you dwelling as an alien by yourself in Jerusalem and so do not know the things that have occurred in her in these days?" He asks: "What things?"

"The things concerning Jesus the Nazarene," they answer. "Our chief priests and rulers handed him over to the sentence of death and impaled him. But we were hoping that this man was the one destined to deliver Israel."

Cleopas and his companion explain the astounding events of the day—the report about the supernatural sight of angels and the empty tomb—but then confess their bewilderment regarding the meaning of these things. The stranger reprimands them: "O senseless ones and slow in heart to believe on all the things the prophets spoke! Was it not necessary for the Christ to suffer these things and to enter into his glory?" He then interprets for them passages from the sacred text that pertain to the Christ.

Finally they arrive near Emmaus, and the stranger makes as if he is going on. Wanting to hear more, the disciples urge: "Stay with us, because it is toward evening." So he stays for a meal. As he says a prayer and breaks bread and hands it to them, they recognize that he is really Jesus in a materialized human body. But then he disappears.

Now they understand how the stranger knew so much!

"Were not our hearts burning," they ask, "as he was speaking to us on the road, as he was fully opening up the Scriptures to us?" Without delay, they get up and hurry all the way back to Jerusalem, where they find the apostles and those assembled with them. Before Cleopas and his companion can say a thing, the others excitedly report: "For a fact the Lord was raised up and he appeared to Simon!" Then the two relate how Jesus also appeared to them. This makes four times during the day that he has appeared to different ones of his disciples.

Jesus suddenly makes a fifth appearance. Even though the doors are locked because the disciples are in fear of the Jews, he enters, standing right in their midst, and says: "May you have peace." They are terrified, imagining that they are seeing a spirit. So, explaining that he is not an apparition, Jesus says: "Why are you troubled, and why is it doubts come up in your hearts? See my hands and my feet, that it is I myself; feel me and see, because a spirit does not have flesh and bones just as you behold that I have." Still, they are reluctant to believe.

To help them grasp that he really is Jesus, he asks: "Do you have something there to eat?" After accepting a piece of broiled fish and eating it, he says: "These are my words which I spoke to you while I was yet with you [before my death], that all the things written in the law of Moses and in the Prophets and Psalms about me must be fulfilled."

Continuing what, in effect, amounts to a Bible study with them, Jesus teaches: "In this way it is written that the Christ would suffer and rise from among the dead on the third day, and on the basis of his name repentance for forgiveness of sins would be preached in all the nations—starting out from Jerusalem, you are to be witnesses of these things."

For some reason Thomas is not present at this vital Sunday evening meeting. So during the days that follow, the others joyfully tell him: "We have seen the Lord!"

"Unless I see in his hands the print of the nails," Thomas

protests, "and stick my finger into the print of the nails and stick my hand into his side, I will certainly not believe."

Well, eight days later the disciples are again meeting indoors. This time Thomas is with them. Although the doors are locked, Jesus once more stands in their midst and says: "May you have peace." Then, turning to Thomas, he invites: "Put your finger here, and see my hands, and take your hand and stick it into my side, and stop being unbelieving."

"My Lord and my God!" Thomas exclaims.

"Because you have seen me have you believed?" Jesus asks. "Happy are those who do not see and yet believe." Luke 24: 11, 13-48; John 20:19-29.

■ What inquiries does a stranger make of two disciples on the road to Emmaus?

■ What does the stranger say that causes the hearts of the disciples to burn within them?

■ How do the disciples discern who the stranger is?

■ When Cleopas and his companion return to Jerusalem, what exciting report do they hear?

■ What fifth appearance does Jesus make to his disciples, and what occurs during it?

■ What happens eight days after Jesus' fifth appearance, and how is Thomas finally convinced that Jesus is alive?

130

At the Sea of Galilee

THE apostles now return to Galilee, as Jesus had earlier instructed them to do. But they are uncertain about what they should do there. After a while, Peter tells Thomas, Nathanael, James and his brother John, and two other apostles: "I am going fishing."

"We also are coming with you," the six reply.

During the whole night, they fail to catch anything. However, just as it is getting light, Jesus appears on the beach, but the apostles do not discern that it is Jesus. He shouts: "Young children, you do not have anything to eat, do you?"

"No!" they shout back across the water.

"Cast the net on the right side of the boat and you will find some," he says. And when they do, they are unable to draw in their net because of all the fish.

"It is the Lord!" John cries.

On hearing this, Peter girds on his top garment, for he has taken his clothes off, and plunges into the sea. He then swims about a hundred yards to shore. The other apostles follow in the little boat, dragging the net full of fish.

When they arrive onshore, there is a charcoal fire, with fish lying on it, and there is bread. "Bring some of the fish you just now caught," Jesus says. Peter goes aboard and pulls the net ashore. It contains 153 large fish!

"Come, take your breakfast," Jesus invites.

None of them have the courage to ask, "Who are you?" because all of them know that it is Jesus. This is his seventh postresurrection appearance, and his third to the apostles as a group. He now serves breakfast, giving each of them some bread and fish.

When they finish eating, Jesus, likely looking toward the large catch of fish, asks Peter: "Simon son of John, do you love me more than these?" No doubt he means, Are you more

attached to the fishing business than to the work that I have prepared you to do?

"You know I have affection for you," Peter responds.

"Feed my lambs," Jesus replies.

Again, a second time, he asks: "Simon son of John, do you love me?"

"Yes, Lord, you know I have affection for you," Peter answers earnestly.

"Shepherd my little sheep," Jesus commands again.

Then, yet a third time, he asks: "Simon son of John, do you have affection for me?"

By now Peter is grieved. He may be wondering if Jesus doubts his loyalty. After all, when Jesus was recently on trial for his life, Peter three times denied knowing him. So Peter says: "Lord, you know all things; you are aware that I have affection for you."

"Feed my little sheep," Jesus commands a third time.

Jesus thus uses Peter as a sounding board to impress upon the others the work that he wants them to do. He will soon leave the earth, and he wants them to take the lead in ministering to those who will be drawn into God's sheepfold.

Just as Jesus was bound and executed because he did the work that God commissioned him to do, so, he now reveals, Peter will suffer a similar experience. "When you were younger," Jesus tells him, "you used to gird yourself and walk about where you wanted. But when you grow old you will stretch out your hands and another man will gird you and bear you where you do not wish." Despite the martyr's death awaiting Peter, Jesus urges him: "Continue following me."

Upon turning about, Peter sees John and asks: "Lord, what will this man do?"

"If it is my will for him to remain until I come," Jesus answers, "of what concern is that to you? You continue following me." These words of Jesus came to be understood by many of the disciples to mean that the apostle John would never die. However, as the apostle John later explained, Jesus did not say that he would not die, but Jesus simply said: "If it is my will for him to remain until I come, of what concern is that to you?"

John later also made this significant observation: "There are, in fact, many other things also which Jesus did, which, if ever they were written in full detail, I suppose, the world itself could not contain the scrolls written." John 21:1-25; Matthew 26:32; 28:7, 10.

- What shows that the apostles are uncertain about what they should do in Galilee?
- How do the apostles recognize Jesus at the Sea of Galilee?
- How many times has Jesus now appeared since his resurrection?
- How does Jesus emphasize what he wants the apostles to do?
- How does Jesus indicate the manner in which Peter will die?
- What comments of Jesus about John were misunderstood by many of the disciples?

131

Final Appearances, and Pentecost 33 C.E.

A T SOME point Jesus makes arrangements for all 11 of his apostles to meet him at a mountain in Galilee. Other disciples are apparently told about the meeting, and a total of more than 500 people assemble. What a happy convention this proves to be when Jesus appears and begins teaching them!

Among other things, Jesus explains to the large crowd that God has given him all authority in heaven and on earth. "Go therefore," he exhorts, "and make disciples of people of all the nations, baptizing them in the name of the Father and of the Son and of the holy spirit, teaching them to observe all the things I have commanded you."

Think of it! Men, women, and children all receive this same commission to share in the disciple-making work. Opposers will try to stop their preaching and teaching, but Jesus comforts them: "Look! I am with you all the days until the conclusion of the system of things." Jesus remains with his followers by means of the holy spirit, to help them fulfill their ministry.

Altogether, Jesus shows himself alive to his disciples for a period of 40 days following his resurrection. During these appearances he instructs them about the Kingdom of God, and he emphasizes what their responsibilities are as his disciples. On one occasion he even appears to his half brother James and convinces this onetime unbeliever that He is indeed the Christ.

While the apostles are still in Galilee, Jesus evidently instructs them to return to Jerusalem. When meeting with them there, he says to them: "Do not withdraw from Jerusalem, but keep waiting for what the Father has promised, about which you heard from me; because John, indeed, baptized with water, but you will be baptized in holy spirit not many days after this."

Later Jesus meets again with his apostles and leads them out of the city as far as Bethany, which is located on the eastern slope of the Mount of Olives. Amazingly, despite everything he has said about his soon departing for heaven, they still believe that his Kingdom will be established on earth. So they inquire: "Lord, are you restoring the kingdom to Israel at this time?"

Rather than try again to correct their misconceptions, Jesus simply answers: "It does not belong to you to get knowledge of the times or seasons which the Father has placed in his own jurisdiction." Then, stressing once again the work they must do, he says: "You will receive power when the holy spirit arrives upon you, and you will be witnesses of me both in Jerusalem and in all Judea and Samaria and to the most distant part of the earth."

While they are still looking on, Jesus begins rising heavenward, and then a cloud obscures him from their sight. After dematerializing his fleshly body, he ascends to heaven as a spirit person. As the 11 continue gazing into the sky, 2 men in white garments appear alongside them. These materialized angels ask: "Men of Galilee, why do you stand looking into the sky? This Jesus who was received up from you into the sky will come thus in the same manner as you have beheld him going into the sky."

The manner in which Jesus has just left the earth is with-

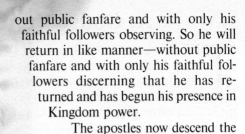

out public fanfare and with only his faithful followers observing. So he will return in like manner—without public fanfare and with only his faithful followers discerning that he has returned and has begun his presence in Kingdom power.

The apostles now descend the Mount of Olives, cross the Kidron Valley, and enter Jerusalem once again. They remain there in obedience to Jesus' command. Ten days later, at the Jewish Festival of Pentecost 33 C.E., while about 120 of the disciples assemble in an upper room in Jerusalem, a noise just like that of a rushing stiff breeze suddenly fills the whole house. Tongues as if of fire become visible, and one sits upon each of those present, and the disciples all begin to speak in different languages. This is the outpouring of the holy spirit that Jesus had promised! Matthew 28:16-20; Luke 24:49-52; 1 Corinthians 15:5-7; Acts 1:3-15; 2:1-4.

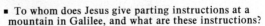

- To whom does Jesus give parting instructions at a mountain in Galilee, and what are these instructions?
- What comfort does Jesus provide for his disciples, and how will he remain with them?
- For how long after his resurrection does Jesus appear to his disciples, and what does he teach them?
- To what person who was evidently not a disciple before Jesus' death does Jesus appear?
- What two final meetings does Jesus have with his apostles, and what occurs on these occasions?
- How is it that Jesus will return in the same manner as he departs?
- What occurs at Pentecost 33 C.E.?

132

At God's Right Hand

THE pouring out of holy spirit at Pentecost is evidence that Jesus has arrived back in heaven. The vision granted shortly afterward to the disciple Stephen also proves that He has arrived there. Just before being stoned for his faithful witnessing, Stephen exclaims: "Look! I behold the heavens opened up and the Son of man standing at God's right hand."

While at God's right hand, Jesus awaits the command from his Father: "Go subduing in the midst of your enemies." But in the meantime, until he takes action against his enemies, what does Jesus do? He rules, or reigns, over his anointed disciples, guiding them in their preaching activity and preparing them to become, by resurrection, associate kings with him in his Father's Kingdom.

For example, Jesus selects Saul (later better known by his Roman name, Paul) to spearhead the disciple-making work in other lands. Saul is zealous for God's Law, yet he is misguided by the Jewish religious leaders. As a result, not only does Saul approve of Stephen's murder but he goes to Damascus with authorization from the high priest Caiaphas to bring back to Jerusalem under arrest any men and women he finds there who are followers of Jesus. However, while Saul is en route, a bright light suddenly flashes around him and he falls to the ground.

"Saul, Saul, why are you persecuting me?" a voice from an invisible source asks. "Who are you, Lord?" Saul asks.

"I am Jesus, whom you are persecuting," comes the reply.

Saul, who has been blinded by the miraculous light, is told by Jesus to enter Damascus and await instructions. Then Jesus appears in a vision to Ananias, one of his disciples. Regarding Saul, Jesus tells Ananias: "This man is a chosen vessel to me to bear my name to the nations as well as to kings and the sons of Israel."

Indeed, with Jesus' backing, Saul (known now as Paul) and other evangelizers have tremendous success in their work of preaching and teaching. In fact, about 25 years after Jesus' appearance to him on the road to Damascus, Paul writes that the "good news" has been "preached in all creation that is under heaven."

After the passing of many more years, Jesus provides a series of visions to his beloved apostle, John. By means of these visions that John describes in the Bible book of Revelation, he, in effect, lives to see Jesus return in Kingdom power. John says that "by inspiration" he was transported forward in time to "the Lord's day." What is this "day"?

A careful study of Bible prophecies, including Jesus' own prophecy regarding the last days, reveals that "the Lord's day" began in the history-making year 1914, yes, within this generation! So it was in 1914 that Jesus returned invisibly, without public fanfare and with only his faithful servants being aware of his return. In that year Jehovah gave Jesus the command to go subduing in the midst of his enemies!

Obeying his Father's order, Jesus cleansed the heavens of Satan and his demons, hurling them down to the earth. After seeing this occur in vision, John hears a heavenly voice proclaim: "Now have come to pass the salvation and the power and the kingdom of our God and the authority of his Christ!" Yes, in 1914 Christ began ruling as King!

What good news this is for worshipers of Jehovah in heaven! They are urged: "Be glad, you heavens and you who reside in them!" But what is the situation for those on earth? "Woe for the earth and for the sea," the voice from heaven continues, "because the Devil has come down to you, having great anger, knowing he has a short period of time."

We are in that short period of time right now. People are presently being separated either to enter God's new world or to suffer destruction. The truth is, your own destiny is now being determined by how you respond to the good news of God's Kingdom that is being preached earth wide under Christ's direction.

When the separating of people has been finished, Jesus Christ will serve as God's Agent to rid the earth of Satan's entire system of things and all those who support it. Jesus will accomplish this removal of all wickedness in the war that is called in the Bible Har–Magedon, or Armageddon. Afterward, Jesus, the greatest Person in the universe next to Jehovah God himself, will seize Satan and his demons and bind them for a thousand years in an "abyss," that is, a state of deathlike inactivity. **Acts 7:55-60; 8:1-3; 9:1-19; 16:6-10; Psalm 110:1, 2; Hebrews 10:12, 13; 1 Peter 3:22; Luke 22:28-30; Colossians 1:13, 23; Revelation 1:1, 10; 12:7-12; 16:14-16; 20:1-3; Matthew 24:14; 25:31-33.**

- After Jesus ascends to heaven, where is he located, and what does he await?
- Over whom does Jesus rule after ascending to heaven, and how is his rule manifest?
- When did "the Lord's day" begin, and what took place at its beginning?
- What separating work in progress today affects every one of us personally, and on what basis is the separating being done?
- When the separating work is finished, what events will follow?

WHEN the Warrior-King Jesus Christ removes Satan and his unrighteous world, what cause for rejoicing there will be! The peaceful Thousand Year Reign of Jesus begins at last!

Under the direction of Jesus and his associate kings, the survivors of Armageddon will clean up the ruins left by that righteous war. Likely, earthly survivors will also bear children for a time, and these will share in the delightful work of cultivating the earth into a gorgeous parklike garden.

In time Jesus will bring forth untold millions from their graves to enjoy this beautiful Paradise. He will do this in fulfillment of his own guarantee: "The hour is coming in which all those in the memorial tombs will . . . come out."

Among those Jesus resurrects will be the former evildoer who died beside him on the torture stake. Recall that Jesus promised him: "Truly I tell you today, You will be with me in Paradise." No, that man will not be taken to heaven to rule as a king with Jesus, nor will Jesus again become a man and live on the Paradise earth with him. Rather, Jesus will be with the former evildoer in the sense that He will resurrect him to life in Paradise and see to it that his needs, both physical and spiritual, are cared for, as illustrated on the next page.

Think of it! Under Jesus' loving attention, the entire human family—Armageddon survivors, their offspring, and the thousands of millions of resurrected dead who obey him—will grow toward human perfection. Jehovah, by means of his royal Son, Jesus Christ, will reside spiritually with humankind. "And," as the voice John heard from heaven says, "he will wipe out every tear from their eyes, and death will be no more, neither will mourning nor outcry nor pain be anymore." No person on earth will suffer or be sick.

By the end of Jesus' Thousand Year Reign, the situation

will be just as God originally purposed when he told the first human pair, Adam and Eve, to multiply and fill the earth. Yes, the earth will be filled with a righteous race of perfect humans. This is because the benefits of Jesus' ransom sacrifice will have been applied to everyone. Death because of Adam's sin will be no more!

Thus, Jesus will have accomplished all that Jehovah asked of him. Therefore, at the end of the thousand years, he will hand over the Kingdom and the perfected human family to his Father. God will then release Satan and his demons from the abyss of deathlike inactivity. For what purpose?

Well, by the end of the thousand years, most of those living

in Paradise will be resurrected ones who have never had their faith tested. Before dying, they had never known God's promises and so could not demonstrate faith in them. Then, after being resurrected and taught Bible truths, it was easy for them in Paradise, without any opposition, to serve God. But if Satan was given opportunity to try to stop them from continuing to serve God, would they prove loyal under test? To resolve this question, Satan will be released.

The revelation given to John reveals that after Jesus' Thousand Year Reign, Satan will prove successful in turning an undetermined number of people away from serving God. But then, when the final test is finished, Satan, his demons, and all those whom he succeeds in misleading will be destroyed forever. On the other hand, the fully tested, loyal survivors will live on to enjoy the blessings of their heavenly Father throughout all eternity.

Clearly, Jesus has played, and will continue to play, a vital role in accomplishing God's glorious purposes. What a grand future we may enjoy as a result of all that he accomplishes as God's great heavenly King. Yet, we cannot forget all that he did while he was a man.

Jesus willingly came to earth and taught us about his Father. Beyond this he exemplified the precious qualities of God. Our hearts are moved when we consider his sublime courage and manliness, his unparalleled wisdom, his superb ability as a teacher, his fearless leadership, and his tender compassion and empathy. When we recall how he suffered indescribably as he furnished the ransom, by which alone we may gain life, surely our hearts are moved with appreciation for him!

Truly, what a man we have seen in this study of the life of Jesus! His greatness is obvious and overwhelming. We are moved to echo the words of the Roman governor Pontius Pilate: "Look! The man!" Yes, indeed, "The *man,*" the greatest man who ever lived!

By our accepting the provision of his ransom sacrifice, the burden of sin and death inherited from Adam can be removed from us, and Jesus can become our "Eternal Father." All who would gain everlasting life must take in knowledge not only of God but also of his Son, Jesus Christ. May your reading and study of this book assist you to take in such life-giving knowledge! **1 John 2:17; 1:7; John 5:28, 29; 3:16; 17:3; 19:5; Luke 23:43; Genesis 1:28; 1 Corinthians 15:24-28; Revelation 20:1-3, 6-10; 21:3, 4; Isaiah 9:6.**

- What will be the happy privilege of Armageddon survivors and their children?
- Who will enjoy Paradise in addition to Armageddon survivors and their children, and in what sense will Jesus be with them?
- What will be the situation at the end of the thousand years, and what will Jesus do then?
- Why will Satan be released from the abyss, and what will eventually happen to him and all who follow him?
- How can Jesus become our "Eternal Father"?